REMEMBERING WOODSTOCK

Dedicated to Richard Bryers (1963–2002),
for whom music was a way of life.

Remembering Woodstock

Edited by

ANDY BENNETT
University of Surrey, UK

ASHGATE

Published by
Ashgate Publishing Limited
Gower House
Croft Road
Aldershot
Hampshire GU11 3HR
England

Ashgate Publishing Company
Suite 420
101 Cherry Street
Burlington, VT, 05401–4405
USA

Ashgate website: http://www.ashgate.com

British Library Cataloguing in Publication Data
Remembering Woodstock. – (Ashgate popular and folk music series)
   1. Woodstock Festival (1969 : Bethel N.Y. 2. Woodstock Festival : 1969 : Bethel, N.Y.) – Influence 3. Rock concerts – New York (State) – Bethel – History
   I. Bennett, Andy, 1963–
   781.6'6'07974735

Library of Congress Cataloging-in-Publication Data
Remembering Woodstock / edited by Andy Bennett.
        p. cm – (Ashgate popular and folk music series)
   Includes bibliographical references.
   ISBN 0-7546-0713-5 (alk. paper) – ISBN 0-7546-0714-3 (pbk.:alk. paper)
   1. Woodstock festival. I. Bennett, Andy, 1963– II. Series.

ML38.W66R46 2003
781.66'079'74735–dc22
2003062698

ISBN 0 7546 0713 5 (HBK)
ISBN 0 7546 0714 3 (PBK)

Typeset by SetSystems Limited, Saffron Walden, Essex.
Printed and bound in Great Britain by T. J. International Ltd, Padstow, Cornwall.

Contents

List of figures and table

Figures

Table

Notes on contributors

Dave Allen is Deputy Head of the Department of Creative Technologies at the University of Portsmouth. He teaches principally on the Entertainment Technology BSc. He has also taught Cultural Studies, English and Creative Studies and Education at the university. His research has normally focused on visual arts education but in the 1960s he was briefly a professional musician and, since then, has been an active semi-professional performer, broadcaster and occasional writer on popular music.

Andy Bennett is Senior Lecturer in Sociology at the University of Surrey. Prior to studying for his PhD at Durham University he spent two years in Germany working as a music teacher with the Frankfurt Rockmobil project. He has published articles on aspects of youth culture, popular music and local identity in a number of journals including *British Journal of Sociology*, *Sociology*, *Sociological Review*, *Media Culture and Society* and *Popular Music*. He is author of *Popular Music and Youth Culture: Music, Identity and Place* (2000, Macmillan) and *Cultures of Popular Music* (2001, Open University Press) and an editor of *Guitar Cultures* (2001, Berg). Andy is Chair of the UK and Ireland branch of the International Association for the Study of Popular Music (IASPM), co-convener of the British Sociological Association Youth Study Group and a member of the Editorial Boards for the journals *Leisure Studies* and *Sociology*.

Gerry Bloustien is a Senior Lecturer and Program Director in Communication, Culture and Media, at the University of South Australia. She has published internationally on youth and popular culture, her recent work on *Buffy* stemming from her own enthusiasm for, and ongoing fascination with, the role of fantasy and play in everyday life. She is the editor of *Musical Visions*, a lively collection of contemporary debates about Australian popular music from indigenous and non-indigenous practitioners and academics, and *Envisioning Ethnography*, a special edition of social analysis on the complexity of visual ethnographic methods. Her book, *Girl Making* (Berghahn Books, New York, 2003) is a cross-cultural ethnography on the processes of growing up female.

Dave Laing was formerly Reader in Media Studies at the University of Westminster and popular music journalist. He is author of *The Sound of* *our Time* (Sheen and Ward, 1969) and *One Chord Wonders: Power and Meaning in Punk Rock* (Open University Press, 1985).

Country Joe McDonald has been a songwriter and performing musician since the mid-1960s. He is a long-time resident of Berkeley, California from where he formed the band Country Joe and the Fish. They were involved in the San Francisco 'scene' of the 1960s and recorded a number of albums including *Electric Music for the Mind and Body* and *I Feel Like I'm Fixin' to Die*. The band appeared at the Monterey and Woodstock festivals and his solo performance of 'Fixin'-to-Die' is particularly well known. Since the 1970s Country Joe McDonald has continued to write, record and perform, often solo but also with a variety of other musicians. He is an active supporter of service veterans and has a considerable interest in nursing. He runs a website about Florence Nightingale.

George McKay is Professor of Cultural Studies at the University of Central Lancashire, UK. He has written on the cultural history of protest and popular music in books such as *Senseless Acts of Beauty: Cultures of Resistance since the Sixties* (Verso, 1996) and edited *DiY Culture: Party & Protest in Nineties Britain* (Verso, 1998). His book *Glastonbury: A Very English Fair* (Gollancz, 2000) is a cultural history of pop festivals in Britain. His book *Circular Breathing: The Cultural Politics of Jazz in Britain* will be published by Duke University Press in 2005. He has also written on Americanization and cultures of anti-Americanism. He is also co-editor of *Social Movement Studies: Journal of Social, Cultural and Political Protest* (Carfax).

Allan F. Moore is Professor of Popular Music, and Head of the Department of Music and Sound Recording at the University of Surrey. Recent books include a revised edition of *Rock: The Primary Text* (Ashgate) and two edited collections for Cambridge: *The Cambridge Companion to Blues and Gospel Music* and *Analyzing Popular Music*. A member of the editorial boards of the journal *Popular Music* and *Twentieth-Century-Music* (both Cambridge), he is currently writing a series of programmes on notable performances in popular music for BBC Radio 4. But he's never been to Woodstock.

John Street is Reader in Politics at the University of East Anglia. His books include *Rebel Rock* (Blackwell, 1986) and *Politics and Popular Culture* (Polity, 1997). He is a co-editor (with Simon Frith and Will Straw) of the *Cambridge Companion to Pop and Rock* (Cambridge University Press, 2002) and a member of the editorial board of the journal *Popular Music*.

Simon Warner is Senior Teaching Fellow in the School of Music at the University of Leeds, where he leads on the BA in Popular and World Musics. A rock reviewer with *The Guardian* from 1992–95, he now writes regularly for the webzine *Pop Matters* (PopMatters.com) and also makes frequent BBC contributions on television and radio. He published *Rockspeak: The Language of Rock and Pop* (Blandford) in 1996. His research interests focus on rock journalism and the relationships formed between popular music and literature. A volume on the latter subject, *Text and Drugs and Rock 'n' Roll*, has just been commissioned by Continuum.

Sheila Whiteley is Professor of Popular Music at the University of Salford, Greater Manchester. She is also Associate Dean (Academic Enterprise) for the Faculty of Arts, Media and Social Sciences, and Chair of the Creative and Cultural Industries Committee. She was General Secretary (1999–2001) of the International Association for the Study of Popular Music and is now Publications Officer. Her publications include *The Space Between the Notes: Rock and the Counter Culture* (Routledge, 1992), *Women and Popular Music: Sexuality, Identity and Subjectivity* (Routledge, 1998) and *Too Much Too Young: Popular Music, Age and Gender* (Routledge, 2003). She was editor of *Sexing the Groove: Popular Music and Gender* (Routledge, 1998) and contributed chapters to *Reading Pop. Approaches to Textual Analysis in Popular Music* edited by Richard Middleton (Oxford University Press, 2000) and *'Every Sound There Is'. The Beatles' Revolver and the Transformation of Rock and Roll* edited by Russell Reising (Ashgate, 2002)

General Editor's preface

The upheaval that occurred in musicology during the last two decades of the twentieth century has created a new urgency for the study of popular music alongside the development of new critical and theoretical models. A relativistic outlook has replaced the universal perspective of modernism (the international ambitions of the 12-note style); the grand narrative of the evolution and dissolution of tonality has been challenged, and emphasis has shifted to cultural context, reception and subject position. Together, these have conspired to eat away at the status of canonical composers and categories of high and low in music. A need has arisen, also, to recognize and address the emergence of crossovers, mixed and new genres, to engage in debates concerning the vexed problem of what constitutes authenticity in music and to offer a critique of musical practice as the product of free, individual expression.

Popular musicology is now a vital and exciting area of scholarship, and the Ashgate Popular and Folk Music series aims to present the best research in the field. Authors will be concerned with locating musical practices, values and meanings in cultural context, and may draw upon methodologies and theories developed in cultural studies, semiotics, poststructuralism, psychology and sociology. The series will focus on popular musics of the twentieth and twenty-first centuries. It is designed to embrace the world's popular musics from Acid Jazz to Zydeco, whether high tech or low tech, commercial or non-commercial, contemporary or traditional.

Professor Derek B. Scott
Chair of Music
University of Salford

Acknowledgements

The idea for this book came from a one-day conference held at the University of Kent in 1999 to mark the 30th anniversary of the Woodstock festival. I am grateful to all those who participated in the conference and to my former colleagues at the University of Kent for their support in organizing the event. Thanks must also go to Heidi May and Derek Scott for their belief in this project and for giving me the time and space to assemble the papers that appear in the book. Finally, a special thanks to Country Joe McDonald, veteran of the late 1960's music scene and the original Woodstock festival, for his input into this book.

In Chapter 5, 'Reporting Woodstock' we would like to acknowledge permissions to use work from the following publications:

Extracts from the *New York Times*. Copyright © 1969 New York Times Co. Reprinted by permission.

Extracts from 'The 10th largest city in the United States' by Steve Lerner, from the *Village Voice*, 21 August 1969. Copyright © 2003 Village Voice Media, Inc. Reprinted with the permission of the Village Voice.

Extracts from 'It was like balling for the first time' by Jan Hodenfield, from *Rolling Stone*, 20 September 1969. Copyright © 1969 Rolling Stone LLC. All rights reserved. Reprinted by permission.

Extracts originally published in *Melody Maker*, 30 August 1969. Reprinted by permission.

Extracts originally published in *New Musical Express*, 23 August 1969. Reprinted by permission.

Extracts from *The Guardian*. Copyright © The Guardian, 1969. Reprinted by permission.

Lyric extracts from Country Joe McDonald's '(I Feel Like I'm) Fixin' To Die' reproduced in Chapters 2 and 4 by permission of McDonald Music Co. 2003.

Every effort has been made to trace all the copyright holders, but if any have been inadvertently overlooked the publishers will be pleased to make the necessary arrangement at the first opportunity.

Abbreviations and acronyms

BBFC	British Board of Film Censors
CBD	Central business district
CCC	Clear Channel Communications
IT	*International Times*
MPA	Motion Picture Association of America
NJF	National Jazz Federation
NME	*New Musical Express*
PPV	pay-per-view
SNCC	Student Nonviolent Coordinating Committee
TAZ	temporary autonomous zone
WOMAD	World of Music, Arts and Dance

Introduction

Andy Bennett

The subject of many books, documentaries and a three and a half hour film of the event, Woodstock has acquired legendary status as both the *defining* and *last great moment* of the 1960s, a decade which saw large-scale social upheavals and significant cultural transformations. Over 30 years after the event, Woodstock remains, in the popular imagination, the point at which the creative and political energies of the 1960's counter-cultural movement briefly united in a three-day spectacle of 'peace, love and music'. The purpose of this book is to consider how and why Woodstock has achieved such iconic status. Examining a variety of issues, from Woodstock's influence on the organization of the popular music industry to its role as purveyor of myths concerning the power of music to shape and inform political action, the chapters in this book unravel the fiction and fact about Woodstock and the popular perceptions that surround it.

The Woodstock festival, officially titled the Woodstock Aquarian Music and Art Fair, took place between 15 and 18 August 1969, near the town of Bethel in upper New York State on land owned by local farmer Max Yasgur. Permission to stage the festival on Yasgur's land was hastily secured after the originally planned site, at the town of Woodstock itself, fell through only weeks before the event was due to take place. The plan to stage the Woodstock festival was hatched by Michael Lang and Artie Kornfeld who, having secured advance funding from two young New York business partners John Roberts and Joel Rosenman, became key organizers of the event. In addition to attracting some of the biggest rock artists of the 1960s, among them Jimi Hendrix, Janis Joplin and The Who, Woodstock also became a platform for new rising stars in the rock world, notably Carlos Santana and the recently formed 'supergroup' Crosby, Stills and Nash. At the height of the festival there were some 450 000 people in attendance. Estimates made by the New York State police suggest that a further 1.5 million people failed to get to the event because of traffic congestion on roads and highways leading to the festival site. Writing ten years after the event, Young and Lang suggested that: 'The Woodstock Festival synergized a way of life which had been growing through the Sixties: antiwar, antiestablishment, pro-drugs, non-competitive, and individualistic' (1979, p. 5).

Woodstock and the 1960s

As Young and Lang's observation suggests, in order to fully appreciate the socio-cultural significance of Woodstock, one needs to view it in the broader context of the late 1960s. This was a period of considerable social and cultural transformation, especially among the young. If the post-war youth market of the 1950s and early 1960s had succeeded in giving youth its own identity (see, for example, Chambers, 1985), from the mid-1960s onwards this identity was set to become ever more radical. The visual image of youth, together with the lifestyle sensibilities, leisure preferences and general outlook of young people became increasingly distinct from those of the parent culture. As with the 1950s, the cultural statements of youth were effected largely through musical and stylistic resources. But it was the changing nature of music and style during the 1960s that gave such statements a distinctive edge over what had gone before (Bennett, 2001). Music became increasingly experimental and, with the aid of improvements in electronic amplification and sound effects, became 'a "total" effect', particularly when listened to under the influence of drugs such as marijuana and, more notably, the synthetically produced lysergic acid diethylamide or LSD (Reich, 1971, p. 24). LSD was originally developed by Swiss chemist Albert Hoffman during the 1930s (see Edelstein, 1985) but remained relatively unknown until the mid-1960s when it became heavily promoted by counter-cultural spokespeople such as Ken Kesey (author of *One Flew Over the Cuckoo's Nest*) and Timothy Leary, a former Harvard University professor sacked from his post following revelations that he had encouraged students to take LSD and drop out of their academic studies (see Edelstein, 1985). Leary would later become famous through his slogan 'turn on, tune in and drop out' which he preached to audiences at counter-cultural gatherings throughout the US (Hall, 1968). Kesey, on the other hand, gave out free samples of LSD at specially organized events known as 'happenings', which combined 'light shows, avant garde films, live music, tape loops and lurid poster art' with psychedelic music performed by the then relatively unknown San Francisco band, the Grateful Dead (Bennett, 2001).

While drug culture was giving rise to new ways of experiencing musical sounds and effects, the lyrical content of popular music also took on increasingly radical dimensions as the 1960s progressed. Songwriters and lyricists saw it as their artistic responsibility to respond directly to current social and political issues which, during the mid-1960s, were becoming increasingly more turbulent. As Billig notes:

> In the mid-1960s, the cultural climate changed. It was a time of open dissent, especially on the college campuses . . . With weighty issues of revolution in the air, how could da-doo-ron-ron express the serious feelings of a new age? And

so the new, mass intellectual music was born. Rock poetry was, if nothing
else, a reaction against the seeming triviality of rock's first era. (Billig, 2000,
p. 114.)

A particularly prominent liaison between rock music and protest centred
around the Vietnam War. From the mid-1960s onwards a strong anti-
Vietnam War movement put increasing pressure on the US government to
end the war and withdraw from Vietnam. Anti-war demonstrators in the
US and Western Europe opposed the seemingly senseless nature of the
Vietnam War, which, it was argued, had 'sunk into an apparently endless
slough of mud and dead bodies' (Snowman, 1968, p. 149). Similar concerns
were expressed concerning what was deemed to be the oppressive action of
the US government and its overt blocking of the self-determination of a
small country in the interest of its own corporate concerns.

The anti-Vietnam War protest was supported by many musicians who
demonstrated their allegiance to the protest's cause both in their music and
through their dominant media profiles to speak out against the war. In 1969
Beatle John Lennon and his wife Yoko Ono staged a ten-day bed-in at the
Queen Elizabeth Hotel in Montreal, Canada in the cause of world peace.
As Brown and Gaines write:

> The climax of the Montreal bed-in was Saturday night sing-in, attended by,
> among others, Tommy Smothers, Timothy Leary, Rabbi Abraham Feinberg,
> and the entire Canadian chapter of the Radha Krishna Temple. The event
> was photographed by three camera units [including] one from the BBC, one
> from the BCBC . . . A new song written by John called 'Give Peace a Chance'
> was recorded live in two sessions in the hotel bedroom. (Brown and Gaines,
> 1983, p. 316.)

A more direct criticism of the Vietnam War was Country Joe MacDonald's
'I-Feel-Like-I'm Fixin'-to-Die-Rag', a powerful anti-Vietnam War song (see
also Chapters 2, 4 and 8) with a sing-along chorus made world-famous
through its inclusion in the Woodstock film (see Chapter 4). According
to Gleason, 'Fixin'-to-Die' summed up perfectly the counter-culture's anti-
war message (1972, p. 139). It was direct, hard-hitting and highly damning
of the US government which, it was argued, were sending thousands of
healthy young men to their deaths in a war which had only an economic
rationale. Similarly, the promotional film to the Doors' anti-war song
'The Unknown Soldier' showed singer Jim Morrison being blindfolded
and shot, a scene intended to parody the 'summary executions of . . .
untried opponents' featured in US media reports about the Vietnam war
(Snowman, 1984, p. 163). Other popular music artists also delivered powerful anti-war messages. For example, Joni Mitchell's song 'Woodstock',
dedicated to the Woodstock festival, contains a reference to bombers

turning into Butterflies, the bombers in question being those attacking North Vietnamese targets.

If the foreign policy of the US government was one issue that mobilized the counter-culture into action, both in the US and across Europe, then domestic affairs also became a focus for forms of direct and radical protest. Across Europe, students occupied university campuses and demonstrated for better facilities. In Paris, university students and workers joined forces to protest about workers' rights and the conditions in factories. As Halliday observes:

> What started as the action of small revolutionary groups swelled into the most significant mass contestation of the State since the Commune, arousing large numbers of the French working class [who] joined in huge demonstrations in solidarity with the students: a general strike was initiated, then, despite the reluctance of trade union leadership, it turned into factory occupations by nearly ten million workers . . . the militant students continued to play a key role during and after the insurrection they had ignited. Action groups were set up to help workers produce propaganda materials . . . Links between workers and students were formed which were to form the basis for future common actions. (Halliday, 1969, p. 320.)

In the US, attention focused on the issue of civil rights. In October 1966 the Student Nonviolent Coordinating Committee (SNCC) was established to enable students to become organized in the battle for civil rights (see Buckman, 1970, pp. 134–35). However, neither the SNCC nor President Kennedy's Civil Rights Bill, passed in 1964, served to alleviate the abject poverty and 'total political impotence' of African Americans (ibid., p. 135). Increasing racial discrimination and harassment across the US led to inner-city riots, some of the most violent examples being in New York's Harlem district and in the black quarters of Rochester, Philadelphia. Civil rights organizations were superseded by the Black Power movement. Embracing the basic tenets of the Muslim faith and its central figure Mohammed, this movement was supplied with much of its political rationale by Stokely Carmichael, who Snowman describes as the movement's 'most articulate and charismatic leader' (1984, p. 154). Commenting on the underlying rationale for the rise of the Black Power movement, Snowman observes:

> All the other ethnic minorities in the United States . . . had achieved a measure of political and economic power only after a period in which they faced the rest of society with a united – and closed – front. Blacks, therefore, owed it to themselves to buy black, to sell black, to vote black – to think black. (Snowman, 1984, pp. 154–55.)

The music of black artists in the US also took a more radical turn during the late 1960s. James Brown's 'Say It Loud, I'm Black and I'm Proud' and Aretha Franklin's 'Respect', for example, accurately corresponded with the mood and feeling of the Black Power movement. As Billig notes, 'With black pride, there was an increasing feeling that African Americans should support and protect their own culture. Music had to be specifically black to appeal to black audiences' (2000, p. 110). Another important black American artist of the late 1960s was guitarist and songwriter Jimi Hendrix. Born in Seattle, Washington, Hendrix took up music professionally having been discharged from the US paratroopers following an injury. Hendrix achieved initial success in 1966 when, under the management of former Animals bassist Chas Chandler, he travelled to London, formed the Jimi Hendrix Experience along with Noel Redding and Mitch Mitchell, and had a hit with 'Hey Joe' (Redding and Appleby, 1990). By the late 1960s Hendrix had 'become passionately involved in the gangs of Harlem [and] in the growth of the Black Muslim Church' (Palmer, 1976, p. 253). Such interests were also largely behind Hendrix's decision in 1969 to form an all-black group, the Band of Gypsies. Eric Burdon of British rhythm and blues group, The Animals, said of Hendrix:

> If you want to see what an American black is going through today, where his mind is at, go and see Hendrix . . . and you'll realise why there are race riots in America and why the country is so close to civil war. He's a wizard on the guitar, but his music is so disturbed and so explosive. He is exorcising generations of anger. (Burdon cited in Palmer, 1976, p. 253.)

Along with Richie Havens and Sly Stone, Hendrix was one of the few African-American artists to appear at the Woodstock festival, and included in his set a searing rendition of the American national anthem, its heavily amplified and harmonically distorted sound resonating with the social and political climate within and outside the US during the late 1960s (see Chapter 2).

Remembering Woodstock

As noted above, for many, Woodstock was both the defining moment of the late 1960s and the swansong of the counter-cultural movement that characterized the era. Since the late 1960s the spirit of Woodstock has lived on in the films, books and articles dedicated to the event. Together with the memories and anecdotal reflections of those who made it to the festival, or remember it taking place, such documents of the event have played their part in mythologizing Woodstock as a key icon of the 1960s.

The chapters in this book examine various aspects of the Woodstock festival, both in terms if its role and place in the history of post-Second World War popular culture and its continuing hold on the popular imagination of those who look back on the 1960s today. Dave Laing (Chapter 1) considers how the concept of Woodstock, no matter how haphazard and spontaneous it appeared at the time, became a template for future rock festivals, which, learning from the successes and mistakes of the Woodstock organizers, turned the festival into a highly lucrative concern, as evidenced by the 25th and 30th anniversary Woodstock festivals of 1994 and 1999 respectively. Laing further considers how this increasing commercialization of the festival event contradicts with carnivalesque sensibility of those who attend festivals, and for whom the festival experience is an opportunity to temporarily suspend the mundane predictability of normal everyday experience.

In Chapter 2 Sheila Whiteley focuses on the original 1969 festival and considers the key musical moments of the event. Examples considered by Whiteley include Country Joe MacDonald's crowd-raising performance of his anti-Vietnam war song 'Fixin'-to-Die' and Jimi Hendrix's rendition of the American national anthem, 'The Star Spangled Banner'. As Whiteley observes, each of these artists utilized their performances at Woodstock as a means of projecting key counter-cultural messages back on to the crowd and to a wider public who would later hear about Woodstock and watch the film of the event.

John Street (Chapter 3) examines the political myths and popular memories that have grown up around the Woodstock festival over the years. As Street observes, such myths have been powerfully promulgated by the combined effort of authors and journalists whose reflections, both positive and negative, have informed ways of thinking about Woodstock and what the event stood for culturally and politically. Street further observes how participation in the myth of Woodstock has widened considerably since the mid-1990s due to a proliferation of Woodstock websites and mailing lists.

In Chapter 4 Andy Bennett looks at the way in which Woodstock is represented in the film of the event, noting how the artistic and editorial licence of the film-makers played its part in creating the cinematic version of the festival seen by global cinema audiences. Bennett also considers the significance of the film as a source of nostalgia, both in relation to the Woodstock festival itself and to the late 1960s more generally.

Simon Warner's chapter presents a compelling retrospective on Woodstock through its retelling of the festival through original journalistic accounts drawn from sources such as the *New York Times*, *Rolling Stone* and *Village Voice*. Drawing on interviews held with those attending the festival, festival site workers and locals from the nearby town of Bethel, Warner illustrates the conflicting opinions and understandings of Woodstock, even as the event was taking place.

Focusing on the musical performances at Woodstock, Allan Moore (Chapter 6) presents a critique of the often cited 'spontaneous' moments of musical genius that unfolded on the festival's main stage over the three days of the event. As Moore reveals, although many of the performances appear to have essentially been created on the spot, inspired by power and emotion of the event, they were the result of honing through previous performances, and in some cases show signs of having been quite meticulously rehearsed beforehand.

George McKay (Chapter 7) offers an historical account of the Beaulieu Jazz Festivals in Britain between 1956 and 1961, noting how these events set important precedents for future rock and pop festivals in Britain and elsewhere. According to McKay, many of the conventions of festival behaviour, both on-stage and off, made famous through Woodstock, actually grew out of these earlier jazz festivals which were, in many ways, the Woodstocks of their day.

Dave Allen's chapter considers the significance of Woodstock in terms of its illustration of a transitional stage between the more politically oriented folk-influenced acoustic music of the first part of the 1960s and the heavily amplified commercially-oriented rock of the second part of the decade. As Allen notes, although both types of music were more or less equally featured at Woodstock, this would be the last 'rock' festival where this would occur, future events being dominated by electric rock bands. In the case of Woodstock, argues Allen, the presence of so much acoustic music gave credence to the 'back-to-land' and political sensibilities of the audience, a feature which would become less central to the ethos of rock festivals during the 1970s.

In the final chapter Gerry Bloustien examines the legacy of Woodstock as this is understood and experienced in early twenty-first century Australia. Focusing on the annual WOMAD festival in Adelaide (known as Womadelaide), Bloustien considers how the retro-hippie look of many festivalgoers and the rural location of the event are an attempt to recreate, albeit in an idealized fashion, the original atmosphere of Woodstock, or at the very least celebrate the essence of the Woodstock message in a contemporary local context.

The book ends with a personal account by veteran Woodstock performer Country Joe McDonald with Dave Allen. McDonald recounts his early years, his time in the US navy and his first forays into music-making, before going on to discuss his appearances at Woodstock and how these shaped his subsequent career.

References

Bennett, A. (2001), *Cultures of Popular Music*, Buckingham: Open University Press.
Billig, M. (2000), *Rock 'n' Roll Jews*, Nottingham: Five Leaves.
Brown, P. and Gaines, S. (1983), *The Love You Make: An Insider's Story of the Beatles*, London: Pan Books.

Buckman, P. (1970), *The Limits of Protest*, London: Victor Gollancz.

Chambers, I. (1985), *Urban Rhythms: Pop Music and Popular Culture*, London: Macmillan.

Edelstein, A.J. (1985), *The Pop Sixties*, New York: World Almanac Publications.

Gleason, R.J. (1972), 'A Cultural Revolution', in R.S. Denisoff and R.A. Peterson (eds), *The Sounds of Social Change*, Chicago: Rand McNally and Company.

Hall, S. (1968), 'The Hippies: An American "Moment"', Working Paper, Birmingham Centre for Contemporary Cultural Studies, University of Birmingham.

Halliday, F. (1969), 'Students of the World Unite', in A. Cockburn and R. Blackburn (eds), *Student Power: Problems, Diagnosis, Action*, Harmondsworth: Penguin.

Palmer, T. (1976), *All You Need is Love: The Story of Popular Music*, London: Futura.

Redding, N. and Appleby, C. (1990), *Are You Experienced? The Inside Story of the Jimi Hendrix Experience*, London: Pan Books Ltd.

Reich, C.A. (1971), *The Greening of America*, Middlesex: Allen Lane.

Snowman, D. (1968), *USA: The Twenties to Vietnam*, London: B.T. Batsford Ltd.

Snowman, D. (1984), *America Since 1920*, London: Heinemann.

Young, J. and Lang, M. (1979), *Woodstock Festival Remembered*, New York: Ballantine Books.

Chapter 1

The three Woodstocks and the live music scene

Dave Laing

Writing in 1980 in *The Rolling Stone Illustrated History of Rock and Roll*, John Morthland described a failed attempt to stage a commemorative event a decade after the first Woodstock festival and confidently asserted that 'if any proof was needed that rock festivals were a thing of the past, surely this was it' (Morthland, 1980, p. 338). Unfortunately for him, rock festivals were to become very much a thing of the present and future to the extent that they remain one of the dynamic aspects of popular music in the early twenty-first century.

For example, Woodstock 1969 was only the first of three successful Woodstock festivals. Both the 25th and the 30th anniversaries of that event were marked by large-scale outdoor music events held in different parts of upstate New York to the Yasgur's farm site. This chapter will discuss the three Woodstock events in the context of the evolution of live music and its business over the period linking 1969 to 1999 and beyond.

In particular, the chapter examines three aspects of this evolution: the evolution of music festivals and their status as carnivalized spaces; the development of the live music business, especially the move from entrepreneurship to corporatization; and finally the 'deterritorialization' of the live event through sound recordings, films and television. These will be discussed after descriptions of the anniversary Woodstock events.

Woodstock anniversaries

The Woodstock 25th anniversary festival (Woodstock II) was held 12–14 August 1994 in Saugerties, New York. Some aspects were similar to the original festival.

First, the weather was unseasonal, with the 840-acre site turning into acres of mud. In 1969 the *Rolling Stone* magazine's article about the Woodstock festival was headed 'The View From The Mud' (Lombardi, 1974, p. 611) although Robert Draper's subsequent unauthorized history of the magazine suggested that its reporting team were able to escape the mud and return to their hotel rooms (Draper, 1990, p. 104). In 1994 it was mud in the mosh pit (not a survival from 1969!) that was said to be responsible for many of the 750 casualties taken to local hospitals with minor injuries.

Second, although some 190 000 people paid $135 each for tickets to Woodstock II, a large proportion of the audience (estimated at 100 000) got in without paying. Numerous others with tickets were unable to get into the show because of a lack of parking spaces! Reporting on the event in *Billboard* magazine, Melinda Newman wrote: 'though it's only 10 miles from our hotel to the parking lot, it took an hour to get there. There are 1000s of people walking along the road balancing laundry baskets full of beer on their shoulders. Down the road, people are cutting holes in the fence and sneaking in for free' (Newman, 1994, p. 17).

The differences between 1969 and 1994 were equally striking. First, unlike the first Woodstock, the 1994 event was heavy with corporate sponsorship – principally from PolyGram Diversified Entertainment, a subsidiary of a major record company, that co-produced the event and from Pepsi which contributed $3 million. The amplification set-up included 500 loudspeakers, 200 microphones and 12 miles of audio cable. The event consumed 9 megawatts of electricity. Production costs were over $30 million, including fees of over $300 000 for leading performers: these included 1969 survivors Crosby, Stills and Nash but also grunge favourites Green Day and hard rockers Aerosmith. Revenues from ticket sales ($25.6 million), sponsorship ($3 million-plus) and concessions ($2 million) covered these costs.

And Woodstock II had a crucial extra audience beyond the muddy fields of Saugerties. There were to be (as in 1969) the albums of the festival and the movie of the event. But on the two days of the event itself there was syndicated television coverage to 290 000 pay-per-view (PPV) customers watching in real time in the US and in recorded form to 26 foreign networks serving 98 countries. Woodstock II reached Europe on the French network MCM, Premiere, BSkyB and the BBC. The festival was taped and relayed by satellite to 30 African countries on M-Net and other networks. Poly-Gram Diversified Entertainment received a further $12.5 million for these television rights (Financial Times Music and Copyright, 1994). Apart from the weather and the discomfort of the audience – a British journalist commented that it was what the Flanders battlefield must have been like – this was as perfectly managed a media event as the 1990s could effect. The event was synergized and cross-collateralized. The fans in the muddy field were extras for the PPV coverage.

In contrast, the financial structure of the first Woodstock festival was highly unorthodox and shrouded in confusion. Elliott Tiber was a youthful local motel manager who describes in his memoir, *Knock On Woodstock*, how he helped the long-haired festival organizer Michael Lang run the gauntlet of a queue of hostile farmers to deposit $250 000 in cash at the local bank (Tiber, 1994, p. 138) and Robert Stephen Spitz explains how the organizers' debts could be paid off only by selling the film rights to Warner Bros which in turn made very large profits from the movie's $50 million-plus box office takings (Spitz, 1979, p. 488). Marc Eliot, however, challenges this image of hippie idealism mixed with financial incompetence. Using anonymous testimony, Eliot claims that 'to those more directly involved, those three days in the Catskills symbolised what to them sixties rock had become: the selling of progressive idealism for corporate profit' (Eliot, 1990, p. 147).

Before any live albums from the 1994 event could be issued, the television coverage and the publicity immediately boosted sales of the current albums by Woodstock II performers Sheryl Crow, Green Day, Nine Inch Nails and others. But the biggest boost was for an act who couldn't make it to Woodstock II. Four albums by Jimi Hendrix re-entered the US charts in August 1994. In addition, Warner Bros, owners of the audio-visual rights to the 1969 festival and PolyGram's rival, took advantage of the publicity surrounding the 1994 event to issue a director's cut of *Woodstock: The Movie* as well as CD-ROMs and CDs (with previously unreleased tracks) of the first Woodstock.

If Woodstock II retained some of the aura surrounding the 1969 event, despite its entanglement with the corporate rock, the 1999 festival (Woodstock III) was almost totally free from the idealism of 1969.

Woodstock III took place 23–25 July at Griffiss Park, a former US airforce base near Rome in New York State. Nobody seemed to notice the coincidental link to Joni Mitchell's song *Woodstock* whose lyrics (inspired by the original event) referred to a dream in which the singer saw bombers becoming butterflies.

None of the artists from the 1969 event took part, except for Jimi Hendrix, a laser projection of whose 1969 performance was presented as the closing sequence of the festival! Otherwise, only the promoters, Michael Lang and John Scher, provided a link to the previous Woodstocks. Lang was an organizer of the original event and Scher had been the PolyGram executive in charge of the 1994 festival. With tickets costing $135, Woodstock III drew a similar number of paying customers to the 1994 event – 190 000 people paid a total of $28.9 million, making it the biggest concert event of 1999 – but this time the freeloaders were fewer – only 25 000. However, this was still only about half of the 400 000-plus who attended the first Woodstock festival.

Faced with the fragmentation of American pop, the 1999 organizers decided to introduce extra stages and to acknowledge the fragments. The bill included a smattering of black acts (James Brown, Ice Cube, Kid Rock), singer-songwriters (Alanis Morrissette, Elvis Costello), and 'traditional' metal (Metallica, Megadeth). But the dominant musical element was contemporary rock and rap metal, personified by such acts as Korn, Rage Against the Machine, Limp Bizkit and Red Hot Chili Peppers.

The conditions at the site were characterized by high temperatures (26–34°C), even higher prices (hamburgers cost up to $20) and by riots, assaults and arson. On the final day, fires were started on the site and rapes occurred during violent scenes in the mosh pit while Limp Bizkit was performing (Rothman, 1999). When John Scher appealed for calm, the band's frontman Fred Durst gave the crowd an ambiguous message: 'They want us to ask you to mellow out. They said too many people are getting hurt. Don't let nobody get hurt, but I don't think you should mellow out' (Smith, 2000, p. 2).

The event was covered live by MTV and was available throughout on pay-per-view television for $89.95. In October, the double album, *Woodstock 99*, was issued by Sony. One disc consisted of rock material; the other included examples of all the other music styles. The album was not a hit.

Woodstock and the outdoor music festival

The Woodstock festival was part of a distinct history of (non-classical) outdoor music festivals in the US stretching back to the early twentieth century.

The earliest festivals were rural events, often celebrating local styles and skills in music and folk dance. The first such event was probably the Georgia Old Time Fiddlers Convention held in Atlanta in 1913. According to Atlanta music historian Wayne W. Daniel: 'From forty to a hundred picturesque musicians flocked to the city auditorium to clown and fiddle – each hoping to win the title of state fiddling champion, a gold medal and a monetary prize of about fifty dollars' (Daniel, 1990, p. 23). A three-time winner of the convention was Fiddlin' John Carson, generally held to be the first hillbilly or white rural musician to make a commercial recording, in 1923.

The final Atlanta convention was held in 1935, its demise being blamed on the corrosive influence of radio and the phonograph on traditional rural fiddling styles. But similar events survived into the 1960s. In that decade, the *New York Times* critic Robert Shelton attended an Old Time Fiddlers Convention at Union Grove North Carolina. The event had been first held in the 1920s and, almost half a century later, was still characterized by 'the scrape of the fiddle, the ring of the banjo and the cry of the human voice' (Shelton, 1975, p. 26).

Another antecedent of the modern outdoor festival was the Mountain Dance and Folk Festival of Asheville, Carolina. This was founded in 1928 by Bascom Lamar Lunsford, 'a local lawyer, collector, balladeer, banjo picker and square dancer' as an adjunct to the city's annual Rhododendron Festival (Cantwell, 1994, p. 32). Although Lunsford was 'conservative in politics and manner' and, in selecting performers for his festivals, 'would not book a hellraiser or a rogue, types not unknown either in folk music or in mountain society, and certainly not a convict or a tramp', he inspired the foundation of a National Folk Festival first held in St Louis in 1934 (ibid, p. 33).

The folk revival of the 1960s gave rise to hundreds more festivals at campuses and elsewhere. In an associated genre, the first of hundreds of bluegrass music festivals was held at Roanoke, Virginia in 1965 (Rosenberg, 1974, p. 19). Although the types of music featured may have changed, the character and atmosphere of such events continues to imbue hundreds of annual festivals in North America and Europe in the early twenty-first century. The following description of a typical weekend bluegrass festival in Georgia in the 1970s could apply equally to numerous folk music, blues or cajun music events in the present day:

> Amateur and professional bands took turns performing on stage in sets that varied in length from fifteen minutes to an hour, depending on the number of bands engaged to perform. Friday night and Saturday night shows frequently lasted until after midnight. Fans began arriving Friday and most did not leave until the last note was sounded on Sunday. Festivals were touted as family affairs and all ages attended, while the adjacent campgrounds – a must at any festival – were filled with all styles and sizes of tents, pickup campers, vans and motor homes. Before, during and after the stage entertainment, amateur musicians gathered in small groups around the parking lots and campgrounds for impromptu jam sessions. (Daniel, 1990, p. 223.)

The informality and democratic tenor of such events was common to the plethora of 'free festivals', 'human be-ins' and other gatherings that drew fans of the new rock music from 1965 onwards in California (Rycroft, 1998), but also in England and elsewhere. Such events were the prelude to the pivotal years of 1967–69 when Woodstock was preceded by the small-scale and idyllic Monterey Pop and followed by the nightmarish Altamont.

While much of the Woodstock audience came with a 'free festival' attitude, the direct precursors of Monterey and Woodstock as music shows were the jazz and folk festivals held at Newport, Rhode Island from the 1950s (see Hentoff, 1962, pp. 82–95). These differed from the more free-form folk events in their precise programming of numerous well-known musicians performing in series over several days.

In the 1950s this was a novel method of presenting music to audiences used to the single evening performance at a concert or jazz club featuring at most a few acts. In his account of the foundation of the jazz festival in 1954, John Hammond emphasizes this unknown and untried element: 'a jazz festival implied a number of concerts performed over several days to essentially the same audience, something no one had tried before' (Hammond, 1981, p. 336).

Like Woodstock was to be, the Newport festivals had been regarded with suspicion by local dignitaries and authorities because of the way in which they imported an aura of oppositional lifestyle and even the occasional riot to the conservative East Coast State of New Hampshire. These festivals also continued well into the 1960s, overlapping with the emergent rock scene. The 1965 Newport Folk Festival was the site of one of rock music's formative moments when Bob Dylan's electric music was almost silenced by an irate Pete Seeger who had to be restrained from unplugging the amplification system. The folk festivals also epitomized an anti-commercial ethic by paying a common fee of $50 to all performers from 'Bob Dylan to prisoners from a Texas chain gang' (Cantwell, 1994, pp. 308–309).

Such economic egalitarianism in the festival business did not survive the commercial boom that Monterey unleashed. According to *Rolling Stone*, between June 1967 and July 1970 'approximately 2.5 million young people attended about 30 festivals in the US and a further 30 were planned after Woodstock which didn't happen' (Lombardi, 1974, p. 611). Rock festivals also spread to other countries. Some Woodstock organizers helped put together the Mount Fuji event in Japan in 1971, several events of the early 1970s were hailed as 'the Italian Woodstock', Woodstock inspired the Roskilde festival in Denmark, first held in 1971 and still running, while in England there were the second and third Isle of Wight Festivals of 1969 and 1970 which drew audiences of 80 000 and 200 000 respectively (Hinton, 1995). The 1969 Isle of Wight event was widely regarded as sharing the 'love and peace' vibe of Woodstock itself:

> A 2,000 watt amplification system ensured that not only the audience but the prisoners in Parkhurst and the monks at Quarr monastery heard the music. All leave for the island's 150 police was cancelled, but as a senior officer commented 'everything has been very good tempered. The kids have been well behaved and there has been no serious trouble'. (Clarke, 1982, p. 37.)

Some authors have regarded Woodstock as unequivocally negative in terms of the supposed community of interest between performers and audiences. Simon Frith wrote that the event 'dramatised the total separation between rock's performers and consumers' (Frith, 1981, p. 222) while the arch miserabilist Martha Bayles fulminated against the 'hugely powerful amplification systems capable of filling sports arenas – or, in the case of Woodstock, acres of farmland'. 'Needless to say', she added, 'there was (and is) a mismatch between such systems and the virtues of Afro-American music' (1994, p. 223).

These comments, however, fail to acknowledge the importance of the 'carnivalesque' or 'dionysian' dimension of outdoor festivals. This dimension is closely linked to the fact that, for most audience members, the key thing is to be present at the event as such, not necessarily to see or experience a particular act. The latter is the motivation to attend a concert, not a festival. The carnivalesque dimension is evident in numerous testimonies from participants in events stretching from the rock festivals of the 1960s to the raves of the 1990s. For example: 'Everyone was dancing. In front of the stage, amidst the dense crowds there, people were dancing, their heads held high above their heads' and 'a beautiful, androgynous girl . . . is dancing on top of a van. Her fingers stab and slice, carving cryptograms in the dawn air, and her mouth is puckered in a pout of indescribable, sublime impudence.' These very similar descriptions are separated by over 20 years. The first speaker is describing the 1970 Isle of Wight Festival, quoted in the late Jeremy Sandford's *Tomorrow's People* (Sandford and Reid, 1974, p. 62). The second is Simon Reynolds' eyewitness account of the 1992 outdoor rave at Castlemorton in the West of England (Reynolds, 1998, p. 139).

The carnivalesque dimension, of course, need not be the dominant element of a festival and it is necessarily less ritualized and less formal than the annual carnival celebrations of the Americas, notably Brazil, Trinidad and New Orleans (for Trinidad see Mason, 1998). However, it shares with them the impetus towards the reversal of everyday systems and structures, a theme that cultural theorists have also discovered in the idea of carnival to be found in the works of the Russian critic Mikhail Bakhtin. Sue Vice, for example, points to the emphasis on the fluidity of the boundary between performers and audience – 'the whole point of carnival . . . is that the viewer is also a participant' (Vice, 1997, p. 187) – while Neil Nehring has usefully applied Bakhtin's 'carnival' to recent musical trends such as Riot Grrrl (Nehring, 1997, pp. 172–77).

The 'temporary autonomous zone' (TAZ) is another concept that has been applied to outdoor music events. The idea of TAZ was introduced by the anarchist writer Hakim Bey (Bey, 1991) and was used by James Ingham in his discussion of illegal Chicago house and Jamaican dub warehouse parties in the northern English town of Blackburn in the late 1980s. Incorporating a quotation from Hillegonda Rietveld (Rietveld, 1993), Ingham writes that TAZ is 'a useful analytical concept that allows us to acknowledge that virtual sound worlds can bring people together in fluid associations driven by desire and imagination in which music can function "to pump a desire into human bodies to move, to dance and let go"' (Ingham, 1999, p. 112).

During the 1980s and 1990s a number of other festivals were proclaimed to embody the spirit of Woodstock. Among the most prominent of these are the US touring festivals Lollapalooza and Lilith Fair. Each was founded by a musician rather than a promoter. Canadian singer-songwriter Sarah McLachlan founded Lilith Fair in 1997 as a 35-concert tour featuring a total of 60 women performers (O'Brien, 2002, p. 470). Lollapalooza was the brainchild of Perry Farrell, the 'dionysiac guru' (Hoskyns, 1996, p. 329) and leader of Jane's Addiction. A 1993 article in the British music paper *Melody Maker* was introduced by the statement that Lollapalooza 'is to the 90s what Woodstock was to the 60s – a miniature Utopia, a meeting of the tribes and a perfect opportunity for hundreds of alienated 10-somethings and 20-somethings to get off their heads to the greatest subcultural noise of the day . . .' (Stud Brothers, 1993, p. 28).

In Europe, both the Glastonbury Festival and WOMAD (World of Music, Arts and Dance) have been compared to Woodstock. In his study of the Glastonbury event, George McKay links the modern festival to a pioneering festival of music and dance organized at Glastonbury by the radical composer Rutland Boughton between 1914 and 1926 (McKay, 2000). With 112 000 paying customers, the contemporary Glastonbury rock festival has its own roots in the free festival movement of the late 1960s and early 1970s and, so far, has retained its idealism not least through the donation of profits to such bodies as Oxfam and the Campaign for Nuclear Disarmament.

Since its foundation in 1982 by enthusiasts for 'world music', over 120 WOMAD festivals have been held. From the outset it was intended to include more than on-stage performances by professional musicians. Its early history is related by Peter Jowers (Jowers, 1993). For example, a 1988 event at Bracknell in the UK was advertised as including concerts, sessions, workshops, lanterns and kites, 'late night extras' and children's entertainment. In WOMAD's 20th anniversary year, outdoor events were held in Spain, Italy, Greece, the UK, Singapore and Australia (see also Gerry Bloustien's account of WOMADelaide in Chapter 9).

The growth and corporatization of the rock concert business

The second music industry context in which Woodstock can be set is the formation of a specific rock performance business hewed out of a more traditional and often antagonistic showbusiness world in the US.

The importance of Woodstock as a catalyst for this process is exemplified by the career of the British group Ten Years After. The band's performance at Woodstock was highlighted in the film of the festival in which the group's guitarist Alvin Lee was seen playing a marathon solo (see also Chapter 6). In the previous year, 1968, the group was persuaded to come to the US with only one concert – in San Francisco – guaranteed. In eight weeks they did just six gigs. But, after Woodstock, Ten Years After were in constant demand for US national tours.

All this coincided with a fundamental change in the concert circuit, led by a new agency, Premier Talent, founded by Frank Barsalona, a former employee of GAC, one of the major booking agencies. In the mid-1960s, Barsalona was frustrated by the attitude of the older generation of agents who thought that rock music was a mere gimmick or craze and refused to see it as a new business opportunity. As a result, he decided to wage the cultural battle within the concert industry by going solo with Premier Talent. His progress was slow but, by 1970–71, he had built up a national circuit of ballrooms and 'underground' venues for rock acts to tour, mainly composed of the remnants of a number of small venues established locally in the late 1960s. In 1966 Bill Graham opened the Fillmore Auditorium in San Francisco for weekly dance parties featuring local bands such as Jefferson Airplane and The Grateful Dead (Glatt, 1993). The following year saw the opening of the Boston Tea Party by Don Law in Boston (Goodman, 1997), the Kinetic Playhouse run by Aaron Russo in Chicago, the Psychedelic Supermarket in New York and Middle Earth in London. These were joined in 1968 by Philadelphia's Electric Factory.

These early rock promoters were very much one-person organizations. For example, the British-based Mel Bush Organisation consisted of Bush himself, 'his sister whom he described as his "assistant and right arm" and three secretaries to take care of the paper work' (Gold, 1976, p. 102). Bush told an interviewer: 'I run my life on simple philosophies, common-sense philosophies, like a small goldmine is worth a lot more than a big empire. I can make more money for myself with four people, than if I had a great big company with big overheads, which on a piece of paper was worth two million pounds, but I couldn't put my hands on any cash' (ibid.).

This 'go it alone' common-sense philosophy derives from a recognition that, unlike other figures in the music business, the promoter owns nothing beyond the contract for the next concert. In particular, the promoter has no intellectual property from which earnings might flow over a longer period than the one night of a gig. If the gig is recorded, the rights to that recording inevitably belong to the artist's record company. If the concert is being filmed or relayed to free-to-air or pay-per-view television, the revenues will almost always flow to the artist manager or, again, to the record company. In this situation, the entrepreneurial promoter may try to diversify in order to offset the possible losses from too few ticket sales. In his biography of Bill Graham, John Glatt recounts how Graham soon moved into managing some of the leading San Francisco acts. This was followed by the formation of a booking agency and a record label (Fillmore Records with Santana and Tower of Power) and by a move into merchandising. The latter turned out to be the most lucrative of the diversifications. Graham began by selling copies of the posters for his gigs (and by denying the poster artist any share in the proceeds). Eventually his subsidiary, Winterland, owned the rights to manufacture and distribute official merchandise such as t-shirts, posters and souvenirs of such artists as Fleetwood Mac, Rod Stewart and Crosby, Stills and Nash (Glatt, 1993, pp. 177–78).

This development coincided with a shift in power relations between the buyers and sellers of talent in the market place. Memoirs of the era contain the laments of the club owners and local promoters who had become accustomed to setting fees to artists based on their own costs. Now they were faced with the demand that they pay the fees fixed by the acts and their agents (such as Premier). They knew the market value of the music from record sales and from the artists' popularity on the newly arrived FM radio stations. After Woodstock, Jimi Hendrix's fee went up to $75 000 from the $18 000 he was paid for playing the festival.

Jon Landau made the point that this price inflation made it certain that Woodstock 1969 would be the last time that 'everyone was together in one place' (Landau, 1972). In a pre-PPV and cable television era, no promoter could afford to pay all those acts and, indeed, many of them would not have agreed to share top billing with each other. The next gathering of the stars of rock was 16 years after Woodstock, at the 1985 Live Aid concerts and, of course, these were only possible in economic and cultural terms because of the charity motivation.

The sharply rising fees of Hendrix and other counter-cultural acts contributed to the disappearance of the first generation of rock venues across the US. During 1971, first the Electric Factory was closed, then the Boston Tea Party and, finally, the two Fillmores, in San Francisco and New York. The failure of these venues did not, however, mean that the entrepreneurs who managed them were out of a job. Bill Graham, Don Law and the rest merely moved from being club managers to being free-ranging promoters. No longer tied to staging shows in their old 3000-seat halls, these regional rock moguls could hire the appropriately sized venue for each act that they were contracted to promote.

While the promoters were all-powerful in their home regions, tours as a whole continued to be controlled by Premier Talent and other booking agencies based in New York or Los Angeles. In the early 1970s attempts were made to dislodge the powerful agents from their role as tour organizers. The first successful challenger was Rolling Stones road manager Pete Rudge who booked the group's 1972 tour himself. This was followed by the iconoclastic Bill Graham who became the first local promoter to mastermind a national tour with Bob Dylan and the Band in 1974, a move that brought Graham into disfavour with the rest of the live music business (Glatt, 1993, pp. 157–59).

Despite these isolated challenges to the established order, the basic functions of the booking agency and the local entrepreneurial promoter in the rock concert business remained virtually unchanged throughout the 1970s and 1980s. However, by 1994, the year of Woodstock II, several other changes were taking effect. These included the entry of major music corporations into the sector and the growing importance of two additional sources of income for the concert industry: merchandising and sponsorship.

Woodstock II itself epitomized the new role of entertainment corporations with PolyGram's promotion subsidiary taking a lead role in organizing the event with Woodstock Ventures, a company owned by Michael Lang and other survivors of 1969. PolyGram Diversified Entertainment was itself a joint venture with John Scher, one of the rugged entrepreneurs of the New York live music scene and a survivor from the very early days of underground rock promotion.

But PolyGram was only one of several record industry companies eagerly looking for a piece of the live music action. Sony, the Japanese consumer electronics company had bought CBS Records in 1988. Soon afterwards, in 1991, it formed Sony Signatures to compete in the increasingly lucrative merchandising market. Over the next eight years this subsidiary became the licensee for official merchandise for numerous top rock acts, crowned by The Beatles for whose rights Sony paid $20 million to Apple Records in 1995. Sony also became directly involved in venue ownership and concert promotion. In 1994 it pooled its venues with those of Blockbuster (the video retail group) and Pace Concerts to form the Pavilion Group.

Merchandising was also an attractive proposition for two other big record companies. BMG and MCA entered this sector by acquiring existing companies dealing in t-shirts, caps, posters and other merchandise. In 1991 BMG bought almost 90 per cent of Nice Man, a company founded by Tom Johnson, whilst the MCA group bought the highly successful Winterland Productions merchandising company from Bill Graham Presents.

By the time of Woodstock III, the concert business had undergone further transformation. Although the record and music publishing corporations (PolyGram, Sony, MCA, BMG) might have been expected to have consolidated their positions by greater horizontal integration of the music business through further acquisitions in live music, in fact, for the most part, the opposite occurred. PolyGram, Sony and MCA withdrew from the sector, while BMG retained its merchandising arm but turned its attentions to the Internet and its ill-judged purchase of Napster. With hindsight, it can be seen that the *volte face* of these major companies derived from their panic in the face of falling record sales. Their first thought was to raise cash and preserve profits by selling off 'non-essential' parts of their companies – even if, in comparison to the record business, live music was in good financial shape!

Instead, the ecology of the music concert business was fundamentally revolutionized by the predatory actions of two very different companies that began the final stage of corporatization of the concert business. SFX was a small radio broadcasting company that suddenly swept down on the industry, purchasing numerous venues and promotion companies in Europe as well as North America. The second company, Ticketmaster, was a 'first mover' in a new technologically-driven segment of the sector – the purchase of concert and sports event tickets by telephone rather than in person. Between 1997 and 1999 SFX acquired many of the surviving regional promoters in the US. These included the Pavilion Group, Bill Graham Presents in California, Cellar Door in New England and Delsener Slater in New York. SFX also bought into leading black music and Hispanic promoters and began a concerted attack on the European scene: in the UK it bought the 20 theatres run by the Apollo Leisure group as well as concert promoter MCP; in Sweden it purchased EMA Telstar, the company responsible for almost all the major music events in the Nordic countries.

Ticketmaster was a small company bought in 1982 by Fred Rosen who set about buying up local ticketing companies throughout the US. By the late 1980s Ticketmaster dominated the business and Rosen, who believed that ticket prices were far too low, was able to impose high service charges to be paid by ticket buyers that would help 'to double the cost of tickets to every American music and sporting event' (Glatt, 1993, p. 246). In 1989, for example, Rolling Stones tickets cost $28, of which $5.50 went straight to Ticketmaster. The company made enemies among fans and artists and, in 1995, the band Pearl Jam took their campaign against the rapacious Rosen to Congress. The US Department of Justice announced that it would investigate Ticketmaster's alleged monopolistic practices but concluded weakly in 1996 that these were acceptable because, in theory, other companies could compete with Ticketmaster.

While Woodstock was the single event with the largest ticket sales in 1999, total ticket sales in the US reached a record level of $1.5 billion, compared with the previous highest total of $1.4 billion in 1994, the year of Woodstock II. Of equal significance, SFX was involved as promoter or co-promoter of 120, or 60 per cent, of the top 200 shows in 1999. In that year the two predators on the live music business joined forces when SFX granted Ticketmaster exclusive rights to sell tickets at all its venues and concerts.

The SFX proportion of the top 200 shows rose to 75 per cent in 2000, the year that SFX was bought by Clear Channel Communications (CCC), the largest radio station owner in the country and a leader in the field of 'outdoor advertising' through billboards and other hoardings. CCC had grown swiftly as a radio station owner after the US government abolished ownership restrictions in 1996. By 2000 it had a dominant position in radio and live music in many US cities. In New York, for example, it owned four radio stations and controlled four important concert halls and clubs featuring music. The company was able to 'cross-promote' its concerts through its radio stations and also through advertising billboards. Because of its control of these sectors it could (and did) undercut the deals offered to leading artists by rival promoters.

The deterritorialization of Woodstock

Although the significance of a performance lies in its unique 'presence' for the audience as witness, it is also the case that none of the Woodstocks was solely a 'live' event. For both cultural and financial reasons, simulacra of each were created through the application of broadcast and recording technology.

The filming of the first Woodstock took place against the background of an awareness that previous concert films failed to 'capture the emotional, as well as the musical, excitement of the event' (Spitz, 1979, p. 352). Such films were unable to simulate the experience of 'presence' for a cinema audience. For the promoters of Woodstock, the solution to this dilemma was to hire a documentary film-maker who was as unorthodox as themselves (coincidentally the Maysles Brothers, directors of the Altamont film *Gimme Shelter* and D.A. Pennebaker, director of the earlier Bob Dylan documentary *Don't Look Back*, were also avant-garde film-makers). The director of the Woodstock movie, Michael Wadleigh, found a bold technical means to capture the excitement of the event – split-screen editing where two different images appeared simultaneously on-screen (see also Chapter 4). The result was a three-hour film that attracted critical acclaim as well as being a box-office blockbuster. The review in the film industry 'bible', *Variety*, was ecstatic: 'the film is a milestone in artistic collation of raw footage into a multipanel, variable-frame, dazzling montage that engages the senses with barely a let-up' (Elley, 1991, p. 682).

The film, of course, did more than simply recreate the experience of witnessing Woodstock. The significance of the filmed version of both Woodstock and its 'alter ego' Altamont (in the film *Gimme Shelter*) in fixing dominant meanings of the festivals has been strongly argued by Robert Duncan. According to Duncan, the Woodstock movie defined the event as a 'myth of eternal youth ... of cherubic innocence triumphant' while *Gimme Shelter* showed 'the maggoty underside of the acid utopia, a countermanding anti-myth to Woodstock's myth of innocence' (Duncan, 1984, p. 29). An earlier concert film had a different sort of impact on at least one viewer. The ethos of the Newport Festival was spread internationally by the highly successful 1957 documentary *Jazz On A Summer's*

Day. Its success in capturing the ambience of the event inspired an English folk fan, Ken Woollard, to found the Cambridge Folk Festival (Laing and Newman, 1994, p. 6).

In addition to the movie there was the audio recording of the event. Many accounts of rock music have emphasized the contrast between the 'live' event and the recorded artefact. Such accounts often proceed on the basis that rock, unlike jazz or traditional musics, is primarily a recorded music and that the role of performance is to recreate recordings in almost the same way that radio provides a different context for the consumption of recordings. In the context of this type of argument, the production of 'live recordings' takes on a special significance, both avowing and disavowing the separation of the 'unique' live event from the potential for repetition of the recording.

At the end of the 1960s the 'live' album, recorded at a concert or festival performance, was becoming an established part of the recorded music industry. Motown Records had routinely issued live albums by artists such as The Supremes and Stevie Wonder in the mid-1960s while the *Beach Boys Concert* album had topped the US album chart in 1964. In Britain, live albums had been made by rhythm and blues-based bands such as the Rolling Stones (1966), the Yardbirds (1965), Cream (1968), and Ten Years After (1968). By 1970, when the *Woodstock* triple-album was issued, the live album concept was increasing in popularity. In the weeks that *Woodstock* was in the British Top 20 it was side by side with *Live At Leeds* by The Who, the first Elvis Presley live album and *Steppenwolf Live*.

Although a video and book of Woodstock II were issued in 1995, along with new versions of the 1970 film and album, at Woodstock II the deterritorialization of the live event had acquired a new dimension through live television coverage. The absent audience could now move closer to the experience of 'being there' through PPV. Live television coverage was also a feature of Woodstock III but, in addition, the process of superimposing a simulacrum on to the live event was underway. Those physically present were not only able to view the 1970 movie in a 24-hour movie theatre sited in a flight hangar but were subjected to the repetition of a 1969 performance on the 1999 stage. The laser projection of the Hendrix performance (a prosthetic 'live' event comparable to the contemporaneous Elvis Presley shows where a live band accompanied the singing of a filmed Elvis), enabled participants in Woodstock 1999 to 'experience' the climax of the original event.

Conclusion

Historians of the music industry have generally had a blind spot where the 'live' music sector is concerned. The reader will look in vain for any reference to Woodstock in Russell Sanjek's standard text *American Popular Music and Its Business* (Sanjek, 1988) or for any discussion of the stadium rock scene in *Hit Men*, Fredric Dannen's classic muck-raking account of the record industry in the 1980s and 1990s (Dannen, 1990). While this is reprehensible, it is also understandable in the sense that, in general, the overlap between the personnel of the record business and the concert business has been occasional and casual, even though both are intertwined in the lives and business affairs of most professional musicians.

In part, the intention of this chapter has been to begin to redress that imbalance by using the most famous event in rock history as a starting point for a discussion of the development of rock music performance events (in particular, the role of the outdoor festival) and of the business structures associated with them.

Robert Spitz's exhaustive account of the 1969 Woodstock Festival shows how what would later be separated out as idealism and business were entwined in the process of the festival's organization. Perhaps the subsequent delinking of those two elements explains why the event was able to provoke such divergent reactions as those of the anti-capitalist dystopian Marc Eliot and the social idealist Jan Hodenfield who wrote, in *Rolling Stone*, that 'an army of peaceful guerrillas established a city bigger than Rochester NY and showed itself imminently ready to turn back on the already ravaged cities and their inoperable "lifestyles" imminently pre-pared to move onto the mist-covered fields and into the cool, still woods' (Draper, 1990, pp. 105–106). That dichotomy reappeared in later years, this time as a division between those who cited Woodstock as the prede-cessor of such idealistic efforts as Lollapalooza, Glastonbury and Lilith Fair and those who saw it as a fatal moment of the 'selling out' of rock.

As this chapter has shown, the history of live music events since 1969 provides considerable evidence to support each view. If the idealism of Woodstock has been reinvented in the remarkable growth in the number and popularity of outdoor festivals, it is undeniable that the profit motive has inspired and informed much of the subsequent evolution of the rock concert business. Such a dichotomy in the world of live music can be interpreted through the model offered in the late 1960s by Ian Birchall, an English socialist writer, cited in my first book on music, published in the year of Woodstock. He wrote of pop music that 'it is (like any art form in a commercial society, only more so) squeezed out between two conflicting pressures'. The pressures were those of 'the publishers and manufacturers' and of 'working class youth seeking to express their experience in modern society' (cited in Laing, 1969, pp. 189–90). In the live music scene of the late twentieth and early twenty-first centuries, the equivalent 'conflicting pressures' are those of corporatization and the carnivalesque.

References

Bayles, M. (1994), *Hole In My Soul: The Loss of Beauty and Meaning in American Popular Music*, Chicago: University of Chicago Press.

Bey, Hakim (1991), *T.A.Z. Temporary Autonomous Zone, Ontological Anarchy, Poetic Terrorism*, New York: Autonomedia.

Cantwell, R. (1994), *When We Were Good: The Folk Revival*, Cambridge, MA: Harvard University Press.

Clarke, M. (1982), *The Politics of Pop Festivals*, London: Junction Books.

Daniel, W.W. (1990), *Pickin' On Peachtree: A History of Country Music in Atlanta, Georgia*, Urbana and Chicago: Illinois University Press.

Dannen, F. (1990), *Hit Men: Power Brokers and Fast Money Inside the Music Business*, New York: Random House.

Draper, R. (1990), *The Rolling Stone Story*, Edinburgh: Mainstream.

Duncan, R. (1984), *The Noise: Notes from a Rock'n' Roll Era*, New York: Ticknor and Fields.

Eliot, M. (1990), *Rockonomics: The Money Behind the Music*, London: Omnibus Press.

Elley, D. (ed.) (1991), *The Variety Movie Guide*, London: Hamlyn.

Financial Times Music and Copyright (1994), 'The Greatest Gainer from Woodstock '94: PolyGram', 14 September, p. 2.

Frith, S. (1981), *Sound Effects: Youth, Leisure and the Politics of Rock 'n' Roll*, New York: Pantheon.

Glatt, J. (1993), *Rage and Roll. Bill Graham and the Selling of Rock*, New York: Birch Lane Press.

Gold, M. (1976), *Rock On The Road*, London: Futura.

Goodman, F. (1997), *The Mansion on the Hill: Dylan, Young, Geffen, Springsteen and the Head-On Collision of Rock and Commerce*, New York: Times Books.

Hammond, J. with Townshend, I. (1981), *John Hammond on Record: An Autobiography*, London: Penguin.

Hentoff, N. (1962), *The Jazz Life*, London: Peter Davies.

Hinton, B. (1995), *Message to Love. The Isle of Wight Festivals, 1968–70*, Chessington: Sanctuary.

Hoskyns, B. (1996), *Waiting For the Sun: Strange Days, Weird Scenes and the Sound of Los Angeles*, New York: St Martin's Press.

Jowers, P. (1993), 'Beating New Tracks: WOMAD and the British World Music Movement', in S. Miller (ed.), *The Last Post: Music after Modernism*, Manchester: Manchester University Press.

Ingham, J. (1999), 'Listening Back From Blackburn: Virtual Sound Worlds and the Creation of Temporary Autonomy', in A. Blake (ed.), *Living Through Pop*, London and New York: Routledge.

Laing, D. (1969), *The Sound Of Our Time*, London: Sheed and Ward.

Laing, D. and Newman, R. (1994), *30 Years of the Cambridge Folk Festival*, Ely: Music Maker Publications.

Landau, J. (1972), *It's Too Late To Stop Now*, San Francisco: Straight Arrow Books.

Lombardi. J. (1974 /1969), 'The View From The Mud', in B. Fong-Torres (ed.), *The Rolling Stone Rock 'N' Roll Reader*, New York: Bantam.

McKay, G. (2000), *Glastonbury: A Very English Fair*, London: Gollancz.

Mason, P. (1998), *Bacchanal! The Carnival Culture of Trinidad*, London: Latin America Bureau.

Morthland, J. (1980), 'Rock Festivals', in J. Miller (ed.), *The Rolling Stone Illustrated History of Rock and Roll*, New York: Random House.

Nehring, N. (1997), *Popular Music, Gender, and Postmodernism: Anger is an Energy*, Thousand Oaks, London and New Delhi: Sage.

Newman, M. (1994), 'Three Days of Music, Mud and Myth: A Woodstock 1994 Survivor's Diary', *Billboard*, 27 August.

O'Brien, L. (2002), *She Bop II: The Definitive History of Women in Rock, Pop and Soul*, London: Continuum.

Reynolds, S. (1998), *Energy Flash. A Journey Through Rave Music and Dance Culture*, London: Picador.

Rietveld, H. (1993), 'Living the Dream', in S. Redhead (ed.), *Rave Off: Politics and Deviancy in Contemporary Youth Culture*, Aldershot: Avebury Press.

Rosenberg, N.V. (1974), *Bill Monroe and the Bluegrass Boys: An Illustrated Discography*, Nashville, TN: Country Music Foundation Press.

Rothman, R. (1999), 'Politics of the Pit', *Village Voice*, 3–9 November.

Rycroft, S. (1998), 'Global Undergrounds: The Cultural Politics of Sound and Light in Los Angeles 1965–1975', in A. Leyshon, D. Matless and G. Revill (eds), *The Place of Music*, New York and London: Guilford Press.

Sandford, J. and Reid, R. (1974), *Tomorrow's People*, London: Jerome Publishing.

Sanjek, R. (1988), *American Popular Music and Its Business. Vol III 1900 to 1984*, New York: Oxford University Press.

Shelton, R. (1975), 'It Happened In America', in D. Laing, K. Dallas, R. Denselow and R. Shelton, *The Electric Music. The Story of Folk into Rock*, London: Methuen.

Smith, R.J. (2000), 'Into The Mosh Pit', *The Guardian*, 8 September, pp. 2–3.

Spitz, R.S. (1979), *Barefoot in Babylon: The Creation of the Woodstock Music Festival, 1969*, New York: Viking Press.

Stud Brothers (1993), 'Woodstock on Wheels', *Melody Maker*, 10 July, pp. 28–30.

Tiber, Elliott (1994), *Knock on Woodstock*, New York: Festival Books.

Vice, S. (1997), *Introducing Bakhtin*, Manchester: Manchester University Press.

Ward, B. (1998), *Just My Soul Responding: Rhythm and Blues, Black Consciousness and Race Relations*, London: UCL Press.

Chapter 2

'1, 2, 3 What are we fighting 4?' Music, meaning and 'The Star Spangled Banner'

Sheila Whiteley

Woodstock, like the deaths of Jimi Hendrix, Jim Morrison, John Lennon and Janis Joplin, is inevitably associated with personal nostalgia. 'I was there' is a phrase that many would like to lay claim to – and, indeed, half a million or so old hippies can do just that. In August, 1969, however, I was in California having made the trek to San Francisco with Jervis (now my ex-husband) and my two-year old daughter Bryony. While our travels across America were very much a part of our love of the music and a shared commitment to many of the ideals of the counter-culture, the impact of Woodstock itself was to shape my future career as a musicologist. To show, rather than simply explain what I mean, I quote briefly from Michael Wadleigh and Bob Maurice's film *Woodstock*, which was released by Warner Bros in 1970.

> *Interviewer:* What is it that the musicians have got? Are you a musician or something?
> *Organizer:* No.
> *Interviewer:* What is it that the musicians have that they can communicate so well with the kids?
> *Organizer:* Music.
> *Interviewer:* I mean, they've always had music. There's always music.
> *Organizer:* Music has always been a major point of communication. I mean, now the lyric and the type of music is a little bit more involved in society than it was.
> *Interviewer:* I need something, let me tell you, a kind of voice-over while I'm showing this music's on. If you could voice-over while there's music playing . . . What that music is saying, kind of . . . You know, what it's about.
> *Organizer:* It's about what's happening now and if you listen to the lyric and you listen to the rhythm and what's in the music and then what's going on in the culture . . .
> *Interviewer:* Great!

But, as the video reveals, there is no voice-over, no 'what that music is saying', no explanation of how the musical communication works, what it *means.* Rather, there is a cut to the building of Woodstock itself, the more straightforward dimension of erecting a stage – something that is immediately accessible, *where* the musicians perform, rather than a blow-by-blow analysis of meaning.

It is, by now, something of a cliché to point out that different contextualizations of music foreground different sensibilities. Watching the *Woodstock* video in the quietness of my room is distinct from being there, from being immersed in the live performance. The experience of seeing a group perform live at a rock festival is different from seeing the same group perform in a concert hall, or on television. They are different performing contexts and this, in turn, affects the reception and interpretation of the musical content.

> At one extreme, one finds that the performer can be fully taken in by his own act; he can be sincerely convinced that the impression of reality which he stages is the real reality. When his audience is also convinced about the show he puts on – and this seems to be the typical case – then for the moment at least, only the sociologist or the socially disgruntled will have any doubts about the 'realness' of what is presented. (Goffman, 1971, p. 28.)

As Simon Frith observes:

> . . . the term 'performance' defines a social – or communicative – process. It requires an audience and is dependent, in this sense, on interpretation; it is about meanings. To put this another way, performance art is a form of rhetoric, a rhetoric of gestures in which, by and large, bodily movements and signs (including the use of the voice) dominate other forms of communicative signs, such as language and iconography. And such a use of the body (which is obviously central to what's meant here by performance art) depends on the audience's ability to understand it both as an object (an erotic object, an attractive object, a repulsive object, a social object) and as a subject, that is, as a willed or shaped object, an object with meaning. (Frith, 1996, p. 205.)

I make no apology for quoting Frith at some length, nor for requoting Goffman whose perception of performance as conveying 'the real reality' is something that has shaped my own writing on the Rolling Stones and their performance at Altamont (see Whiteley, 1997). It is also apposite to my discussion of Jimi Hendrix and his performance at 'the counter-culture's great white Bacchanalia – Woodstock' (Hicks, 1970 [1996], p. 209). For many, this is where he reached 'his highest level of artistic maturity . . . and not surprisingly his work there was also his most politically deep and significant' (ibid.). But, as the interviewer so tellingly wanted to know: 'What that music is saying . . . You know, what it's about.'

There is little doubt, as Woodstock's organizer, Michael Lang, observed at the time, that you need to listen to the lyrics, to the rhythm, to *what's in the music* and then relate the music to what is going on in the culture. In other words, there is an implied homology between the cultural and musical characteristics. Culturally, the late 1960s was characterized by resistance and radical dissent, with the most significant social criticism coming from young people, in the main partly drawn from the university campus population, from philosophers such as Herbert Marcuse and Norman Brown, from poets and writers such as Allen Ginsberg – not least his poem 'Howl' – and Jack Kerouac whose book, *The Dharma Bums* (1958), provided 'the first handy compendium of all the Zen catch phrases' that became such an integral part of the 1960s youth catechism (Roszak, 1969, p. 131). Finally, there was the godfather of hallucinogenic experience, Timothy Leary. As counter-cultural theorist Theodore Roszak observed at the time:

> For better, or worse, most of what is presently happening that is new, provocative, and engaging in politics, education, the arts, social relations (love, courtship, family, community), is the creation either of youth who are profoundly, even fanatically, alienated from the parental generation, or of those who address themselves primarily to the young. (Roszak, 1969, p. 1.)

I do not propose to discuss these points in any detail but, instead, highlight some of the major areas of conflict. Possibly the most significant here is the opposition to the Vietnam War which is generally identified as the one great unifier of the counter-culture in that it demonstrated a concern for the developing world and, in particular, the racial and economic exploitation of other races. While confrontation was particularly acute in the US where there was both an increasing rejection of parental values and a lack of commitment by draftee servicemen, European students identified the war as symptomatic of the corruptions of advanced consumer capitalism. As such, the focal activity directed against the war was associated with wider social and moral issues. In particular, there was a growing recognition that a political system that perpetuated inequality and a general lack of freedom was untenable, and that its institutions (parliament, the national assembly, the Church, universities, business, the media and leisure itself) were corrupt and therefore in need of radical change.

   The second half of the 1960s produced an escalation of student protest and rebellion in most of the industrially developed countries, including Japan. These revolutionary phenomena possessed similar features which came to a head in the years 1968–69. In Russia, Czechoslovakia and Yugoslavia, students and intellectuals demanded very precise freedoms to study and to discuss, without the formal constraints of communist doctrine. In comparison, those students in capitalist countries, who were influenced by the ideas of neo-Marxism and various liberation movements, aimed at the destruction of capitalism to make a world free from war, poverty and exploitation. There were also local grievances such as impersonal teaching and overcrowding, pedantic academicism and bureaucratic administrations, but these were only the outward manifestations of a demand for deeper social and political changes (Whiteley, 2000, pp. 22–23).

While there was no single song that summed up its central values, both the social and political denominations of youth protest shared a common belief that rock could articulate its concerns. As stated in the *Woodstock* interview cited earlier, 'Music has always been a major point of communication . . . now the lyric and the type of music is a little bit more involved in society than it was.'

I want to turn briefly to one such example from Woodstock that clearly shows this sense of communication and how the lyrics relate to the values of the counter-culture and its rejection of the US's involvement in the Vietnam War, Country Joe's 'Fixin'-to-Die'. In particular, the question is raised: *'What are we fighting for?'* Ideally, we would all join in, for what is important here is the way in which participation in the music, as either performer or audience, establishes a common cultural and political bond. As Steve Gilbert explained in a recent e-mail:

> There's a nice paradox in Country Joe's 'Fixing to Die Rag' – dystopia/ utopia, the light nature of the rag-time tune juxtaposed with the deadliness of the subject matter. I was around then, and getting drafted to go to die was the prime object of fear – hence the dark jokes to relieve the anxiety. I see it as a manifestation of the old-time tendency – an off-shoot of the folk revival that was generally around during that era, as in the Beatles' 'When I'm Sixty-Four', 'Your Mother Should Know', 'Maxwell's Silver Hammer'. There was another American song from the same period 'I'm Just a Good Old American Boy' that fits pretty much the same pattern, with a similarly ironic sense of humour. As for 'Fixin' to Die', I don't hear it as a rag *per se*, but as a parody of the ragtime songs that permeated the 'teens and early 1920s, such as 'Alexander's Ragtime Band' and 'Twelfth Street Rag'.[1]

Steve also draws attention to *The Yale Record*, a special issue which contained 'Lyndon Johnson's Lonely Birds' Club Band' with lyrics parodying several songs, such as:

> If I get shot up during the war
> Many months from now . . .
> Will you still knead me, will you still feed me . . .
>
> Lovely Lynda (Bird Johnson) needs a mate
> But agents have come between us,
> Will you demilitarise your zones for me?

Finally, there was (in its entirety):

> I read the news, today, Oh God.

Returning to Country Joe's apocryphal question: 'What are we fighting for?', I want briefly to focus in on the word 'we'. The 'we', in this context, clearly refers to more than the crowd at Woodstock who, with their long hair and pipes of peace, were more likely to be the drop-out draftees. The 'we' refers to the citizens of America and, as such, focuses attention on national identity. I have already commented briefly on the Vietnam War, and I now want to consider another great conflict, that of the civil rights movement and how this relates to the American flag, 'The Star Spangled Banner'.

In common with the cultural and political upheavals associated with student protest, the mid-1960s had witnessed increasing unrest as the earlier liberal civil rights movement (at its simplest, the black American's pursuit of equality in law and opportunity) had given way to Stokeley Carmichael's demand for Black Power. At the time of Woodstock, the deaths of Malcolm X (21 February 1965) and Martin Luther King (4 April 1968), together with the systematic repression of black radicalism, had led to a watershed in the battle for civil rights. The promotion of black pride, black unity and self-empowerment which had characterized such mainstream soul hits as James Brown's 'Say It Loud, I'm Black and I'm Proud' and Nina Simone's 'Young Gifted and Black', and which had offered solutions for social, economic and political oppression through a rejection of white American goals and values, had been countered by a systematic embourgeoisement of the black middle classes. For those remaining in the inner cities, however, increasing economic and political oppression led, inevitably, to an intensification of racial pressures. 'The confusion and disillusionment of the period were evident in Marvin Gaye's 'What's Going On?' and 'Inner City Blues' (Garofalo, 1992, p. 237), and (in another Woodstock band) Sly and the Family Stone's album, *There's a Riot Goin' On*, all of which were released in 1971.

New York was the first metropolitan area to fall into virtual economic bankruptcy. The effects of overpopulation and unemployment had led to the securing of a federal loan with harsh repayment conditions. This, in turn, led to dramatic cuts in social and public services, and widespread housing problems. Initial attempts at urban renewal resulted in the upwardly mobile relocating to the suburbs while the poorer inhabitants – largely black and Hispanic households – were forced to relocate to inferior housing; around 60 000 homes in the South Bronx were demolished in the 1960s and early 1970s to make way for the construction of the city's urban expressway. With white residents and business owners moving to the northern sections of the Bronx and Westchester, large numbers of houses were left vacant, only to be exploited by the professional slumlords. The residents who remained were, by and large, impoverished black and Hispanic families, inarticulate, with limited community education and little or no political voice.[2]

In 1969 questions were raised; for example, 'Just who does the national flag refer to – who is included, who is excluded from the codes of nationalism, citizenship and equality of opportunity which relate to the United States of America?'. Here I would refer to such songs as Isaak Hayes' 'Chains', Len Chandler's mid-1960s freedom song 'Move on over, or we'll move on over you', and Gil Scott Heron's 'The Revolution Will Not Be Televised', all of which express a revolutionary ethos, raising consciousness and energizing change.

If the national flag symbolizes national identity[3] and the 'what-goes-without-saying', then for the black American it also symbolized, in Roland Barthes' words, 'the ideological abuse which, in my view, is hidden there' (1973, p. 126). This identification of inclusion/exclusion is equally evident in a country's national anthem and, in the case of 'The Star Spangled Banner' (which is sung each morning by American schoolchildren) this works to build a feeling of belonging to one's country and what this means in terms of patriotic sentiment – America right or wrong, and certainly an unflinching commitment to one's duty which may necessitate sacrifice or even death. It is significant to note, in this context, the stand made by black American athletes at the 1972 Olympic Games in Munich, Germany. This time, when the national anthem was played, they stood with one arm raised in the Black Power salute and with their feet bare, symbolizing their history as slaves in a country characterized, ostensibly, by equality.

The words 'symbolic' and 'symbolized' are significant here. In many ways bare feet, the Black Power salute and the American national anthem suggest a conflicting symbolism. It is certainly salutary to consider just how many young black men were conscripted to the war in Vietnam – to fight for *their* country – while so many rights were being denied them – a point I will return to later.

Clearly, the words of 'The Star Spangled Banner' overflow with patriotic emotion. It was written by Francis Scott Key and reflects his feelings when watching the British bombardment of Fort McHenry on the night of 13–14 September 1814, prior to the attack on Baltimore: 'While the bombardment continued, it was proof that the fort had not surrendered. But suddenly the bombardment ceased, and it was not known whether the fort had surrendered or the attack upon it had been abandoned' (Fuld, 1966, p. 435). At dawn, having paced the deck all night, he turned his telescope to the fort and saw that the flag was still there. On his way to shore, to secure the release of a friend under the flag of truce, he finished the poem, arriving at Baltimore from the ship on the evening of 17 September. A broadsheet of the poem was printed the next day under the title 'Defence of Fort McHenry' and a copy was given to every individual at the fort. The opening phase – 'O, say can you see by the dawn's early light' – is one we are all familiar with and establishes a heroic narrative which links flag to nation. No small wonder, then, that the gigantic shell-holed 'The Star Spangled Banner' continues to be a leading attraction at the Smithsonian Institution, Washington, DC.

The meaning of the music, however, is more problematic. Music means everything and nothing simultaneously. It is an abstract form, a rhythmic and dynamic arrangement of sounds within a structured whole. However, the melody of the American national anthem does follow certain well-established compositional procedures for songs that are intended for mass singing: a memorable tune with balanced phrases and contrasting sections which follow the shift in emphasis, the change of mood in the lyrics; a melody that stays within a limited and singable vocal range; and a move to an emotional climax as the song nears its end. In common with the British national anthem, 'The Star Spangled Banner' is in 3–4 time – a waltz – but with an equal emphasis on each beat of the bar that moves it towards a march, appropriate to its militaristic associations. In this connection it is, of course, a clear advantage that the tune works equally well within a purely instrumental genre.

The melody itself is not unique to 'The Star Spangled Banner'. It was originally known as *The Anacreontic Song* (but with F natural rather than F sharp in bar 3) and had been published in London, 1779–80.[4] By 1820 it had been used as the setting for about 50 printed American poems, almost all of a patriotic nature, including one by Key to commemorate Stephen Decatur's triumph in the war with Tripoli in which the phrase 'By the Light of the star-spangled flag of our nation' appears.[5]

The melody, then, brings with it a history of patriotic fervour. Those at Woodstock may well have been unaware of this, but nevertheless immediately felt its status and sentiment – 'what-goes-without-saying'. Certainly for Americans it is the most familiar of all songs, one which speaks of 'the land of the free', the 'home of the brave' – sentiments that are intended to inspire a nation at war.

Turning now, to the video of Hendrix's performance of 'The Star Spangled Banner' – considered by so many to be the most complex and powerful work of American art to deal with the Vietnam War and its effects on successive generations of the American psyche – it is important to note that this was not his only performance but, rather, his best known (Shaar-Murray, 1989, p. 224). It is also significant that Woodstock was a festival dedicated to celebrating 'Three Days of Peace with Music'. As such, Hendrix's choice of 'The Star Spangled Banner' as the climax to his set was no spontaneous gesture. Rather, as Bob Hicks comments in his memorial article to Hendrix, 'he sculpted an electronic musical monument as carefully composed and finely rehearsed as any orchestral concert piece. It was a chillingly contemporary work, a vision of cultural crisis, of structural breakdown and chaos, screeching to an almost unbearable tension which must, somehow, burst' (Hicks, 1970 [1996], p. 209).

Hendrix was certainly aware of the problems confronting black service-men in Vietnam. He, himself, had earlier been conscripted to the 101st Airborne Division (aka 'Screaming Eagles') which had been assigned to Vietnam in 1965. By this time, Hendrix had been honourably discharged following a training injury in the autumn of 1962, but he certainly knew the score as far as the position of black GIs were concerned: they represented 2 per cent of the officers and were assigned 28 per cent of the combat missions (Shaar-Murray, 1989, p. 23). On New Year's Eve 1969, he had dedicated 'Machine Gun' to 'all the soldiers that are fightin' in Chicago, Milwaukee and New York . . . oh yes, and all the soldiers fightin' in Vietnam'[6] and 'The Star Spangled Banner' is equally focused in its onomatopoeic evoca-tion of the sounds of jungle warfare.

To begin with, Hendrix does not use the guitar in a traditional sense. Rather, he moves straight into crackling feedback 'manipulating the position of his body in relation to the mike and amplifiers' in order to get an overload which is then re-routed through the mike monitors' (Hen-derson, 1990, p. 245). This then generates an independent sound against which Hendrix plays the opening refrain – slightly out of pitch on '. . . the dawn's early light'. Even though the words are not sung, they are as familiar to the audience as the British national anthem is for me, and the feedback and sustain provide a commentary on the flag itself as, at the words 'broad stripes and bright stars', the sounds plummet and waiver. The attack, however, comes at the evocative 'rocket's red glare' where Hendrix creates the sound of a fighter plane 'coming out of a deep dive, the impact of bombs striking the earth and the cries of the Cambodian peasants' (ibid.). The straight melody finally comes through on 'gave proof through the night', and the anthem ends to the sounds of feedback and sustain and a final ear-shattering grind as the guitar strings are treated to a crude bottleneck slide against the mike stand. As Charles Shaar-Murray writes:

> . . . the ironies were murderous: a black man with a white guitar; a massive, almost white audience wallowing in a paddy field of its own making; the clear, pure, trumpet-like notes of the familiar melody struggling to pierce through clouds of tear-gas, the explosions of cluster-bombs, the screams of the dying, the crackle of flames, the heavy palls of smoke stinking with human grease, the hovering chatter of helicopters . . . It is utterly appropriate that Francis Ford Coppola hired Randy Hansen, a young guitarist whose act used to consist of note-for-note Hendrix reproductions in full wig and make-up, to contribute sedulously Hendrix-derived overkill to the soundtrack of an ambush scene in his 1979 Vietnam exorcism *Apocalypse Now*. (Shaar-Murray, 1989, p. 24.)

I would certainly agree with Hicks' accolade that:

> ... one man with one guitar said more in three and a half minutes about that particularly disgusting war and its reverberations than all the novels, memoirs and movies put together. It is an interpretation of history which permits no space for either the gung-ho revisionism of Sylvester Stallone and Chuck Norris or the solipsistic angst of Coppola and Oliver Stone. Rather it taps directly into the Vietnam experience to present 'a compelling musical allegory of a nation tearing itself apart. (Hicks, 1970 [1996], p. 195.)

So, what did the music mean, and did the crowd understand? While it is obviously impossible to say that those listening to Hendrix shared my interpretation, it is nevertheless suggested that the majority would have engaged with his performance, recognizing his style and possibly making some assumptions as to his personal philosophy and feelings about the civil rights movement and those engaged in the Vietnam War. Clearly, the melody itself is still recognizable, but the sheer volume of noise, the distortion, the blue note bends and swerves, sustain and feedback aurally attack the original three–four metre, the neatly balanced phrases, the uplift of the melodic line and, as such, the connotations of heroism associated with 'The Star Spangled Banner' are undercut by a mood of devastation. I would also add that this was no spontaneous improvisation. Rather, it was a thought-through personal statement with all the trademarks of Hendrix's performance style – the loud, sustained and full texture, the use of expressive timbral nuance, the avoidance of a rigid rock beat. It is also significant that he played alone and that there was no introduction to the song. Rather, he went straight in, suggesting an underlying confidence that the audience would recognize the significance of those first few bars. Hendrix, I believe, understood all too well who was paying the price in Vietnam and, as Bob Hicks (ibid.) observed, it was no wonder that he burned himself out: 'He looked too deep, too soon.' In his performance of 'The Star Spangled Banner' he showed us, and continues to show us, at least part of what he saw.

Notes

1. Steve Gilbert is a subscriber to 'Rocklist', a US e-mail network of academics dedicated to the discussion of popular music to which I belong. His response to my question concerning the significance of 'Fixin'-To-Die' is quoted in full here. Thanks Steve.
2. New York was not atypical: Cleveland, Chicago and Los Angeles were other examples of societies where technological advancement and modernisation resulted in urban deprivation and instability (see Whiteley, 2000, p. 174).
3. See Roland Barthes' relevant discussion of secondary signification in the photo

taken from the cover of the French magazine *Paris Match* (1955): 'I am at the barber's, and a copy of *Paris Match* is offered to me. On the cover, a young Negro in French uniform is saluting, with his eyes uplifted, probably fixed on the fold of the tricolour. All this is the meaning of the picture. But, whether naively or not, I see very well what it signifies to me' (Barthes, 1973, p. 11). As Barthes observed, he felt compelled to 'track down, in the decorative display of *what-goes-without-saying* the ideological abuse which, in my view, is hidden there' (ibid., p. 126).

4. The Anacreontic Society was a 'convivial' society in London in which concerts were given and songs were sung by its members. *The Anacreontic Song* was published 1779–80 by Longman and Broderip, 26 Cheapside, London, and the first edition states that the song is 'Sung at the Crown and Anchor Tavern in the Strand – the words by Ralph Tomlinson Esq., late President of the Society'. The price was 6d (old pence) (see Fuld, 1966, p. 434).

5. It is not insignificant that the choice of 'The Star Spangled Banner' as America's national anthem in 1931 provoked criticism by the Music Supervisor's Conference of America as reflecting a nation at war rather than a nation committed to peace and goodwill. Hendrix, then, was not alone in his attack on its overt militarism (see Fuld, 1966, p. 434).

6. Jimi Hendrix, Fillmore East, New York City, New Year's Eve (1969), cited in Shaar-Murray (1989, p. 22).

References

Barthes, R. (1973), *Mythologies*, London: Paladin.

Frith, S. (1996), *Performing Rites: On the Value of Popular Music*, Oxford: Oxford University Press.

Fuld, J.J. (1966), *The Book of World Famous Music: Classical, Popular and Folk*, New York: Crown Publishers Inc.

Garofalo, R. (1992), 'Popular Music and the Civil Rights Movement', in R. Garofalo (ed.), *Rockin' the Boat: Mass Music and Mass Movements*, Boston, MA: South End Press.

Goffman, E. (1971), *The Presentation of Self in Everyday Life*, Harmondsworth: Penguin.

Henderson, D. (1990), *The Life of Jimi Hendrix: 'Scuse Me While I Kiss the Sky*, rev. edn, London: Omnibus Press.

Hicks, B. (1970 [1996]), 'Jimi Hendrix: A Memorial (Northwest Passage, 29th September 1970)', in C. Potash (ed.), *The Jimi Hendrix Companion: Three Decades of Commentary*, New York: Schirmer.

Kerouac, Jack (1958), *The Dharma Bums*, London: Penguin.

Roszak, T. (1969), *The Making of a Counter-Culture: Reflections on the Technocratic Society and its Youthful Opposition*, London: Faber and Faber.

Shaar-Murray, C. (1989), *Crosstown Traffic: Jimi Hendrix and Post-war Pop*, London: Faber and Faber.

Whiteley, S. (1997), 'Little Red Rooster v. The Honky Tonk Woman: Mick Jagger, Sexuality, Style and Image', in S. Whiteley (ed.), *Sexing the Groove: Popular Music and Gender*, London: Routledge.

Whiteley, S. (2000), *Women and Popular Music: Sexuality, Identity and Subjectivity*, London: Routledge.
Woodstock: Three Days of Music, Peace and Love. A Once-in-a-Lifetime Celebration, Warner Bros. Inc.: A Warner Communications Company (1970).

Chapter 3

'This is your Woodstock': Popular memories and political myths

John Street

Introduction

From the stage at Live Aid in 1985, opening the Philadelphia end of the media spectacle, Joan Baez announced to those watching: 'Good morning you children of the 80s. This is your Woodstock and it is long overdue.' With her history of political activism, her career as a singer of radical folk songs and her association with Bob Dylan, it seems fairly clear what Baez meant. She didn't mean, we can assume, 'Here are some great rock acts; I hope you enjoy them'. She meant, instead, that Live Aid was a major cultural and political event. Live Aid was a revival of the spirit of 1960s cultural politics. She wasn't just looking out at a sea of pop fans, at an audience; she was looking out at a political movement. Baez's Woodstock was the moment when all the dreams of flower power idealism coalesced into a single gesture that was to define a generation. Woodstock represented the triumph of 'peace and love'. The music, the musicians and the fans had somehow forged an alternative community (a 'Woodstock Nation'), one that opposed the dominant ideology. As the journalist Pete Hamill wrote at the time, 'the politics of Woodstock were anti-authoritarian, anti-establishment, anti-war' (quoted in Garofalo, 1997, p. 380). Live Aid, Baez appeared to suggest, offered the same prospect for the children of the 1980s. It was a blow against the empire of materialist individualism presided over by Margaret Thatcher and Ronald Reagan.

That, at least, is what it seems that Baez meant. But her pronouncement raises a number of interesting questions. Did her audience, for instance, draw the same inferences? What did 'Woodstock' mean to them? After all, Live Aid took place almost a generation later and was being witnessed by many more people than either gathered at Yasgur's Farm or saw the movie. And if 'Woodstock' meant something to the Live Aid audience, does it mean the same thing now, in the twenty-first century? In addition, Baez's pronouncement not only raises the question of whether Woodstock was the sort of event assumed by Baez – was it all 'peace and love'? – but also begs the question of what exactly 'Live Aid' was. In short, it may be that 'Woodstock' still has a place in popular memory and still features in the narratives of pop history, but *how* it features needs to be examined more closely. This chapter is an attempt to explore the memories and meanings of Woodstock, to see how its myths and realities form part of past and present cultural politics, and to explore the significance of it and Live Aid for the power of popular culture.

Remembering Woodstock

Woodstock lives on in a number of different ways and in a number of different places. It is not preserved and enshrined in a single form in a single place like a dinosaur skeleton in a natural history museum: its history is notoriously fuzzy. There is, after all, no agreement as to how many people there were actually there. Was it 500 000 (Friedlander, 1996; Osgerby, 1998); or 400 000 (Ward et al., 1987; Clarke, 1998), or 300 000 (Larkin, 1993; Shaar-Murray, 1989)? If there is no consensus on the number of people attending, there seems little chance of a unanimous view on any other aspect of the event. And while, in principle, it may be possible to establish a more accurate account of how many people were there, it would not get us much closer to understanding Woodstock. 'Woodstock' exists not as a single historical entity, but as a multiplicity of symbols and signs. It exists in many incarnations. It has to be understood as signifying many different experiences and ideas and moments. What follows is not an attempt at producing a definitive list, but merely a way of illustrating some of them by looking at the way in which the memory of Woodstock is preserved.

Woodstock on the web

'Woodstock' lives today, as do many past events, as a website. What is intriguing about current Woodstock websites is the aura of 'heritage' that pervades them. They are less concerned with the minute details of the performances in 1969, but rather with preserving the spirit of those days. The sites want to retain the mystique and aura of those distant days, to evoke the bucolic pleasures of communing with nature and with each other. There are web pages devoted, for example, to preserving the venue (a site of special cultural significance, as it were) for future generations. Other websites advertise memorabilia and memories (those of the Incredible String Band, for example). At the Woodstock Store (www.woodstock69.com/woodstock_gift.htm) you can buy, framed or unframed, a 'Set of Original

Single Day Woodstock Tickets', as well as Woodstock Zippo lighters and souvenir programmes of the event.

More intriguing are the memories recorded on the web by people whose mantra is 'I was there' (www.woodstock69.com/woodstock_mem.htm). They talk about meeting friends, of braving the cold, of the way they got there ('in my Fiat convertible') and the tiny details that sketch the experience for them (one person gave up smoking at Woodstock because the 'coolest' girl refused his offer of a Kool cigarette), but they also talk of the larger meaning Woodstock assumes in their lives. Woodstock was, Diana Vincelli writes, 'a turning point in life'. Juan Morales says of Woodstock that it epitomized the 'social changes in human freedom and expression ... we learned not to be ashamed of our bodies in the nude, we smoked grass to expand our horizons with the music, we spent time with our kids ... it was LIFE!!' Susan Harnisch-Jones reports: 'If Woodstock did anything for me, it gave me STRENGTH to state my beliefs.' In many accounts, Woodstock exists as a utopian moment: 'There was a feeling of community, a spirit of cooperation that touched everyone who was there. It may only have existed for a few days, but it lives on in some form in all of us' (Chris S.). Another insists: 'Woodstock was not a concert. This was a coming together ... Many people dropped out, stopped wearing and eating decaying animals, began to respect our setting' (Dr Jan Pitts). 'In my mind', writes Jimmy Wage, 'Woodstock was the biggest time I've ever had and most likely will ever have in my life.'

These accounts, written long after the event, are evidence both of the fact that Woodstock is being preserved on the web and of how it is being remembered, as a utopian moment, as a turning point, and as a highlight in lives being lived now. In all of these memories, the music features remarkably little. Even those who played at the festival say little about the sounds (the keyboard player of Sha Na Na, for example, remembers the 'COLD'). Instead, it is the political and social significance of Woodstock that animates the memories and the personal narratives in which it is located. As one of the visitors to the website argues, the same music as was heard at Woodstock was to be heard at many other festivals that summer (Jan Pitts): 'How could the music have had anything to do with it?' she asks. 'Some people never even found the main stage ... There was something much greater that pulled us together at Woodstock that day in August.'

Woodstock in the mass media

'Woodstock' also exists as a trope within contemporary journalism. It is a shorthand for describing any number of events at which people gather in large numbers, especially festivals: 'China's answer to Woodstock'; 'a Woodstock-style happening organised by the Social Democrats in Bonn';

'It's like Woodstock, only with advertisements'; 'like Woodstock . . . hopelessly planned'. When ex-President Bill Clinton addressed the Hay-on-Wye literary festival, he described it as 'the Woodstock of the mind'. 'Woodstock' also stands for a life-changing cultural event – the Sex Pistols' first gig, the opening of the club, Shoom: 'the event that was the Woodstock of its generation' (Tom Horan, *Daily Telegraph*, 30 March 2002). But its application does not end there. It is used to mark fashion design – 'Woodstock bikinis in Marie Claire', 'Country Joe fringes'. Or as one reporter noted of the tennis player André Agassi, 'he looks like he missed the last train to Woodstock . . . he's a tennis flower child gone to seed'. Woodstock is also used to describe film technique – 'Woodstock-like split-screen' – as well as to mark careers – 'Woodstock veteran' (Arlo Guthrie), 'the darling of the Woodstock set' (Joni Mitchell). It provides, too, a way of identifying eras and generations: 'It was the post-Woodstock, late-hippie, pre-Glitter period'; 'America's post-Woodstock generation'; 'Woodstock generation folkie parents'. 'Woodstock' is also used to authenticate a particular aesthetic: 'Kula Shaker try to emulate Jimi Hendrix at Woodstock'; 'a bit like Woodstock, only not so boring'.[1] Dismissing the band Queen, Michael Coveney wrote 'the whole point was that they were some camp old shambolic showbiz outfit miles removed from the true spirit of Elvis, the Beatles, the Stones, Woodstock, even Cliff Richard' (*Daily Mail*, 15 May 2002). In this case, Woodstock is used as a standard of worth, but it also represents the opposite. A review of Carlos Santana in *The Times* is headed 'Woodstock? It's still here, man' (10 June 2002).

If the website memories of Woodstock are almost exclusively devoted to its utopian, life-changing power, the mass media represent it as an altogether more ambiguous phenomenon – a symbol of success and failure, of the aesthetically good and bad. A similar picture emerges from popular memory.

Woodstock in the mind

In 1999, 30 years after Woodstock, I conducted a simple survey of 150 university students to see what 'Woodstock' signified for them. I asked them to write down the thoughts and associations that came into their minds when they saw the single word 'Woodstock'(see Table 3.1). I do not pretend that my sample was a representative one. All I wanted to establish was the *different* ways in which 'Woodstock' could exist. 'Drugs' and 'hippies' featured prominently, but so did 'Snoopy's friend'. As one of my respondents wrote: 'Large rock festival in a muddy field, full of people like my Mum and Dad consuming drugs.' Once again, the music seemed relatively insignificant (and some of the artists linked to Woodstock did not actually appear there – for example, Bob Dylan). These memories of the event chime with those recorded by the BBC documentary-maker Pete

Table 3.1 Woodstock and its associations

Word used	No. of uses (%) (n=429)
Drugs	49 (11.4)
Hippies	43 (10.0)
1960s festival	40 (9.3)
Snoopy's friend	36 (8.4)
Mud	32 (7.0)
Rock	32 (7.0)
Free love	26 (6.5)
Jimi Hendrix	20 (4.7)
Peace and love	13 (3.0)
America	12 (2.8)
Naked people	11 (2.6)
Protest/rebellion	7 (1.6)
Vietnam	4 (0.9)
Bob Dylan	4 (0.9)

Source: 2nd/3rd year undergraduates at University of East Anglia, 1999 (n=150).

Everett. One respondent told Everett of their image of Woodstock: 'Everybody took their clothes off at festivals. At Woodstock and even at the Isle of Wight a lot of people took their clothes off. And it was all right' (Everett, 1986, p. 100).

Not all memories are so partial or so trivialized. On one of the Woodstock websites (www.woodstock69.com/woodstock_mem.htm), someone too young to have been there – 'I wasn't even born until '73' – writes: 'Woodstock is no longer a place, but let this place be sacred, for it is where it all came together for so many people . . . It has nothing to do with drugs, or the music, or even Bethel, N.Y. It has to do with the people and their way of thinking, their way of loving and believing.' For this person, Woodstock exists as a symbolic resource, a way of thinking about the 'good life'. This use of Woodstock is not exclusive to its place of origin. According to Greil Marcus, the demonstrators in Tiananmen square justified themselves 'with images of Woodstock' (1993, pp. 380–81).

It is clear that, as with the mass media, Woodstock circulates within popular memory in a variety of forms and significances. It provides a model of a particular way of being and acting, but one that might be embraced or rejected. It is intriguing to see how this same tendency to use Woodstock to symbolize both the good and the bad is also reproduced within the writing of pop history.

Woodstock in pop history

The writing of pop history might be seen to constitute the official memories of Woodstock. What is evident (and not surprising) is that different histories give a different place to Woodstock, some making it central, some peripheral, and some ignoring it altogether. This is quite apart from their inability to agree on how many people were there.

To give an illustration of the different ways in which pop historians have recorded Woodstock, here is Colin Larkin, author of a vast encyclopaedia of pop and rock: 'the festival totally changed the world's attitude towards popular music'. If the Monterey festival represented the 'birth of the new music revolution, Woodstock was its coming of age' (Larkin, 1993, p. 1209). Charlie Gillett (1983, p. 403) sees Woodstock as bringing together the leading figures in rock and launching the careers of those still in the 'minor leagues'. Contrast this with *The Faber Book of Pop and Rock*, edited by Hanif Kureishi and Jon Savage (1995), in which there is no piece devoted to Woodstock, and in which the only references to it are perjorative (the 'Woodstock Nation' was 'a festival fantasy'; 'It [Woodstock] was so weak and stupid, and they believed it'; 'leftovers from the denimed Woodstock era'). In *Rock of Ages: The Rolling Stone History of Rock and Roll* (Ward et al., 1987), Woodstock is unfavourably compared to the 1965 TAMI Show, featuring the Beach Boys, James Brown, and Gerry and the Pacemakers. But, however badly Woodstock is treated in such books, its presence is acknowledged, whereas other similar events in the same year (Blind Faith in Hyde Park, a festival in Atlanta that attracted 140 000, and a three-day festival at Newport) are overlooked. The way in which Woodstock is written about in pop history – and this is symptomatic of the genre – is largely in terms of its musical contribution (the careers it established). This is in striking contrast to the way in which it is remembered in other media, where the emphasis is on its social and political significance. But, then again, this is not reflected in the social and political histories of the period.

Woodstock in social and political history

Eric Hobsbawm's (1995) account of the twentieth century, for instance, makes no mention of Woodstock. In his history of the 1960s, Jonathon Green is wary of the 'hyperbolic assessments' provoked by Woodstock, and sees it serving more to fuel hippy 'fantasies of an alternative culture'. He continues, 'It was the supreme counter-cultural feelgood event', concluding with a more mundane judgement: 'It combined dope and sex and rock'n'roll, . . . love and peace, . . . self-sufficiency and vegetarian cooking' (Green, 1998, p. 436).

This tone is echoed elsewhere in other historical narratives. It is striking how little attention is given to Woodstock in the *political* history of the time, at least in those accounts written by political activists of the traditional kind. Tariq Ali's *Street Fighting Years: An Autobiography of the Sixties* (1987) contains no mention of Woodstock. George McKay, who in his book *Senseless Acts of Beauty* traces the Free Festival movement, argues that Woodstock happened too soon to influence the British festival movement and quotes this pessimistic reading of 1969 from the *International Times*: 'Woodstock is the potentiality but Altamont is the reality' (McKay, 1996, p. 14). Nonetheless, McKay does concede that Woodstock is important to the history of free festivals. What is important about this historical placement of Woodstock is, of course, that it neither reflects Baez's evocation of it nor the intention of those who organized it (they were intending it to be a paying event). In his account of the British underground of the 1960s, Nigel Fountain reports a similar wariness about Woodstock's legacy, quoting one jaundiced commentator: 'Woodstock . . . had a lot to answer for. It caused such damage everyone tried to emulate it' (Fountain, 1988, p. 116).

Michael Clarke, in his study of the politics of pop festivals, accords Woodstock a quite different, if no less unflattering, legacy. Woodstock served to demonstrate to the authorities that a peaceful festival was a possibility and that moral panic was unnecessary. Clarke writes:

> Woodstock was eagerly promoted as the festival of peace and love, a demonstration that large numbers of young people could congregate without violence and disorder despite the forebodings of the authorities and in the context of substantial youth participation in the anti-Vietnam War movement and the civil rights campaign in the USA. (Clarke, 1982, p. 36.)

This first part of this chapter has provided an account of the ways in which 'Woodstock' is remembered and the ways in which it circulates as an idea in contemporary culture. We have seen the conflicting claims, ambiguities and manifold incarnations that define 'Woodstock'. The second part of the chapter turns to another aspect of Joan Baez's pronouncement: the politics of the event itself. Baez was not just appealing to a memory of the event, she was also making claims for the way such events operate politically.

Woodstock, Live Aid and the performance of politics

Joan Baez was not the only person to link Woodstock to Live Aid; many other commentators did the same. Paul Friedlander (1996), for instance, sees a natural continuity between the two. What is revealing is *how* they do this. For some, the division is marked by the difference between the authentic (Woodstock) and the inauthentic (Live Aid), between principle and the cash nexus. One historian of US popular music, Reebee Garofalo, praises Woodstock while damning Live Aid. He writes: 'Woodstock was experienced as participatory, communitarian and non-commercial (indeed anti-commercial), with no great spiritual or physical distance between artist and audience' (Garofalo, 1992, p. 15). Woodstock, he claims, mediated between folk culture values and mass culture commercialism, forging in the process the 'Woodstock nation'. Live Aid, by contrast, was simply 'an unabashed celebration of technological possibilities' (ibid.). Live Aid was neither counter-cultural nor oppositional. Woodstock humanized mass culture, while Live Aid was part of the international star-making system, revealed in its commercial sponsorship (Pepsi) (Garofalo, 1997). Garofalo's arguments echo those of other commentators (for example, Rijven et al., 1985; Marcus, 1989) whose criticisms are as occupied with Live Aid's political failings as with its musical ones. Live Aid is seen to represent the interests of a self-satisfied entertainment elite.

But to voice such scepticism is not necessarily to dismiss Live Aid completely. Take Will Straw, for example. Addressing a group of popular music scholars on the day before the Live Aid event, Straw said: 'I take it for granted that most of us here find the various charity projects tasteless, self-serving for those involved, symptomatic of existing geo-political relations and politically inappropriate, and that we never much liked Bob Geldof anyway' (Rijven, et al., 1985, p. 25). But Straw went on to draw attention to the ways in which musicians' capacity to raise money for, or awareness of, worthy causes should not be overlooked or discounted.

I do not want here to comment at length on the rival political claims to be made for Live Aid or Woodstock, but instead use this discussion as a backdrop to some thoughts about how we might make sense of the politics of Woodstock (and other such events). In doing this, it is important to consider the political rhetoric that shapes such events, and the ways in which politics are acted out and organized into them.

Politics as rhetoric and ideology

One important aspect of politics is the attempt to get people to see their interests and their experiences in one way or another. And one aspect of the contrast made between Woodstock and Live Aid is the attempt to represent them as embodying conflicting sets of ideas. Many of the memories of Woodstock that we discussed earlier, together with the representation of it offered by Garofalo, see it as embodying an ethos of communitarianism and as standing in opposition to the individualism–capitalism of Live Aid. By this account, Woodstock constituted its audience as citizens of a collectivity, while Live Aid represented them as consumers of a service. But although Woodstock may indeed have given voice to a communitarian philosophy, the same can be claimed for Live Aid. Dick Hebdige, for example, argues that Live Aid gave voice to a strongly anti-Thatcherite critique of selfish individualism and appealed to a collective identity which challenged the libertarian politics of the time. He writes of Live Aid as 'the articulation of a different version of "common-sense" drawing on traditions of co-operation and mutual support, rooted in the human(e) values of good fellowship and good neighbourliness' (Hebdige, 1988, p. 219).

Equally, Woodstock's own ideological rhetoric was not confined to the communitarianism of folk memory. The festival was, in contemporary parlance, 'spun', and one of the spin doctors was the Yippie activist Abbie Hoffman. It was reported that Hoffman secured $10 000 from the organizers to promote Woodstock as a radical event (Spitz, 1979, p. 167). Hoffman 'periodically descended upon [Michael Lang's] office shouting anticapitalist war cries' and, in the end, Lang realized: that '[w]e need those cats on our side . . . They're pretty groovy guys to have around, and they have a direct line to the underground which'd be invaluable to us. If they're in our corner, we can't miss' (Spitz, 1979, pp. 164–65). Meanwhile, political radicals at Woodstock printed and distributed leaflets which quoted Eldridge Cleaver and Bob Dylan. Hoffman went on to publish *Woodstock Nation* (a contrast to *Pig Nation*), promoting the event's claim to a radical agenda. It is worth remembering, too, that Woodstock was not originally a 'free festival'; it became one by default. In short, we need to be wary of taking the rhetoric of the events at face value; many conflicting ideologies lie close to the surface.

Politics as organization

A second claim made for Woodstock is that it did not just give voice to a particular world-view, but that this was part of its organizational practice. This is what is implied by Garofalo's comment on the lack of barriers between performers and audience. Once again, it is important to be cautious of mistaking appearance for reality. Robert Spitz's (1979) detailed history of Woodstock, *Barefoot in Babylon*, tells a tale of entrepreneurial endeavour and smart business practice. In a sense, it was the commercial interests appeased, the contracts signed and the deals struck that produced 'Woodstock'. Dave Marsh reports, for instance, how Michael Lang refused to pay acts because the event was now a 'free festival', despite the fact that they had 'collected more than $1 million on film rights, recording rights and ticket sales' (1983, p. 349). Lang also refused to book the then highly politicized John Lennon and the Plastic Ono Band, having been offered their services when he approached Lennon in an attempt to book The Beatles, who would have been a significant commercial draw for the festival. Apart from Spitz's book, however, there is little detailed evidence of how Woodstock was organized, so it is difficult to draw any very certain conclusions about its organizational politics. What we can note, however, is that we should treat any claims for its democratic credentials with scepticism.

Politics as performance

Politics is part of performance as well as rhetoric and organization, and Woodstock provided a number of platforms for performing politics. The most obvious of these were to be found in the songs: for example, Country Joe MacDonald's 'I-Feel-Like-I'm-Fixin'-to-Die' or Richie Havens' 'Freedom', both of which had explicitly political texts. In the same way, the famous stage announcements – about the birth of babies or the beauty of the audience or the free food – these, too, constituted a sense of political community.

But politics can be performed in other ways. There was the moment when Abbie Hoffman was brutally turfed off the stage by Pete Townshend of The Who: 'Townshend put one of his Dr Marten boots squarely into Hoffman's ass, swatted him with his Gibson SG and, as the Yippie fell into the photographers' pit, played on . . . Townshend later described kicking Abbie's ass as "the most political thing I ever did"' (Marsh, 1983, p. 350). Whatever its place in the pantheon of political gestures, Townshend's act, and his claim for it, point to the idea that singing and speaking about politics do not exhaust the ways in which politics becomes part of performance.

One aspect is *who* is performing – who is seen and heard. An example of this is the marginalization of women as performers (particularly in the filmed record of Woodstock). Only two women performed solo (Melanie and Joan Baez), and the other women to be seen were Janis Joplin, Grace Slick of Jefferson Airplane and Licorice McKecknie and Rose Simpson of the Incredible String Band. The women's marginalization was further highlighted by the way in which they disappeared from the film version. Women were not the only people to be made notable by their absence. Sly Stone was one of the few acts with a substantial African-American following, but he too was omitted from the final film (Garofalo, 1997, p. 234).

The significance of these omissions lie self-evidently in the way careers were promoted or thwarted by the decisions of record companies, film producers and impresarios. The 'politics' of Woodstock can be read from the exercise of power to include and exclude access to a particular good (in this case, the opportunity to perform or be seen to perform). But the politics of the event do not end with who is chosen and who is not. There is also a politics of performing: of how those on stage present themselves and model their audience.

In 2002, in Britain, Queen Elizabeth II celebrated her Golden Jubilee. One of the events organized to commemorate this was a concert held in the gardens of Buckingham Palace. It began with guitarist Brian May (of the other Queen) standing on the battlements playing the national anthem. As he postured and grimaced in the evening breeze, his efforts prompted a direct comparison with Hendrix's rendition of 'The Star Spangled Banner'. Hendrix's Woodstock performance has been read as politically radical, as challenging US imperialism and fuelling domestic dissent. Charles Shaar-Murray describes 'the stately unreeling of the melody derailed by the sounds of riot and war, sirens and screams, chaos and alarm' (1989, p. 195). May's version of 'God Save the Queen' was, by contrast, a tribute to the UK's monarchic dynasty. Hendrix's performance is described and analysed in much more detail elsewhere in this book (see Chapter 2). My point here is simply that, by contrasting these two moments in pop history, it is possible to indicate how two very different politics might emerge from similar examples.

These moments in the constitution and politics of a community were underpinned by the more strategic thinking of the organizers. Spitz describes how Lang and others assembled the running order for the event. They 'arrived at a formula for the sequence whereby Friday evening would showcase folk-oriented artists to build the audience's enthusiasm slowly and to ease them into their new surroundings' (Spitz, 1979, p. 177). It was thought that 'presenting an acid rock show the first night might whip the kids into an uncontrollable frenzy, and, at all costs, they wanted to avoid a riotous mood' (ibid.).

All these elements – rhetoric and ideology, organization, performance – helped construct the politics of the event – give it particular meanings – including those upon which Baez drew at Live Aid. They provide a framework for making sense of Woodstock's politics and for comparison with Live Aid. They do not, of course, have any necessary impact on the way people think of either, or how they interpret Baez's pronouncement.

The Political significance of Woodstock

The politics of Woodstock are undoubtedly confused and ambiguous, whether we talk about the memories it evokes, the legacies it left, or indeed its place in the history of the late 1960s. For some, Woodstock fits comfortably into the story of the commercialization of rock. The rock impresario, Bill Graham, once remarked that 'the real thing that Woodstock accomplished was that it told people that rock was big business' (quoted in Wiener, 1984, p. 104). But there are other ways of reading Woodstock's role. Robert Hewison (1988), for example, sees it as clearing a space for practising the hippy ideal. It provided both legitimacy and opportunity for the other ways of being. A similar claim is made by Bill Osgerby who sees Woodstock as instrumental in the formation of group identities which helped sustain commitment to 'alternative lifestyles' (1998, p. 89). These interpretations do not derive from some systematic analysis of the impact of Woodstock or from within some well-developed theoretical framework. There is, to my knowledge, little on the former, and one of the few attempts at such theoretical work, such as that by Ron Eyerman and Andrew Jamison (1998), says nothing about Woodstock. Nonetheless, it is evident that work on the new social movements, like that by Eyerman and Jamison or by Christian Lahusen (1996), does suggest fruitful ways of locating Woodstock within the processes of social and political change.

Eyerman and Jamison argue that there is a need to connect cultural and political processes. Music and musicians serve to articulate – to bear witness to – the political concerns of a movement, while the movement simul- taneously gives meaning to the music. As they write, 'by combining culture and politics, social movements serve to reconstitute both, providing a broader political and historical context for cultural expression, and offering, in turn, the resources of culture – traditions, music, artistic expression – to the action repertoires of political struggle' (Eyerman and Jamison, 1998, p. 7). Wood- stock, by this account, becomes both producer and product of the politics that coexisted with it. This happens, suggests Lahusen (1996), through the distribution and deployment of various forms of capital – economic, social and cultural. Without these resources, events like Woodstock cannot take place. It is not just a matter of money, although this is important, but also of who is connected to who and whether they can be persuaded to participate (and how their participation is viewed by others). In this sense, Woodstock is the consequence of a political process, to be understood and analysed in the way that other such policy outcomes and political movements are to be understood.

Conclusion

To return to Joan Baez for the last time. She was both right and wrong when she announced to that audience in 1985: 'This is your Woodstock.' As we have seen, 'Woodstock' has multiple meanings and is invested with very different political interpretations. Some of these make 'This is your Woodstock' a badge of political pride: you are changing the world; you are challenging the dominant order. It could equally be a badge of shame: you are a pawn in the carefully contrived machinations of a sophisticated marketing exercise. Either of these interpretations might make Baez right, although only the first would do so in the way she intended. She might, though, be wrong. It might be that Woodstock changed the world, whereas Live Aid left it exactly as it found it. Or vice versa. The weight of critical opinion clearly tends to favour the former interpretation, and would prefer not to see Woodstock tainted by association with Live Aid. Arguably, though, Live Aid has, in fact, had the greater impact on both politics and popular music. Woodstock may have politicized rock for a moment, but it was 'rock' very narrowly conceived and 'politics' of almost utopian vacuity. Live Aid, by contrast, created the conditions for the politicization of mass entertainment (think of the millions who saw Live Aid as it happened). It gave political significance to pop very broadly conceived (think of the artists and genres that inhabited those stages in London and Philadelphia). It made a difference (think of the money raised and the lives saved). Without Live Aid, it would be impossible to understand Bono's campaign to end Third World debt, which sees him in earnest conversation with Prime Minister Tony Blair, President Chirac, President Bush and the pope. By comparison, Woodstock exists largely as a folk memory and one that is, at best, confused. Woodstock is recalled, in the words of one of the students I polled, as 'drugs, mud, snoopy, 60s, hippies'. Such myths contribute much to the history and character of popular music, but they bequeath less, it might be argued, to popular music's engagement with politics.

Note

1. This and all the previous quotations in this section are taken from the *Guardian* or *Observer* in 1998, unless otherwise attributed.

References

Ali, T. (1987), *Street Fighting Years: An Autobiography of the Sixties*, London: Collins.

Clarke, D. (1998), *The Penguin Encyclopaedia of Popular Music*, 2nd edn, London: Penguin

Clarke, M. (1982), *The Politics of Pop Festivals*, London: Junction Books.

Everett, P. (1986), *You'll Never be 16 Again*, London: BBC Publications.

Eyerman, R. and Jamison, A. (1998), *Music and Social Movements: Mobilizing Traditions in the Twentieth Century*, Cambridge: Cambridge University Press.

Fountain, N. (1988), *Underground: The London Alternative Press 1966–74*, London: Comedia.

Friedlander, P. (1996), *Rock and Roll: A Social History*, Boulder, Co: Westview Press.

Garofalo, R. (1992), 'Understanding Mega-Events: If We Are the World, Then How Do We Change It?', in R. Garofalo (ed.), *Rockin' the Boat: Mass Music and Mass Movements*, Boston, MA: South End Press.

Garofalo, R. (1997), *Rockin' Out: Popular Music in the USA*, Boston, MA: Allyn and Bacon.

Gillett, C. (1983), *The Sound of the City*, rev. edn, London: Souvenir Press.

Green, J. (1998), *All Dressed Up: The Sixties and the Counterculture*, London: Jonathan Cape.

Hebdige, D. (1988), *Hiding in the Light: On Images and Things*, London: Routledge.

Hewison, R. (1988), *Too Much: Art and Society in the Sixties 1960–75*, London: Methuen.

Hobsbawm, E. (1995), *Age of Extremes: The Short Twentieth Century 1914–1991*, London: Abacus.

Kureishi, H. and Savage, J. (eds) (1995), *The Faber Book of Pop and Rock*, London: Faber.

Lahusen, C. (1996), *The Rhetoric of Political Protest*, Berlin: Walter de Guyer.

Larkin, C. (1993), *The Guinness Encyclopaedia of Popular Music* (Concise Edition), London, Guinness Publishing.

McKay, G. (1996), *Senseless Acts of Beauty: Cultures of Resistance Since the Sixties*, London: Verso.

Marcus, G. (1989), 'We are the World?', in A. McRobbie (ed.), *Zoot Suits and Second-hand Dresses*, Basingstoke: Macmillan.

Marcus, G. (1993), *In the Fascist Bathroom*, London: Penguin.

Marsh, D. (1983), *Before I Get Old: The Story of The Who*, London: Plexus.

Osgerby, B. (1998), *Youth in Britain Since 1945*, Oxford: Blackwell.

Rijven, S., Marcus, G. and Straw, W. (1985), *Rock for Ethiopia*, IASPM Working Paper 7.

Shaar-Murray, C. (1989), *Crosstown Traffic: Jimi Hendrix and Post-war Pop*, London: Faber and Faber.

Spitz, R.S. (1979), *Barefoot in Babylon: The Creation of the Woodstock Music Festival, 1969*, New York: Viking Press.

Ward, E., Stokes, G. and Tucker, K. (1987), *Rock of Ages: The Rolling Stone History of Rock and Roll*, London: Penguin.

Wiener, J. (1984), *Come Together: John Lennon in his Time*, New York: Random House.

Chapter 4

'Everybody's happy, everybody's free': Representation and nostalgia in the *Woodstock* film

Andy Bennett

> ... that film [Woodstock] brought the festival to the rest of the world in a very real sense. I mean, whatever happened in the microcosm up there was brought very viscerally to the rest of the world ... because of the film. (Michael Lang, Woodstock festival co-organizer cited in Lang, 1999, p. 251.)

At the time of its release, the film *Woodstock* was something of a 'must see' for many who had been unable to get to the actual event. Shot entirely on location, the film is one of the very few, and certainly the most comprehensive, visual documents of the Woodstock festival. In addition to the wealth of music featured, although it is widely held that many classic performances never made it on to the final cut of the film (see Logan and Woffinden, 1976),[1] *Woodstock* also purports to capture something of the atmosphere of the festival. Between sequences of performance, young festivalgoers are caught on film dancing, eating, playing in the mud and swimming naked in lakes on the festival site. The film also includes footage from interviews with some of those attending the festival, who openly express their feelings about the Woodstock event, their motivation for being there and their views on the general state of the world as it was during the late 1960s. The often spontaneous phrases caught on film have since become part of a canonized body of knowledge concerning Woodstock, the hippie movement and the late 1960s more generally.

This chapter will examine and evaluate the significance of the *Woodstock* film as both a visual document of the Woodstock festival and a focus for nostalgia concerning the event and the wider socio-cultural context of the hippie movement. The first section of the chapter deals with the making of the film, its status as one of the first 'rockumentaries' and the film-makers' innovative use of the split-screen effect to convey particular representations of the Woodstock festival to the cinema audience. This will be followed by a consideration of the *Woodstock* film's role in constructing the myth of the rock community (Frith, 1981). The final section of the chapter examines how audiences today interpret Woodstock, and how the film evokes feelings of nostalgia typified through the harking back to a 'golden age' of youth culture (Bennett, 2001).

The making of the *Woodstock* film

In his candid account of events surrounding the making of *Woodstock*, associate producer Dale Bell recalls the anxieties of the hastily assembled film crew as they drove out of New York City on their way to the festival site. Bell describes the experience as 'a trip with a destination in the unknown, a synthesis somewhere between vision and technology. Or, perhaps, a potential catastrophe' (1999, p. 59). As Bell explains, while some of the crew were seasoned professionals, skilled in the art of film-making, others had very little experience at all. According to Bell, however, any lack of skill was compensated by the raw enthusiasm possessed by each member of the film crew for the task they were about to undertake. The filming itself was an allegedly challenging experience for all involved. Even acquiring the required amount of raw stock – 'enough to be able to shoot for 175 hours' – with the limited financial resources and finding a way to protect this and other equipment 'from other people and the elements' would prove in itself to be a difficult task (ibid., p. 65). Also, the huge scale of the Woodstock event meant that the relatively small film crew invariably found itself overstretched. As Elen Orson, who was involved in both the on-site filming and the editing of the film, explains how, upon learning that she was at Woodstock, people often 'ask if I had any of the Brown Acid . . . little do they know, there was no time for acid, aspirin, food, or anything; just work' (1999, p. 169).[2]

The editing of the film footage proved similarly arduous. Extensive amounts of footage had to be sorted into batches according to artist and song and then synchronized with the matching soundtrack recording. Orson describes the experience of working on such a huge and complex task with the limited editing equipment available during the late 1960s as 'like slashing your way through the jungle with a machete' (ibid., p. 168). While footage of some artists was relatively easy to edit, with mouth and hand movements providing indicators as to which song, or section of a song, was being performed, other footage proved far more difficult to work with. In commenting on her experience of editing footage of the Indian sitar player Ravi Shankar's performance, Orson notes: 'There were no vocals, no lips to read, no flashy rock-and-roll moves, nothing to establish a point of correspondence. Just five people sitting calmly making many, many hand movements' (ibid., p. 168).

Woodstock was officially released in March 1970 by Warner Bros Pictures who had bought the distribution rights to the film for $1 million (Young and Lang, 1979). Critical responses to the film were mixed. As Denisoff and Romanowski observe: '*Variety* called it "an absolute triumph in the marriage of cinematic technology to reality." *Sight and Sound* considered the Warner Brothers release "a revolutionary hybrid of commercial and underground cinema". Canby thought it was "somewhat less extraordinary than the event it preserves"' (1991, pp. 714–15; see also Schowalter, 2000). Nevertheless, *Woodstock* proved an immense financial success story with worldwide box office takings grossing in excess of $50 million by the beginning of 1979. Indeed, Turbeville has since suggested that *Woodstock* could be seen as a crucial precursor to the music video, the 'box-office success [of the film] alert[ing] record company executives to the increasing power of performance to sell product' (1999, p. 177).

Woodstock as rockumentary

> . . . we all had a great desire to get it right, not to leave it to the network guys or the big studio guys who may or may not understand its value in society. The film had to be made by young hip people who would not interpret, or misinterpret it, but allow it to flow through their hands. (Orson, 1999, p. 168.)

As the above comment by Elen Orson reveals, throughout the shooting and production of *Woodstock* there was a determination on the part of those involved to create an authentic document of the event. According to Orson, there was a common understanding among those involved in the making of *Woodstock* that the integrity of the final product would largely be assured by the connectedness of the film team's involvement in, and empathy with, the hippie culture of the late 1960s. Clearly, however, although a compelling document of the Woodstock festival, the compressing of a three-day event into a three and a half hour film was possible only through the exercise of considerable artistic licence on the part of director, Michael Wadleigh, and his production team. In effect, *Woodstock* is an early example of what is now commonly referred to as a rock documentary or 'rockumentary'.

According to Renov (1993), one of the key aspects of the documentary technique is the manner in which it allows for the recomposition of sound and images in ways designed to produce a particular ordering and presentation of events. Consequently, all documentaries are, by the very nature of their production, selective picturings of events rather than truly representational accounts. The content of a documentary will depend on a range of factors, including technical equipment used, the experience of the film crew, filming conditions and, most importantly, the subjectivity of those involved in the editing and final production stages of the documentary-making process. Thus, as Renov observes:

> Every documentary representation depends upon its own detour from the real, through the defiles of the audio-visual signifier (via choices of language, lens, proximity, and sound environment). The itinerary of a truth's passage (with 'truth' understood as prepositional and provisional) for the documentary is, thus, qualitatively akin to that of fiction ... there is nothing inherently less creative about nonfictional representations, both may create a 'truth' of the text. (Renov, 1993, p. 7.)

Read in the context of this interpretation, it becomes clear that *Woodstock* portrays not so much the 'reality' of the Woodstock event as a series of impressions, selectively picked out from the hours of film footage shot on location, the choice of footage used in the final cut of the film being informed by artistic and/or personal value judgements concerning the quality of fit between the representation and the actual event.

An illustrative example of such artistic licence of the part of the Woodstock production team is Country Joe McDonald's rendition of 'Fixin'-To-Die', a powerful anti-Vietnam War song that assumed anthemic properties as a result of its inclusion in the film (see also Chapters 2 and 8). In the now legendary film sequence of Country Joe's Woodstock performance, subtitled lyrics are added at the bottom of the screen, urging cinema audiences to sing along with the satirical chorus lyric:

> And it's one, two, three what are we fighting for,
> Don't ask me I don't give a damn, the next stop is Vietnam,
> And it's five, six, seven, open up the pearly gates,
> Don't ask me to wonder why, whoopee we're all gonna die . . .

However, it is not only this simple editing trick that enhances the song's inclusion in Woodstock, but also its positioning in relation to the running of the film. As Country Joe MacDonald himself explains elsewhere in this book, his solo performance at Woodstock[3] actually took place at the beginning of the event, the scheduled opening performances by electric groups having been put back because of difficulties in getting their equipment to the festival site. Country Joe volunteered his services, was hastily provided with a guitar and ushered on to the stage. In the final cut of the film, 'Fixin'-to-Die' appears midway into the film, editorial technique transforming a spontaneous and impromptu opening performance into a centrally defining spectacle of the Woodstock event. The moment when Country Joe appears on the cinema screen is dramatically punctuated by his infamous 'F Cheer' crowd-raiser. Due to the artistry of editorial technique, in the film this appears to be a meticulously articulated gesture designed to move an already adrenalized audience on to a higher plane of counter-cultural fervour. As Country Joe explains, however, the reality of the situation was quite different:

> You don't see in the film that I had been on stage for 25 minutes before that, and that no one paid any attention to me. But when I realized that no one was paying any attention, and they were all having a good time talking to each other, then I went, 'Gimme an F!' And then, it seemed to me as though every single person in that audience stopped talking, looked at me and yelled, 'F!' (McDonald, 1999, p. 222.)

A further instance of artistic editing in *Woodstock* is seen in Dale Bell's account of what became known as the 'Port-O-San Sequence'. This involves an interview with a Port-O-San toilet cleaner at the Woodstock festival site. During the course of the interview, the Port-O-San employee offers an apparently spontaneous personal reflection: 'Happy to do this for these kids. I have one here and one in Vietnam.' Bell and fellow members of the film production team felt that this single gesture summed up perfectly the spirit of the Woodstock event and the period in which it took place, and thus elected to include it in the film. In actuality however, the interview sequence only appeared in the final cut of the film due to a degree of creative intervention on the part of the editing team. As Bell recalls:

> When this portrait arrived in the editing room, there never was a question that it would find its way into the documentary portion of the movie . . . Yet it almost didn't make it, not because of the content but because of the sound. In spite of all the patching of cords, pushing of buttons, sliding of dials, they could not isolate the dialogue of the scene from all the junk noise in the background . . . Recalling our use of the bouncing ball over the lyrics in the Country Joe MacDonald [sequence], I suggested that we use subtitles to allow the audience to read along while they listened to the words. The combination might make the audience hear better. We all looked at each other. The mixers, the editors, all harkened to the idea. So it went off to the title company, preserved indelibly. (Bell, 1999, p. 120.)

Another aspect of *Woodstock*'s production that significantly enhances its representational power is the use of the split-screen effect. A short-lived innovation of the late 1960s, made famous through its use in the 1967 feature film *The Thomas Crown Affair* and also used in *Easy Rider*, the other defining film of the counter-cultural movement (see Denisoff and Romanowski, 1991), this technique literally involves the splitting of the screen into two smaller parallel screens, thus enabling two different sequences of film to be viewed simultaneously. The pairing of film sequences in this way allows for a number of different effects to be achieved. In *Woodstock* the split screen is used in two principal ways. First, it facilitates a more effective intercutting between the artists on stage and members of the audience, thus enhancing the feeling of performer/audience communication that many of those who attended believed to be central to the ethos of the Woodstock festival. This, in turn, facilitated the transference of this feeling to those who would later see the film in the cinema. Thus, as Wootton observes, 'intercutting between the stage and spectator can help establish an emotional identification between the "real" spectator participating in the atmosphere of a live event and the passive consumer watching the recorded performance' (1995, p. 95).

The second way in which the split-screen effect is used in *Woodstock* is to provide extra-visual commentary on points and observations made by those interviewed in the film. Thus, for example, an extended account by Woodstock co-organizer Artie Kornfeld on how the counter-cultural generation were rejecting the norms and values of the dominant society is accompanied in the parallel screen by a scene of a young couple retiring into long grasses on the festival site where they are seen to undress and lay down together, presumably to make love.

Woodstock and the myth of the rock community

A further aspect of *Woodstock*'s filmic significance lies in its promotion of sense of 'community', something which was inherently linked to the wider counter-cultural ideology of the late 1960s. As Frith explains, like the folk music revival of the early 1960s, the counter-culture grounded its notion of community in music, or rather in the power of music in bringing people together to share in a common cause. According to Frith, two basic assumptions were inherent in this musicalised construction of community: 'firstly the music was an authentic "reflection of experience"; secondly, the music reflected the experience of a community – there was no distinction of social experience between performers and audiences' (1981, p. 159). That rock music was deemed capable of playing such a pivotal role in the construction of a community has much to do with the way in which it was perceived by those who performed and listened to it during the late 1960s.

Thus, as Frith notes, despite its reliance on systems of mass production and mass communication, which tied it firmly in with the industrial logic of late capitalism, the rock music of the late 1960s enjoyed a status as an authentic, artistic form of expression that set it apart, in the minds of those who performed and listened to it, from commercial chart music (see Willis, 1978; Frith, 1983). This in turn engendered a feeling among rock audiences that their bonding with rock performers was one of 'community', and that the music produced by rock artists was *the* music of the counter-culture in that it communicated a message and cause endorsed by all of those with counter-cultural involvement – audiences and musicians alike. Some initial justification for this belief may have been garnered from the fact that, at least during the early stages of the 1960s rock movement, record companies, confused by the appeal of this new musical style, actively enlisted the help of young 'streetwise' hippies. Thus, as Harron observes:

> The record companies . . . were confused and even alarmed by the strange groups whose music was so profitable. Faced with a new and uncertain market, they were forced to loosen the reins and bring in young outsiders to tell them what would make a hit. (Harron, 1990, p. 184.)

The scenario described by Harron was, however, short-lived. As Frith and Horne note, by the late 1960s, rock groups such as Pink Floyd and Led Zeppelin had become 'so successful in selling high seriousness (for their fans this was the most flattering pop form) that any contradictions between creative and market forces seemed to be resolved' (1987, pp. 73–74). This point is clearly illustrated by Bill Graham, establisher of the Fillmore East (in New York) and Fillmore West (in San Francisco) that hosted perform-ances by some of the major rock acts of the late 1960s: 'An artist would get onstage and say: "Let's get together", . . . and fight and share and commu-nicate. Then he'd get into his jet and fly off to his island and play with his sixteen-track machine. It was hypocrisy' (Palmer, 1976, p. 247).

In every sense then, the notion of a counter-cultural community was a myth, maintained by the sheer belief of those involved that music could, in some way, represent their interests and, ultimately, change the world. This belief was widely shared among counter-cultural devotees, including those involved in the making of *Woodstock*. Moreover, the way in which the festival is represented in the film is clearly intended to portray the feeling of counter-cultural community that many felt the festival epitomized. As Schowalter observes: 'The film's split screen imagery and superimposed cinematography ensure that the viewer is never denied a view of the massive crowd, even as the camera portrays performers' (2000, pp. 88–89). Such shots are countenanced with anecdotal observations by featured performers, notably Arlo Guthrie's report from the stage that the New York State Freeway had been closed due to the congestion caused by cars full of people trying to get to the festival and that the festival site was, to all intents and purposes, a 'city' due to the sheer number of people in attendance. Similar expressions of community are forthcoming from festivalgoers themselves; at one point, an interviewer talks to a group of young men sitting naked in a shallow stream, one of whom reflects on the way in which the festival has provided a means of expression for an alternative counter-cultural voice, summed up in his observation: 'Everybody's happy, everybody's free'.

The activities building up to the festival featured in the film also do much to suggest the intended 'communal spirit' of the event to those watching from the vantage point of the cinema. Thus, as Schowalter observes:

> Seemingly driven by a cause greater than themselves, like worker ants, images of old and young laboring in fields, driving tractors, and building the mammoth stage potentially position the viewer to consider the unquestioned faith, the imperative of pulling 'this thing off'. (Ibid., p. 88.)[4]

Such representation continues as the festivalgoers begin to arrive and set up camp for the three days ahead. To the soundtrack of Canned Heat's 'Goin' Up The Country', itself a celebration of the rustic ideals that underpinned the counter-culture's rejection of technocratic urban living (Roszak, 1969), the viewer is treated to 'a montage of people smoking marijuana, drinking alcohol, and dancing' (ibid.).

Woodstock and nostalgia

As noted at the beginning of this chapter, at the time of its release *Woodstock* was intended to provide an accurate audio-visual document of the festival for a global audience. More significantly, however, the film was, and remains, one of the most compelling exposés of the late 1960s counter-culture and the music that inspired it. In the early years of the twenty-first century the Woodstock festival and the era to which it belonged have assumed an essentially mythical status, the term 'Woodstock' being synony-mous with a series of images – notably, free love, peace, drugs, rurality, and performances by some of the most legendary names in the rock music of the English-speaking world. To view the *Woodstock* film now is to reopen the door on much of what is regarded to have defined the counter-culture of the late 1960s. As such, the film evokes a powerful feeling of nostalgia, not only for those who lived through the era but also those generations born post-Woodstock. The spectacle of long-haired teenagers chanting 'no rain, no rain'[5] during a spell of bad weather at a local music festival in the German town of Lorsch during the summer of 1992 was sufficient to bring home to the author the multi-generational familiarity with, and appeal of, *Woodstock* in this way.

The significance of *Woodstock* as a nostalgic frame of reference depends very much on the existing stock of knowledge regarding the late 1960s that the viewer brings to the film. Elsewhere, I have argued that, for many of those who lived out their teenage years or early twenties during the late 1960s, the era is regarded as a 'golden age'[6] of youth culture, and 'a yardstick by which to compare the youth of the present day' (Bennett, 2001, p. 156). Embedded in such perceptions of the late 1960s are a series of romantic recollections of youth as more politically aware, more worldly and more proactive than contemporary youth. Indeed, the force of such perceptions is such that it has given rise to a number of damning indictments on present-day youth, such as that by Young who claims that the concept of youth culture is 'of historical value only, since the customs and mores associated with it have been abandoned by your actual young person' (1985, p. 246).

Accusations such as these have justifiably been criticized, notably by Lipsitz who argues that 'the enduring hold of the 1960s on the imagination of the present has been pernicious' (1994, p. 17). Similarly, Grossberg (1994) notes how 1960s nostalgia airbrushes out of youth cultural history the strident political statements of punk rockers and rap artists. Nevertheless, for those members of the 'sixties generation' who buy into the myth of the late 1960s as *the* era of youth protest and 'revolution', *Woodstock* serves up all the necessary ingredients for the promulgation of this myth. Subjected to the artistic creativity of the film-maker's lens and the producer's editorial licence, the performers and festivalgoers are represented in ways designed to suggest that Woodstock represented a revolutionary moment in history and the defining moment of the counter-cultural movement. Over the years, this feature of *Woodstock* has become something of a self-fulfilling prophecy, the intended message of the film-makers having been woven into a broader perception of what the late 1960s was essentially about. As such, viewing the film becomes a way of reliving the 1960s dream, *Woodstock* being a permanent document of the late 1960s available for replay at the touch of a button.

If *Woodstock* is, in this sense, about the preservation of the 1960s dream, then it is also, at a more fundamental level, about the preservation of youth itself. As Ross notes, the ageing baby boomer generation has become 'caught up in the fantasy that they are themselves still youthful, or at least more culturally radical . . . than the youth of today (1994, p. 8). To some extent this has been achieved through careful retro-marketing, notably CD and DVD reissues of 1960s music, and by 'come back' or 'reunion' tours of groups who first rose to prominence during that decade. Similarly, Frith draws attention to the use of 1960s music as a marketing technique in advertisements, arguing that this amounts to a playing back to an ageing baby boomer audience of 'old rock values – brash individualism [and] youthful rebellion' (1990, p. 90). Viewed from this perspective, watching *Woodstock* performs an important role, simultaneously revitalizing the spirit of youthful rebellion and transporting the viewer back to that period in time when this began to take hold.

In addition to this reading of *Woodstock* as indicative of a youthful cultural 'golden age', another reading of the film exists – one formed by post-1960s generations for whom the decade is accessible only through its media representation. For such generations, Woodstock is doubly articulated depending on the particular stance taken in relation to the 1960s. As John Street illustrates elsewhere in this book, for contemporary young people, the Woodstock festival, and the 1960s more generally, is viewed either in a tongue-in-cheek way – an era of bad fashions, outrageous hairstyles, drugs, 'free love' and so on – or as a mythical era – characterized by legendary rock performers such as Jimi Hendrix, Janice Joplin and Jim Morrison, whose early deaths have assured them iconic status, with their music, image and charismatic qualities continuing to generate legions of fans in every new generation of music lovers. For both types of contemporary 1960s association, *Woodstock* is a source of ongoing curiosity, a means through which particular images of the 1960s, however stereotypical these may be, find justification. Indeed, Pickering notes how, in late modernity, stereotyping is largely the product of the 'reliance of public knowledge on inadequate and manipulated media representations' (2001, p. 18).

It is perhaps an ironic legacy of *Woodstock* that, in its efforts to portray the event as authentically as possible, the film has become one of the key sources for stereotyping the 1960s. Whether this is done with reverence for the decade, or in a more satirical fashion, all of the key elements needed for the stereotyping of the 1960s are ceremoniously rolled out during the three and a half hour duration of the film. To some extent, this quality of the film may well derive from the editorial decisions made by the film-makers themselves; caught up in the spectacle of the event, and with the perceptions of many present that music was about to 'change the world', it is arguable that *Woodstock* was, from the very outset, a mission statement of the counter-culture. As such, it could be said, the film continuously plays down the mundane in favour of the spectacular, presenting the Woodstock festival as a pinnacle of the counter-culture's musicalized campaign for a new world order based on 'peace, love and understanding'. Whatever the truth about this, it is clear that for post-1960s generations seeking answers about that era from *Woodstock*, these are the sorts of messages most readily forthcoming from the film.

Notes

1. In 1994 Warner Bros released *Woodstock: The Director's Cut*, which purportedly contains classic performances missing from the original film, notably those by Canned Heat, Jefferson Airplane and Janis Joplin (see Romney and Wootton, 1995, p. 167).
2. Orson is referring here to the now legendary sequence in the film where an MC addresses the audience from the main stage, advising them against buying or accepting 'bad acid', identifiable by its brown colour, that was being sold on the festival site (see also Chapter 5).

3. Country Joe MacDonald was the only artist to appear at Woodstock twice – on the first occasion as a solo performer and on the second with his band as 'Country Joe and the Fish'.
4. However, as Meade points out, this aspect of the film is highly 'traditional' in terms of its portrayal of gender roles in that men are shown doing all the heavy manual and organizational work while women 'looked after babies or dished up hot meals' (1972, p. 173).
5. This directly mimics a scene in the Woodstock film where an MC encourages the crowd to chant 'no rain, no rain' in an attempt to drive away the storm that overtook the festival site on the Sunday afternoon.
6. The term 'golden age' was originally coined by Pearson (1983).

References

Bell, D. (1999), 'Tripping North', in D. Bell (ed.), *Woodstock: An Inside Look at the Movie that Shook up the World and Defined a Generation*, Studio City, CA: Michael Wiese Productions.

Bennett, A. (2001), *Cultures of Popular Music*, Buckingham: Open University Press.

Denisoff, R.S. and Romanowski, W.D. (1991), *Risky Business: Rock in Film*, Somerset, NJ: Transaction.

Frith, S. (1981), 'The Magic That Can Set You Free: The Ideology of Folk and the Myth of Rock', *Popular Music*, (1), pp. 159–68.

Frith, S. (1983), *Sound Effects: Youth, Leisure and the Politics of Rock 'n' Roll*, London: Constable.

Frith, S. (1990), 'Video Pop: Picking Up the Pieces', in S. Frith (ed.), *Facing the Music: Essays on Pop, Rock and Culture*, 2nd edn, London: Mandarin.

Frith, S. and Horne, H. (1987), *Art into Pop*, London: Methuen.

Grossberg, L. (1994), 'Is Anybody Listening? Does Anybody Care?: On Talking About "The State of Rock"', in A. Ross and T. Rose (eds), *Microphone Fiends: Youth Music and Youth Culture*, London: Routledge.

Harron, M. (1990), 'McRock: Pop as a Commodity', in S. Frith (ed.), *Facing the Music: Essays on Pop, Rock and Culture*, 2nd edn, London: Mandarin.

Lang, M. (1999), 'A Worldwide Phenomenon', in D. Bell (ed.), *Woodstock: An Inside Look at the Movie that Shook up the World and Defined a Generation*, Studio City, CA: Michael Wiese Productions.

Lipsitz, G. (1994), 'We Know What Time It Is: Race, Class and Youth Culture in the Nineties', in A. Ross and T. Rose (eds), *Microphone Fiends: Youth Music and Youth Culture*, London: Routledge.

Logan, N. and Woffinden, B. (eds) (1976), *The NME Book of Rock 2*, London: Wyndham.

McDonald, C.J. (1999), 'The legacy of "Gimme an F!"', in D. Bell (ed.), *Woodstock: An Inside Look at the Movie that Shook up the World and Defined a Generation*, Studio City, CA: Michael Wiese Productions.

Meade, M. (1972), 'The Degradation of Women', in R.S. Denisoff and R.A. Peterson (eds), *The Sounds of Social Change*, Chicago: Rand McNally and Company.

Orson, E. (1999), 'That Syncing Feeling', in D. Bell (ed.), *Woodstock: An Inside Look at the Movie that Shook up the World and Defined a Generation*, Studio City, CA: Michael Wiese Productions.

Palmer, T. (1976), *All You Need is Love: The Story of Popular Music*, London: Futura.

Pearson, G. (1983), *Hooligan: A History of Respectable Fears*, London: Macmillan.

Pickering, M. (2001), *Stereotyping: The Politics of Representation*, Basingstoke: Palgrave.

Renov, M. (1993), 'Introduction: The Truth About Non-Fiction', in M. Renov (ed.), *Theorizing Documentary*, London: Routledge.

Romney, J. and Wootton, A. (eds) (1995), *Celluloid Jukebox: Popular Music and the Movies Since the '50s*, London: British Film Institute.

Ross, A. (1994), 'Introduction', in A. Ross and T. Rose (eds), *Microphone Fiends: Youth Music and Youth Culture*, London: Routledge.

Roszak, T. (1969), *The Making of a Counter-Culture: Reflections on the Technocratic Society and its Youthful Opposition*, London: Faber and Faber.

Schowalter, D.F. (2000), 'Remembering the Dangers of Rock and Roll: Toward A Historical Narrative of the Rock Festival', *Critical Studies in Media Communication*, **17** (1), pp. 86–102.

Turbeville, D. (1999), 'Our Incredible Shifting Sculpture', in D. Bell (ed.), *Woodstock: An Inside Look at the Movie that Shook up the World and Defined a Generation*, Studio City, CA: Michael Wiese Productions.

Willis, P. (1978), *Profane Culture*, London: Routledge and Kegan Paul.

Wootton, A. (1995), 'The Do's and Don'ts of Rock Documentaries', in J. Romney and A. Wootton (eds), *Celluloid Jukebox: Popular Music and the Movies since the '50s*, London: British Film Institute.

Young, J. and Lang, M. (1979), *Woodstock Festival Remembered*, New York: Ballantine Books.

Young, T. (1985), 'The Shock of the Old', *New Society*, 14 February, p. 246.

Chapter 5

Reporting Woodstock: Some contemporary press reflections on the festival[1]

Simon Warner

Introduction

The legend of the Woodstock festival has been shaped by more than three decades of mediation. Whatever happened in Max Yasgur's field in August 1969 has been mythologized through a number of documents – in print, on screen and in sound recordings – that have attempted to contextualize the occasion as, perhaps, the high water mark of the anti-establishment forces of the 1960s. Michael Wadleigh's 1970 documentary movie, five records' worth of live album sets, television documentaries, video releases, retrospective articles and rock histories have endeavoured to present the festival as the embodiment of the hippie dream. In what we might regard as the standard version, Woodstock has been venerated as a shining example of utopia in action, often contrasted with the bleak horrors that beset Altamont later the same year. In addition, it is worth proposing that the vision of the original event has also been recontextualized in the light of subsequent festivals in 1994 and 1999.

Yet the initial eyewitness accounts of the event may be a more useful place for us to glean an authentic picture of the real Woodstock. Both the mainstream and the alternative press attempted instant reflection on those 'three days of peace, love and music'.[2] For the *New York Times*, the event produced a series of high-profile, front-page reports and some outraged editorial remarks; for *Rolling Stone*, the occasion appeared to offer evidence that the short revolution in society was perhaps taking hold. This account gathers a range of versions of the Woodstock story – from a number of key US and UK newspapers to music and alternative publications which sent reporters to the event. It will endeavour to provide an overview of contemporary accounts which may challenge the mythic status bestowed on the festival by subsequent memoirs.

Newspapers, of whatever provenance, approach their quarry – be it a political crisis, a terrorist attack, a distant war or, indeed, a rock festival –

burdened with their own ideological baggage. Whether the publication represents the voicepiece of establishment 'common sense' or the rallying cry of a marginalized minority, the idea of the value-free report rests more easily in the realms of the imagination than in the avenues of actuality. This suggests that any piece – even this – cannot be truly unshackled from the constraints of pre-mediation. I say this, not by way of apology necessarily, but essentially to warn that a retrospective summary of contemporaneous reflection is also compromised by this writer's own preconceptions, a young English teenager of the time whose own exposure to the happenings at the Woodstock festival only came – and then secondhand at best – when he was old enough to witness the X-certificate-rated[3] British movie release some years after.

Woodstock has been sold primarily by a vocal generation who believed that the event was the apogee of their attainment. Although the festival was riddled by weaknesses in its infrastructure and economic model and, although it did not bring peace to South-east Asia or racial harmony to the streets of black America, the occasion is still venerated as a key moment in the long decade that stretched from early civil rights protests to the fall of Nixon. This chapter attempts to find various balances in the view it provides. It draws on daily newspapers on both sides of the Atlantic, it draws together reports contained in the music press, and gives space to alternative interpretations – both high-profile and fringe – in a bid to paint, if not an accurate, then a panoramic picture of those column inches dedicated in the immediate aftermath to the happenings in upstate New York that summer.

The publications whose reports I draw upon are as follows. From the US, I employ the *New York Times*, the *Village Voice* and *Rolling Stone*. *Creem*, the Detroit-based magazine, was also included in the survey but did not include an account of the event. From the UK, I utilize *The Guardian*, *Melody Maker* and *New Musical Express*. The *Daily Mirror* also featured in the inquiry but, again, did not carry an item. The principal aim was to put together a flavour of the reports that arose from the event in the days, or week, after the occasion. In addition, I have also gathered some latter-day reflections from writers who attended and wrote about the event, who have updated their thoughts for this piece – Greil Marcus of *Rolling Stone* and Tom Smucker of *Fusion*. The chapter presents a broad survey of what was said in these newspapers and magazines, followed by some general analysis, including the recent commentaries mentioned above.

The *New York Times*: 'All the news that's fit to print'[4]

On the bus to Bethel: the build-up to the festival

The *New York Times*, the daily newspaper of the largest city located in the state where the Woodstock festival took place, provides the most substantial reflection on this period. Between 15 August and 24 August 1969, it covered the festival in a range of stories – news articles, features, editorials and readers' letters. Reports ranged from pre-festival anxieties over a decision to prevent New York City police officers performing security roles in an off-duty capacity, to a post-mortem in the Sunday edition the weekend after the festival, which gave an almost unanimous thumbs-up to the gathering.

In between, the tone of the reporting and comment fluctuated in style and message. While the lengthy news accounts which filled column after column from Saturday 16 August through to Tuesday 19 August presented a measured description of the chaotic scenes surrounding the rise and fall of the three-day celebration, the two key editorial responses contrasted significantly in their expression. One letter from a reader eulogized the festival in its wake, while a post-festival news item, which reported comments made by locals, communicated a considerably more hostile feeling towards the event.

One matter the *New York Times* does draw attention to is the somewhat tortured history the festival endured even before the summer of 1969. The promoters had originally hoped to site the event at Woodstock, a community in upstate New York. Unable to find a suitable location, however, they then chose Wallkill for the arts gathering, but further problems ensued as late as July and, eventually, the Catskill Mountain hamlet of Bethel – 60 miles south-west of Woodstock, 15 miles north-west of Wallkill – in Sullivan County would become the resting place of the ultimately misnamed festival. It seems curious, with the benefit of hindsight, that the press continued to refer to a location that was such a significant distance from the actual area where the musical celebrations would occur.

Initial fears about the event were raised in the edition of Thursday 15 August with the news that off-duty police officers would not be released by the New York police department to play the part of 'people handlers' or 'ushers' for the 200 000 fans expected at the Bethel location. Lesley Pomeroy, in charge of security told the *New York Times*: 'Now I don't have security people at all. I've been struck. We're having the biggest collection of kids there's ever been in this country without any police protection' (Fosburgh, 1969, p. 22). Instead, it was revealed, 100 members of the Hog Farm commune – based at Sante Fe in New Mexico – would now try to supervise the earmarked 600 acres of fields and forests, ten miles west of Monticello.

The day before, the first hoards of music fans were beginning to make their way to Bethel. At Port Authority bus terminal in the heart of Manhattan, bus services were leaving every 15 minutes to carry passengers north. Said a manager for the bus company: 'Sometimes over the Fourth of July or Labor Day, we have a big crowd, but never so many thousands going to one place' (ibid.). Reporter Lacey Fosburgh described the clans who were gathering: 'Carrying sleeping bags and tents, canned food and guitars, dressed in beads, leather, bandanas and long gowns, the young people spoke of sleeping out under the stars and possible riots' (ibid.).

There was some antagonism, certainly surprise, shown towards those queuing at Port Authority. 'As some persons waiting for other buses looked with disapproval and occasional disgust at the array of costumes and colours swimming behind the yellow barricades, the young people reclined along the floor and spoke with gusto about marijuana and music, and the weekend ahead' (ibid.). Some members of the Woodstock-bound group commented on the forthcoming event. Said Peter Franklin, an actor with the city's La Mama Theater: 'The cream of the underground will be there. Everybody's coming from all over the country. There'll be drugs and psychedelics and music and riots.' One unidentified 16-year old was more circumspect: 'I know there'll be drugs everywhere and I wonder what it will be like. I wonder what will happen to all of us' (ibid.).

Car chaos, but crowds stay calm

By the Saturday 16 August edition *what* would 'happen to all of us' was becoming clearer. Friday had seen huge traffic jams and growing fears that the security, unconvincingly arranged in the few days before, would be able to deal with the situation. For one thing, estimates were already suggesting that there were around 400 000 people pouring into the vicinity around the festival site – around double the organizers' expectations. The head of security for the event – now described as Wes rather than Les Pomeroy – told the paper: 'Anybody who tries to come here is crazy. Sullivan County is a great parking lot' (Collier, 1969a, p. 1). Midnight on Friday saw lines of cars forming queues some 20 miles in length.

Yet, in the midst of this potential disaster area, a theme of peace and calm was beginning to emerge, to the evident surprise of the authorities: 'The police and the festival's promoters both expressed amazement that despite the size of the crowd – the largest gathering of its kind ever held – there had been neither violence nor any serious incident' (ibid., p. 31). It became apparent, too, however, that the police were taking a diplomatic approach to law enforcement. County Sheriff Louis Ratner commented: 'We don't want any confrontations' (ibid.). The police were not seeking to make mass arrests even though there were clearly many breaches of the law being witnessed. 'So far', recounted Collier, 'there have been about 50 arrests, most of them for possession of drugs such as LSD, barbiturates and amphetamines' (ibid.). A sergeant in the State police put the picture in broader context: 'As far as I know the narcotics guys are not arresting anybody for grass. If we did there isn't enough space in Sullivan or the next three counties to put them in' (ibid.).

The problems of crowd control extended beyond traffic jams and drug infringements, nonetheless. John Roberts, the 24-year old president of Woodstock Ventures, the festival's sponsor, remarked that 'a large percentage of those who have arrived at the festival site today had not paid their $7 for the day's performance. There were so many people crushed in around the gates that the fences came down and we simply could not control who came in.' He said that the organizers were 'going to have to plead – or rather explain – to the crowd that we need their bread and that the people who paid $18 for advance tickets are uptight about the people who haven't' (ibid.).

Nor was it only tensions on the site that were interesting the reporter. In the middle of the town, local residents were expressing their unhappiness at the turn of events. A sign had been erected reading 'Stop Max's Hippie Music Festival. No 150,000 hippies here. Buy No Milk', the latter a reference to the produce of the herd of Max Yasgur, the farmer who had somewhat controversially rented 600 acres of his land to the event organizers.

As the audience waited for the Friday afternoon performance to begin – delays had been caused as workmen struggled to finish constructing the 80-foot wide stage – the crowds were 'diverted by strolling musicians, improvised group performances, and debates among long-haired girls and their bearded boy friends. Their debate topics included Vietnam, campus disorders and the merits of various music groups' (ibid.). On its first day the festival had already overtaken numbers attending a two-day event, the Hampton Rock Festival in Georgia, which had attracted 125 000 in July 1969.

The bands play on – mud, music and 'badly manufactured acid'

By the time Sunday's *New York Times* hit the streets, Barnard Collier was revealing that the crowd had soared to 300 000 young people 'drawn by such performers as Joan Baez, Ravi Shankar, Jimi Hendrix and The Jefferson Airplane, the prospect of taking drugs and the excitement of "making the scene"' (Collier, 1969b, p. 1). They came, he said, 'in droves camping in the woods, romping in the mud, talking, smoking and listening to the wailing music' (ibid.). He added: 'Most of the hip, swinging youngsters heard the music on stage only as a distant rumble. It was almost impossible for them to tell who was performing and probably only about half the crowd could hear a note. Yet they stayed by the thousands, often standing ankle-deep in mud . . .' (ibid.). Michael Lang, aged 24, the producer of the occasion, reiterated the peaceful nature of the gathering: 'It's about the quietest, most well-behaved 300,000 people in one place that can be imagined. There have been no fights or incidents of violence of any kind' (ibid.).

The first 24 hours of the event saw around 1000 people treated for a range of ailments – accidents, exposure – but around a third were needing help for adverse drug reactions. This edition of the newspaper expanded on this thread, reporting that announcements from the stage were drawing attention to the 'badly manufactured acid' that was circulating (ibid., p. 80). Organizers told the crowds:

> You aren't taking poison acid. The acid's not poison. It's just badly manufactured acid. You are not going to die. We have treated 300 cases and it's all badly manufactured acid. So if you think you've taken poison, you haven't. But if you're worried, just take half a tablet. (Ibid.)

By Saturday, buses from New York City to the festival had been cancelled. 'We're not driving to that disaster area', a bus company spokesman stated (ibid.). A journey that should have taken their vehicles two hours and 20 minutes had almost doubled; one bus took 12 hours to get there. Those who did reach the site 'found tens of thousands of tents, campers and makeshift lean-to shacks . . . made of any materials at hand, including trees, wood, ropes, sheets and blankets' (ibid.). Food shortages were a problem but members of one commune passed out 'a free gruel of peanuts, oatmeal, raisins and sunflower seeds' (ibid.). Local farmers complained to police officers that foragers had stripped their land of corn and vegetables. Meanwhile, piles of rubbish began to gather, with scores of men employed, but hard-pressed, to deal with the reservoir of debris.

Financial crisis – the money men count their losses

The financial chaos surrounding the event was outlined in more detail. A festival official revealed that ticket sales had ceased. 'Now it's all a freebee', he commented (Collier, 1969b, p. 80). Promoter John Roberts provided further insight, revealing that, while advance ticket sales had generated $1.3 million and first-day sales of $140 000 had raised the total to just under $1.5 million, expenses would run close to $2 million. 'Financially speaking, of course,' said Roberts, 'the festival is a disaster' (Special correspondent, 1969a, p. 80). Calculations had all been based on 100 000 people attending each day. 'As triple that number appeared, the entire ticket-selling, ticket-taking set-up broke down. Thousands of people streamed in without paying the $7 admission' (ibid.). Roberts pointed out that the theme of the fair was 'three days of peace and music' but it had turned out to be rather 'scary'. He said: 'If we had any inkling that there was going to be this kind of attendance, we certainly would not have gone ahead' (ibid.).

However, Roberts believed that while there had been a business purpose to running the event, there had also been a sociological motivation: 'I had felt for a long time that the polarization of the generations is a very serious threat to our society, and we felt that a cultural exposition created by youth could be of inestimable value in bridging that gap.' The idea for the festival had taken seed the previous February in the minds of two partners in Woodstock Ventures, Michael Lang and Arthur Kornfeld. Said Roberts:

> Ours was going to be in the country. It was going to be away from the urban and suburban areas in a very rustic setting with a lot of room, grass, trees, lakes. It was going to be a youth cultural exposition and that is where the culture of this generation expresses itself more naturally. (Ibid.)

Word of the event had been released in April 1969 when announcements were placed with radio stations in New York City and Boston. Radio advertising was the chief means of promotion although Roberts said the spend had been under $200 000. The main promotional thrust had been provided by DJs talking about the event. 'We got a tremendous amount of excitement and speculation on the radio stations when disk [*sic*] jockeys talked it up in the last couple of months' (ibid.). The huge crowds had confirmed the success of the efforts to spread the news, but the accompanying chaos also brought a downside to the project. 'Would there be another massive outdoor music and art fair?' asked the reporter. 'No, I don't think so', Roberts replied. 'We've had a very adverse situation up here' (ibid.).

On Monday 18 August the *New York Times* reported the exodus of Sunday night and the early hours of Monday as the festivalgoers began to disperse. The front page account spoke of 'at least two deaths and 4,000 people treated for injuries, illness and adverse drug reactions' (Collier, 1969c, p. 1), but the report provided a balanced picture. Dr William Abruzzi, the festival's chief medical officer, remarked again on the absence of violence at the occasion which is 'remarkable for a crowd of this size. These people are really beautiful' (ibid.). The Sunday afternoon had seen a huge storm hit the site, which broke during Joe Cocker's set. The storm had not only raised fears of damage to the stage and the amplification system, but also introduced 'the threat of bronchial disorder and influenza . . . according to staff doctors here. Many boys and girls wandered through the storm nude, red mud clinging to their bodies' (ibid., 1969c, p. 25).

Collier reflected on the feelings of those who had taken part. 'For many', he wrote, 'the weekend had been the fulfilment of months of planning and hoping, not only to see and hear the biggest group of pop performers ever assembled, but also to capture the excitement of camping out with strangers, experimenting with drugs and sharing – as one youth put it – "an incredible unification"' (ibid., p. 1). Drugs had plainly been a feature of that unified experience – some members of the crowd interviewed were suggesting that 99 per cent of those present had smoked marijuana (Special correspondent, 1969b, p. 25). But Max Yasgur, who had earned a $50 000 rent for the land he had provided, said the occasion had taught him that 'if the generation gap is going to be closed, we older people have to do more than we have done' (Special correspondent, 1969c, p. 25).

The music, which had featured surprisingly little in the wider account so far, was summarized by Mike Jahn, describing The Band as a group who play 'a taut fusion of country music and rock with vocals direct from the classic, nasal hillbilly style' (Jahn, 1969, p. 25). Sly and the Family Stone won praise for their ability to combine 'a happy-sounding melody line with an infectious and very danceable soul beat' (ibid.), while Creedence Clearwater Revival performed 'simple, unsophisticated and rollicking music' (ibid.). Janis Joplin's set earned criticism, however, as her new band favoured precision and technical accuracy over the spontaneity and excitement that had characterized her earlier combo. However, The Who gained coverage not for their on-stage bravura but for their insistence that they were paid before they played. Promises that everyone would be paid by the organizers prompted the British group's road manager to retort: 'I've heard that before – we want cash' (Reeves, 1969, p. 25). The band received $11 200 prior to their show.

Yet the prime movers behind Woodstock were beginning to take a more measured view of the monetary crises that had reared their head in recent days. While losses were now believed to be running at between $1 million and $2 million, organizing team Michael Lang, John Roberts, Arthur Kornfeld and Joel Rosenman talked about the three days 'with deep pleasure', saying that they 'created a great event in the development of a new American "youth culture"' (ibid.). In terms of accounting, it was revealed that the sound and lighting rig owned by the promoters was worth over $200 000, and, significantly in retrospect, the writer suggested that a documentary movie that had been made 'for about $150,000 seems to have the potential to become sort of a cinematic Bible for young people' (ibid.). We must assume that this was the footage that would become the 1970 movie release (see Chapter 4).

The Monday edition of the newspaper also included a first editorial comment. Headed 'Nightmare in the Catskills', it said that 'the dreams of marijuana and rock music that drew 300,000 fans and hippies . . . had little more sanity than the impulses that drive the lemmings to march to their deaths in the sea. They ended in a nightmare of mud and stagnation that paralysed Sullivan County for a whole weekend.' It continued: 'Surely parents, the teachers and indeed all the adults who helped create the society which these young people are so feverishly rebelling [*sic*] must bear some responsibility for this outrageous episode' (Editorial, 1969a, p. 34). The sponsors of the event 'who apparently had not the slightest concern for the turmoil it would cause, should be made to account for their mismanagement' (ibid.). But the piece did reflect briefly on the positive – the 'genuine kindness of the residents of Monticello' and 'the fact that the great bulk of the freakish-looking intruders behaved astonishingly well' (ibid.).

'Mr' Hendrix plays amid a 'sea of refuse'

In the Tuesday 19 August edition a post-mortem reflected on the closing musical moments in the early hours of Monday morning – 'When Mr Hendrix appeared he was kept on-stage for at least two hours' (Collier, 1969d, p. 34) – and the aftermath, including the scale of the clean-up. It was claimed that two weeks would be required to shift the sea of refuse – from drink cans to sodden sleeping bags. Yet Max Yasgur's optimistic tone continued to ring. 'What happened at Bethel in the past weekend was that these young people together with our local residents turned the Aquarian festival to a dramatic victory for the spirit of peace, goodwill and human kindness', he said, adding that, on the evidence of the number of drug users at the event, 'there must be 15 to 20 million of them in America' (ibid.). A man who had attended the festival offered a closing thought from the other side of the fence: 'I'm here for the same reason that Indians used to have tribal gatherings. Just being here with people like me makes it all worthwhile. I guess it will reinforce my life style, my beliefs, from the attacks of my parents and their generation' (ibid.).

Returning to issues of law infringement, the report stated: 'In general, the fair was, so far as drugs and nudism, were concerned, beyond the law during the three-day period. Had the police arrested everyone possessing marijuana, however, the narrow lane leading to the fairgrounds would have been crammed with paddywagons and would have undoubtedly triggered demonstrations' (ibid.). Nevertheless, the reflection that an air of calm had pervaded the occasion was repeated. Festival medical director Dr William Abruzzi said that the problems confronted by the 50 physicians on duty were 'typical if you were trying to take care of a city of 300,000 people without buildings'. Yet he stressed that 'we didn't treat one single knife wound or black eye or laceration that was inflicted by another human being' (ibid.).

Interestingly, the second editorial comment on events changed tack somewhat from Monday's principally critical account. As the dust settled, the newspaper suggested that 'the rock festival begins to take on the quality of a social phenomenon, comparable to the Tulipmania or the Children's Crusade. And in spite of the prevalence of drugs . . . it was essentially a phenomenon of innocence' (Editorial, 1969b, p. 42). Attempting an assessment of the motives of those who attended – after all, they could have listened to the music at home – the column proposed that 'they came, it seems, to enjoy their own society, free to exult in a life style that is its own declaration of independence' (ibid.).

By Wednesday 20 August, as coverage diminished, a news story with a different ring put the case of Bethel farmers who attacked the festival as 'a conspiracy to avoid the law' (Narvaez, 1969, p. 37). The festival had failed to respect health codes – sanitary facilities were inadequate – cars had been parked in fields, damage had been done to crops and fences had been removed for firewood. They also expressed concern that the festival may be invited back. Meanwhile a third fatality associated with the event was recorded. On Thursday 21 August a reader's letter referred to the Bethel Music Festival, *not* Woodstock. Ralph B. Levering of Princeton, New Jersey, defended the festival conditions – traffic, noise pollution and so on – as an improvement on New York City. 'Perhaps we should say, in fair comparison', he commented, 'that the festival was beautiful and New York is bearable' (Levering, 1969, p. 40).

The following Sunday, 24 August, brought two contrasting items as the main swell of the festival and its immediate repercussions ebbed away. A Washington-based correspondent Russell Baker penned a satirical question-and-answer piece which gently lampooned the festival. He said that he doubted that President Nixon's promise to bring the nation together had meant this at all. More like his vision was 'a quilting bee at which everybody would drink cider and eat ginger snaps' (Baker, 1969, p. 12). But he made the more serious point that, if these gestures against 'dreary conformity' had been seen in Russia, the West would be delighted. Patrick Lydon's review of the festival came more from the realms of idealism than cynicism. He wrote:

> Out of the mud came dancing, out of electrical failure came music, out of hunger came generosity. What began as a symbolic protest against American society ended as a joyful confirmation that good things can happen here, that Army men can raise a 'V' sign, that country people can welcome city hippies. One of Hendrix's last numbers was 'The Star Spangled Banner'. Yes, most everything happened up on the farm. (Lydon, 1969, p. 16.)

The *Village Voice*: New York City's radical weekly

New York City's radical weekly magazine, the *Village Voice*, also gave time and space to events upstate. On Thursday 21 August the publication made

Steve Lerner's account of the Aquarian Exposition at the Woodstock Music and Art Fair its front-page story. Lerner's report spoke with a more playful voice than the *New York Times*' generally detached commentary. 'Stoned silly most of the time, more than half a million freaks from all over the country made the painful pilgrimage to Max Yasgur's 600 acre farm to play in the mud' (Lerner, 1969, p. 1). He believed that those who turned up were 'looking for a kind of historic coming out party of the East Coast freak population'. Many of those in the crowd were 'the only hippies on their block or in their hometown, and the mass rally served as a confirmation of their lifestyle after months of sitting alone counting their psychedelic beads' (ibid.).

He commented that the gathering at White Lake 'was an ordeal or an ecstatic adventure depending on whether you see the glass as half full or half empty', adding that while much had been made of the trying circumstances facing festivalgoers 'most of those who came accepted the insufferable conditions as part of the challenge of the outing' (ibid.). He continued:

> Now if you can imagine a hip version of Jones Beach transported to a war zone in Vietnam during the monsoon maybe you'll catch a glimpse of what White Lake looked like a day after the long-haired troops occupied the area ... Perhaps most amazing was the physical stamina, tolerance, and good nature of a basically indoor, urban group of people caught in wretched out-door conditions. It showed more dramatically than any planned demonstration could have that hip kids are fundamentally different from the beer-drinking, fist-fighting Fort Lauderdale crowds of yesteryear. (Ibid.)[5]

While the *Voice* report reflected hardly at all on the musical component of the festival – only Hendrix was mentioned as playing at the event – it did offer some insights into the social and political issues raised by the gathering. Capturing a brief exchange between two teenagers, Lerner pointed out how white faces predominated at the gathering:

> 'Do you realize that if we stayed here we'd be the 10th largest city in the United States', a 17 year old blond boy ... suggested. 'Yeah, that would be far-out, man, but would you want to live here?' one of the few black kids who came to the fair said as he surveyed the elbow-to-elbow crowd sitting on a hillside of mud and trash. (Ibid. p. 10.)

Drugs and the 'poison tabs of flat blue acid' were the subject of comment, but Lerner revealed that Hugh Romney – aka Wavy Gravy – of the 'outlandish' Sante Fe Hog Farm Commune had invited 'anyone on a bummer to come up to their tepees and sit around and rap' (ibid.). The report highlighted the ease with which drug peddlers were plying their trade. '"I've got acid here, mescaline, and hash", a dealer with shoulder-length dark hair called to the crowd as he waded through like a popcorn salesman at a football stadium. No one was very worried about being busted in the middle of 400,000 freaks, and dealing was done in the open' (ibid.).

The *Voice* also focused on the festivalgoers' tendency to abandon their clothes and the liberated sexual displays that then occurred:

> Public nudity was also pretty cool and by Saturday couples were swimming together in the lake without anyone stopping to gawk. In a way the nudity seemed more natural and necessary than fashionable, since everyone was constantly getting drenched in the rain and large numbers of people were wearing the only clothes they had with them. By Sunday, however, the bathers had gotten bolder and were sunning themselves on towels and petting each other as if it were the most natural thing in the world. By Monday a few couples were making it in public, guys were walking round with unembarrassed erections . . . (Ibid., p. 10.)

As the festival rolled towards its conclusion and the vast throng began to disperse, 'Hare Krishna disciples with shaved heads, flowing robes, finger cymbals and a vacant faraway look in their eyes weaved through the departing crowds passing out peacock feathers' (ibid), but members of Students for a Democratic Society, trying to sell copies of *New Left Notes* were meeting with little success. '"Hey, man, stop selling papers and join the revolution", an outrageous, toothless dope freak said . . . when he was offered some radical literature' (ibid.). Yet Lerner could not fail to capture a sense of political optimism that had been generated by the previous three days, as one member of the gathering remembered the Democratic Convention demos in Chicago in 1968. 'A young man with red hair and carrying a pair of broken sandals said as he watched the crowd leave: "It's incredible. Last year there were less than 10,000 of us in Chicago and now look at this army." It's difficult to say which was the more revolutionary event' (ibid.).

Rolling Stone: 'All the news that fits'[6]

As the *Voice* finished on the events in Chicago the year before, so a magazine based on the other side of the country, began with it. San Francisco's *Rolling Stone*, located in the city where the hippie vision had begun to materialize around 1965, started its front-page report with a reference to events at that same Democratic Convention:

> Chicago was only the labour pains. With a joyous three-day shriek, the inheritors of the earth came to life in an alfalfa field outside the village of Bethel, New York. Slapping the spark of life into the new-born was American rock 'n' roll music provided by the Woodstock Music and Art Fair.[7]

The writer, Jan Hodenfield, made reference to a recent anti-ballistic missile bill passed by the US Senate which made the possibility of total destruction of the world, he felt, all the more likely. Woodstock, he thought, was a sign that individuals were now ready to turn their back on 'the already ravaged cities and their inoperable "life-styles"' and 'move onto the mist-covered fields and into the cool, still woods' (Hodenfield, 1969, p. 1). He framed one memorable and euphoric response to the recent events:

'It was like balling for the first time,' said one campaigner, her voice shredded, her mind a tapioca of drugs. 'Once you've done it, you want to do it again and again, because it's so *great*.' And they will do it again, the threads of youthful dissidence in Paris and Prague and Fort Lauderdale and Berkeley and Chicago and London criss-crossing ever more closely until the map of the world we live in is viable for and visible to all of those that are part of it and all of those buried under it. (Ibid.)

Rolling Stone provided a lengthy and detailed account of the three days of activity and incident, but was notable for its attempt to wrestle with the multitude of musical acts who spanned the event. Country Joe McDonald's efforts to stimulate audience participation were reported. '[He] did an acoustic set on his own, offering his first number to Janis, at the end eliciting a happy-savages roar when he yelled to the crowd: "Gimme an F" – they answered – "Gimme a U" – they answered – "Gimme a C" – they answered – "Gimme a K" – and they yelled. "Now, what's that spell?" The shout rang out for at least ten miles' (ibid., p. 24). The absence of Bob Dylan, who had made the Woodstock terrain his home, was remarked upon, his 'presence hovering over this three-day jamboree' (ibid.) but of more concern were the black performers missing from the bill:

Sunday's marathon was opened by Joe Cocker, his fingers epileptic butterflies, his harsh voice driving, but grey rather than black, driving home the absence of R and B artists. As with most festivals, white was right. No Sam and Dave. No Wilson Pickett. No Stevie Wonder. No Aretha. No Temptations. No Fats Domino. Which is perhaps understandable when the audience is largely white. But is not explicable when a darkie show such as provided by Cocker is offered as the forgivable alternative. (Ibid. pp. 24–26.)

On the business front, information was released on a press conference, held on the following Thursday, at which the organizers revealed that, despite talk of $2.5 million debts, things were going to be all right. With the assistance of the banks – John Roberts had the most visible connections with the worlds of banking through his family's drug and cosmetic business, the account stated – a recovery would be mounted. 'Additionally, they said, residual rights to movies, records and books are the property of Woodstock Ventures Inc. "You should expect an announcement soon, on the movies and records"' (ibid., p. 26). Furthermore, Mike Lang suggested that there would be another Woodstock fair in August 1970 'maybe even at Bethel' (ibid.).

Elsewhere in *Rolling Stone*, Greil Marcus reserved particular praise for the live contribution of Crosby, Stills, Nash and Young – 'their performance was scary brilliant proof of the magnificence of music and I don't believe it could have happened with such power anywhere else' (Marcus, 1969, p. 18) – but he spent much of his bylined account considering the implications of an occasion like Woodstock and what lessons could be learnt from an event of this scale. He said that there had been 'a staggering line-up of bands – a truly national festival' but proposed that 'the logistical problems are the minor ones' (ibid.). 'The true challenge', he believed, 'is to recognize that Woodstock was truly the Land of Oz and that those who were there will want to find a way back and that those who heard about it will be there to follow' (ibid.). He pointed out that to plan for a future festival for a crowd of 150 000 would be folly as a crowd of one million would arrive; to plan for a million would see 10 million turn up.

Marcus believed that neither advance tickets sales alone nor bands playing for free would be the solution, nor would the tactics of a repressive state. 'We also cannot revert to electrified fences, police dogs, tear gas, and the rest of the contemporary American paraphernalia in an attempt to keep the "legitimate" audience separate from the rest of the rock and roll population.' Instead, he put forward a bolder vision of how the burgeoning phenomenon of the rock festival might be handled. 'Probably an attempt will have to be made to get the record companies to finance the next national festival, whether it's held in Woodstock, Mill Valley, or Toronto. It has to be considered in the same light as the Olympic Games, which is exactly what this festival was, yet more like the Games of 2,500 years ago than those today.' Woodstock, he opined, 'is just the beginning – or the end – and we must now sit down and figure out how to make it work' (ibid.).

A British view: *The Guardian, Melody Maker* and *New Musical Express*

While the principal print coverage of Woodstock was, predictably, carried in the US, there were a number of reports in the UK that are, perhaps, worth our attention if only to get a sense of how far this cultural phenomenon was a national occasion and how far the ripples were picked up on by the sensors of the British media. *The Guardian*, an established voice of liberal reporting since the nineteenth century, did cover the event, by means of a news report and an additional commentary. The *Daily Mirror*, a populist, tabloid newspaper of left-wing sympathies, did not cover the occasion. In *The Guardian* of Monday 18 August 1969, a brief news account, supplied, we must assume, by an agency, reported on numbers attending the festival, described various artists showcased – Baez, Hendrix, Jefferson Airplane, Ravi Shankar and The Who – and outlined various calamities that had befallen the event – mud, hunger and thirst. 'Drug use', it stated, 'appeared to have tapered off' (Unknown author, 1969, p. 2). It made reference to a dozen helicopters – including two army vehicles – that had been utilized to carry the sick to hospital and 100 people arrested on drugs charges but also emphasized there had been 'no reports of violence' (ibid.). A photograph featuring two women in hippie garb was included.

The Guardian's New York-based US correspondent, the renowned journalist and broadcaster Alistair Cooke, provided a more personalized account of the happenings the following day, Tuesday 19 August. Comparing the festival crowds with the forces convened at Gettysburg – Woodstock had twice the number – Cooke spoke of Bethel's relief as the human tide eventually headed away. He also spoke of the fears that locals had expressed before – 'a rural version of the Chicago Democratic Convention riots' (Cooke, 1969, p. 9) was among the predictions – but, despite two deaths, three drug users in a critical condition, and 3000 minor injuries, some 296 000 had been left 'in pretty good shape and incurable high spirits' (ibid.). The piece said that 'the kids had undoubtedly brought credit on their strange breed', but Cooke saved his main praise for:

> ... the sleepless doctors and radiologists, kindly farmers and old ladies, the Stewart Air Force Base, volunteer ambulance drivers, the women of the Jewish community centre near by, and the sisters of the Convent of St Thomas. The beautiful people who assumed that nature would provide were lucky in the availability at such desperate short notice of so much old-fashioned Christian and Jewish charity. (Ibid.)

Two other UK publications should be mentioned – the two most important of the weekly music newspapers produced at the time. The *Melody Maker*, in its 30 August 1969 edition, scooped its rival *New Musical Express*, although hardly gloriously. On its live review pages, column inches had been dedicated to a Woodstock notice, but the reporter Clive Selwood confessed that he had been unable to reach the festival, despite the best efforts of his host, Elektra Records boss Jac Holzman, to charter a private plane. The reporter made several vain attempts to get to the eye of the storm but failed in his various bids. 'We decided to return to the relative peace, quiet and sanity of New York City and struggle back to town. En route we saw all the highways littered with literally thousands of cars whose occupants had apparently abandoned them and set out to walk the last 20 miles' (Selwood, 1969, p. 6). *NME* could claim not even a Pyrrhic victory in the 23 August 1969 edition. New York-based reporter June Harris complained: 'It's been very hard keeping up with the run of summer music festivals in this country. The US is so enormous that it boils down to catching what you can, where you can and when you can' (Harris, 1969, p. 12). In a brief overview she mentioned East Coast events at Newport, Atlantic City and Woodstock but had opted herself to attend an event at Tanglewood, Massachusetts, instead.

Some conclusions: names and numbers

In broad terms, the reports consulted for this overview largely cohere in terms of the main details of the occasion – deaths, injuries and arrests, for instance. Discrepancies over numbers attending are down to the inevitable inaccuracies inherent when the authorities or organizers or press men and women make snap judgements about a crowd that can only be the subject of speculative estimates. The *New York Times'* efforts to keep tabs on the size of the audience reflects the problem – 200 000 are expected on the Thursday before the festival, 400 000 are believed to be 'in the vicinity' by Saturday, when locals are telling 150 000 hippies they are not welcome. By Sunday, a figure of 300 000 was being applied (see Collier, 1969b). The *Village Voice* was content to go with '400,000 freaks' (Lerner, 1969, p. 1), while *Rolling Stone*'s cover carries the heading 'Woodstock: 450,000'. *The Guardian*, probably relying on agency reports, recorded 300 000. Interestingly, the *Melody Maker* reviewer believed he was 'like some 200,000 others' who never got near enough to hear any music (Selwood, 1969, p. 6). When we consider that a figure of half a million has since frequently been used to define the crowd – very likely an inflated number if we are to trust the contemporary estimates – we are now most unlikely to be able to identify a definitive number.[8] Yet it seems reasonable to propose that it was the scale of the attendance that sowed the seeds of the subsequent mythology: the crowds that turned up became the story – they caused the chaos on the roads and in the rural community where they based themselves, and so generated the subsequent news coverage.

How far the music was the myth-maker is harder to discern. Of the publications considered here, only *Rolling Stone* (Hodenfield, 1969; Marcus, 1969) gave sustained and critical attention to the bands and solo performers who took to the stage. The *New York Times* did dedicate some space to the bands (Jahn, 1969; Lydon, 1969) but their columns were primarily given over to the hard news – the human catastrophe, the financial calamity – rather than the event's creative dimensions. Other newspapers and magazines might have mentioned key members of the bill in passing but there was less attention paid to the artistic significance of the show.

The surprising range of references to where the festival took place, and to a lesser degree, the names it was given, provides a certain degree of confusion, too. The *New York Times* refers to its reports as coming from Bethel, NY, *Rolling Stone* locates its report as coming from Woodstock, NY, while the *Village Voice* puts its stress on White Lake. Bearing in mind that the occasion is also referred to as the Woodstock Music and Arts Festival (Fosburgh, 1969, p. 22), the Woodstock Music and Art Fair (Collier, 1969a, p. 1) and Bethel Music Fair (Levering, 1969, p. 40), as an Aquarian festival (Collier, 1969d, p. 34) and also an Aquarian Exposition (Lerner, 1969, p. 1), there was still a lack of unanimity on both geography and title of the gathering in the days surrounding and following the event. As has already been mentioned, Woodstock, the abbreviated name now given to these events, is a misnomer in that none of the festival took place within 60 miles of that location.

Postscript: two writers revisit the scene

Over 30 years later we can safely say that Woodstock *is* Woodstock – history has confirmed that as the festival's name. But what about its meanings? Tom Smucker, who attended the festival in his 'political phase', wrote a piece for *Fusion* magazine in the autumn of 1969 (Eisen, 1970, p. 85). The festival, he said, 'seemed like a chance to resolve the Rock-New Left contradiction in my life. Here was a large, organised . . . attempt to relate politically to a Rock Event.' Yet even then, within weeks, the seeds of cynicism were starting to take hold. 'I have heard and read (and yes, written) so much about Woodstock that I'm sick of it. WMCA has a special Woodstock record collection.[9] *Life* magazine has a special issue. Someone on the block has a "We Proved It at Woodstock" sticker,' he wrote (Eisen, 1970, p. 90). Revisiting his piece, Smucker says:

> Rereading the piece now, and being generous towards my younger self I would agree with the essential points that Woodstock was so big no one got it; the experience of the vast majority of the crowd was 'of itself' not 'of the acts', as the movie rearranged things; and the Left was washed along in the flood with the other debris. However, looking back, I think what I missed was that the crowd knew how to function as a very large crowd not only because of experiences as rock audiences but also because of experiences at marches and demonstrations. So I think there was a Leftist component to the experience the crowd had of itself. (Smucker, 2002.)

Greil Marcus, too, has had cause to reflect on his comments of the time. In a 25th-anniversary piece for *Interview* magazine, weeks before Woodstock 1994 was to take place, he pointed out that the bubble of optimism that ascended from Woodstock quickly burst. In fact he stated that 'on the scale of lost hopes, in years to come rock festivals would seem almost as corrupt as the war'. Yet the legend of the original event 'remained inviolate and unspoiled' despite the connections that might have been made at the time – the link between hippie culture, the Manson Family and murders days before the festival nor the fact that Altamont had originally been presented as Woodstock West. Recalling his 1969 *Rolling Stone* piece, he remarks:

> I did think it was funny, at the time, that while everyone else was writing about the grand social-political implications of Woodstock, I was mainly concerned with the logistics of future large concerts, and besotted with the grandeur of such events – the power of a huge audience to impart huge power to music being played before it. Then came Altamont – where, lying face down in the dirt after having tripped on my way out of that disaster, I heard the Rolling Stones closing the night with 'Gimme Shelter', probably the most powerful performance I've ever heard. Still, the closing section of the piece was, to put it charitably, absurdly naive. But so were the social-political analyses. In *Rolling Stone*, I wrote with a fan's enthusiasm about performances. I have no apology for that. (Marcus, 2002.)

Notes

1. Thanks to Simon Frith, Robert Christgau, Greil Marcus, Tom Smucker, Andy Bennett, Nina Platts and Christine Micklethwaite and *The Guardian* library for their help in compiling this chapter.
2. This phrase 'Three days of peace, love and music' gained global currency when it was used on posters to advertise Michael Wadleigh's 1970 motion picture, *Woodstock*.
3. The cinema version of the Woodstock event was certificated by the British Board of Film Classification on 7 May 1970. At the time, a film carrying an X-certificate could only be viewed by audiences aged 16 or over. However, on 1 July 1970, the BBFC introduced a new system of categorization and X-certificate films were now deemed suitable only for those 18 or over (see BBFC, 2003, online). As a result, an anomaly arose – those over 16 but under 18 could no longer legally view screenings of *Woodstock* following the changes. In the US, the movie was released on 8 February 1970, earning an R-certificate from the Motion Picture Association of America, permitting those under 17 to see it but only if they were accompanied by a parent or adult guardian (see MPAA, 2003, online).
4. The *New York Times*, founded in 1896, carries the phrase 'All the news that's fit to print' on its masthead and the editorial page.
5. Fort Lauderdale has been the destination for college students and their high-spirited Spring Break parties for many decades.
6. *Rolling Stone*, established in 1967, adapted the *New York Times*' catchphrase and replaced it with 'All the news that fits'.

7. This was an uncredited write-up, but was actually penned by Jan Hodenfield (1969, p. 1).

8. In *Woodstock Festival Remembered* by Jean Young and Michael Lang the preface states: 'In August 1969, two million people attempted to get to a 660-acre dairy farm in White lake, New York, about 100 miles north of New York City . . . Five hundred thousand got there' (1979, p. 5). In *Rock of Ages: The Rolling Stone History of Rock and Roll* by Ed Ward, et al., it is stated that '400,000 showed up' (1986, p. 430). Greil Marcus in an article in *Interview* magazine, July 1994, talks of 'the 450,000-strong hippie commune', hazards that 200 000 were shouting 'Fuck the rain!' but points out that only 30 000 remained on the Monday morning.

9. WMCA was a Top 40 radio station, home to, among others, Murray the K, the so-called 'fifth Beatle'.

References

Baker, R. (1969), 'Observer: Still More on the Famous Musical Weekend', *New York Times*, Section N, 24 August.

British Board of Film Classification (2003), 'History of the BBFC: 1970 – AA' http://www.bbfc.co.uk/website/2000About.nsf/History-1970?OpenPage [accessed 5 March 2003].

Collier, B.L. (1969a), '200,000 Thronging to Rock Festival Jam Roads Upstate', *New York Times*, 16 August.

Collier, B.L. (1969b), '300,000 at Folk-Rock Fair Camp Out in a Sea of Mud', *New York Times*, 17 August.

Collier, B.L. (1969c), 'Tired Rock Fans Begin Exodus', *New York Times*, 18 August.

Collier, B.L. (1969d), 'Quiet Returns to Bethel as a 19-Hour Concert Closes Rock Fair', *New York Times*, 19 August.

Cooke, A. (1969), 'Grooving on the Sounds', *The Guardian*, 19 August.

Editorial (1969a), 'Nightmare in the Catskills', *New York Times*, 18 August.

Editorial (1969b), 'Morning after at Bethel', *New York Times*, 19 August.

Eisen, J. (ed.) (1970), *The Age of Rock 2: Sights and Sounds of the American Cultural Revolution*, New York: Vintage.

Fosburgh, L. (1969), '346 Policemen Quit Music Festival', *New York Times*, 15 August.

Harris, J. (1969), 'Tanglewood Festival Features The Who', *New Musical Express*, 23 August.

Hodenfield, J. (1969), 'It Was Like Balling For the First Time', *Rolling Stone*, 20 September.

Jahn, M. (1969), 'Rock Audience Moves to Dusk-to-Dawn Rhythms', *New York Times*, 18 August.

Kopkind, A. (1970), 'Woodstock Nation', in J. Eisen (ed.), *The Age of Rock 2: Sights and Sounds of the American Cultural Revolution*, New York: Vintage.

Lerner, S. (1969), 'The 10th Largest City in the United States: Warm Wind at White Lake', *Village Voice*, 21 August.

Levering, R.B. (1969), ' "Beautiful" Festival', Letters to the Editor, *New York Times*, 21 August.

Lydon, P. (1969), 'A Joyful Confirmation that Good Things Can Happen Here', Arts, *New York Times*, 24 August.

Marcus, G. (1969), 'The Woodstock Festival', *Rolling Stone*, 20 September.

Marcus, G. (1994), 'So What Was It About Woodstock '69 That Made It Historic?', *Interview*, July.

Marcus, G. (2002), e-mail to Simon Warner, 'Reporting Woodstock', 9 December.

Motion Picture Association/Motion Picture Association of America (2003), 'Movie ratings' http://www.mpaa.org/movieratings/search/index.htm [accessed 5 March 2003].

Narvaez, A.A. (1969), 'Bethel Farmers Call Fair a Plot to "Avoid the Law"', *New York Times*, 20 August.

Reeves, R. (1969), 'Fair's Financier Calls it "Success"', *New York Times*, 18 August.

Selwood, C. (1969), 'Woodstock', *Melody Maker*, 30 August.

Smucker, T. (1970), 'The Politics of Rock: Movement vs Groovement', in J. Eisen (ed.), *The Age of Rock 2: Sights and Sounds of the American Cultural Revolution*, New York: Vintage. Originally published in *Fusion*, 17 October, 1969.

Smucker, T. (2002), e-mail to Simon Warner, 'Reporting Woodstock', 16 August.

Special Correspondent (1969a), 'Promoter Baffled that Festival Drew Such a Big Crowd', *New York Times*, 17 August.

Special Correspondent (1969b), 'Bethel pilgrims smoke "grass" and some take LSD to "groove"', *New York Times*, 18 August.

Special Correspondent (1969c), 'Farmer with Soul', *New York Times*, 18 August.

Unknown author (1969), 'Rock Enthusiasts Suffer Hunger and Thirst', *The Guardian*, 18 August.

Ward, E., Stokes, G. and Tucker, K. (1986), *Rock of Ages: The Rolling Stone History of Rock and Roll*, London: Penguin.

Young, J. and Lang, M. (1979), *Woodstock Festival Remembered*, New York: Ballantine Books.

Chapter 6

The contradictory aesthetics of Woodstock

Allan F. Moore

Theory

The phrase 'Woodstock Nation' says it all. A convenient shorthand, certainly. A falsehood, even more so. However, the articulation of the concept of a self-determined ethnicity to an event whose purpose was music reminds us that in the late 1960s it was possible to maintain the illusion that certain musical practices acted as a universalizing social force. The strength of this association must not be underestimated. While popular music in the industrialized West in the 1930s and 1940s had been a leisure pursuit, and in the 1950s and early 1960s had become crucial to subcultural identification ('Teddy Boys', 'Mods') as the available stylistic patterns multiplied, the revulsion felt by affluent youth at US imperialism in Southeast Asia coincided with an ever more radical approach to music-making and selling, such that we talk about a single 'counter-culture', identifiable by its 'sound'. These days, the 'sound of the '80s' is recognized as no more than a marketing ploy for selling back-catalogue compilations for nostalgic reassurance. 'The sound of the '60s', though, continues to evade its metonymicity.

Why should this be? Part of the fault, of course, clearly lies with the musicians themselves, who forgot that they were just workers and believed themselves to be leaders. As critic Lester Bangs observed sourly: 'Popular music . . . has absolutely nothing to do with anything except making money and getting rich. Some popular musicians start out with revolutionary rhetoric, but all they want is cars and girls and champagne.' Promoter Bill Graham also shares this view: 'An artist would get onstage and say: "Let's get together" and fight and share and communicate. Then he'd get into his jet and fly off to his island and play with his sixteen-track machine. It was hypocrisy . . . how many musicians went onstage and said: "Don't take acid, it ruins your head"? Not one. Not one' (both quoted in Palmer, 1976, pp. 270, 247–48).[1] Musicians, then, had no business adopting any kind of political rhetoric, no duty to reflect back to their audience the feelings and beliefs that audiences appeared to be expressing. But hang on, isn't that simply to accept that, once such listeners have the benefit of becoming mature, they will see that popular music, for all its illusion of magic, is just another enterprise? This is political rhetoric, but it is a defence of the 'high art' position (it is unpopular music that has nothing to do with making money). No, the phrase 'Woodstock Nation' says it all. The relation between music and society is not so simple, and we need to take a step back to observe how and why this is the case.

As a theoretical issue, understanding how music relates to the society from which it issues remains a vexed problem. Robert Walser suggests that the problem dissolves, declaring that 'you only have the problem of connecting music and society if you've separated them in the first place' (Walser, 2003). Tempting though this line of argument is, the observation that our culture behaves as if 'music' and 'society' operate separately (we use music to escape, in some way or other) doesn't permit us simply to claim that it shouldn't. The Romantic aesthetics to which our music practices are heir are founded, after all, on the assumption of the autonomy – the separation from the outside world – of the musical experience. Raymond Monelle, on the other hand, argues that the two spheres cannot be related or, at least, that they relate only at one remove: 'Music does not signify society . . . it does not signify "reality" . . . codes [only] signify each other' (2000, p. 19). This, too, seems unsatisfactory, if only because we do not inhabit a society with any skill in seeing its own illusory nature. Nicholas Cook's theory of multimedia proposes three possible types of relationship between the media involved, one of which is conformance, where both media correspond to each other, where they effectively tell the same story, in the process each amplifying the narrative pursued by the other (Cook, 1998, p. 100ff). Cook may seem a strange source to use, but he insists that 'multimedia' is defined, in part, by the emergence of new meaning greater than that of the individual media. In other words, the media act on each other. In this sense, it seems to me that 'music' and 'society' can be considered simply different media, and this relationship of conformance can stand for how 'music' and 'society' may interact.

Correspondence theories have been around a long time, wherein features in both 'music' and 'society' appear capable of analogous interpretation. This cannot be taken too far: the semiotician Charles Morris notes that while Stravinsky's *Rite of Spring* does not denote any particular thing, its field of reference is not sufficiently wide to include 'a quiet brook, or lovers in the moonlight, or the self's tranquility. "Primitive forces in elemental conflict" . . . is the approximate signification of the music' (quoted in Merriam, 1964, p. 233). We may describe such a signification as working with a *realist* aesthetic, wherein aspects of the real world (the world we believe we inhabit, naturally) conform to, or appear to work in parallel with, aspects of the art which we create to express that inhabiting. However, as Monelle argues, the world we inhabit is not simply a natural one – a realization which caused a crisis of consciousness in the early part of the last century, and which gave birth to a new, modernist aesthetic. The constructed nature of our world was here made apparent in the absence of naturalism structuring the art created to express that new consciousness: Kandinsky's abstract watercolours; Joyce's attack on chronological time; the unadorned functionalism of the Bauhaus; the fragmentation of melodic gesture in Schoenberg. Under modernism we should therefore expect some sort of rupture between features of our world and its expression.[2]

Consciousness

What did the world look like to the Woodstock generation, to the Wood-stock Nation? Theodore Roszak pointed to the attempt, in the early poetry of Allen Ginsberg, to extract the 'impulse' of the creative act, irrespective of its aesthetic quality, and without the imposition of rational reworking: 'what the counter culture offers us, then, is a remarkable defection from the long-standing tradition of skeptical, secular intellectuality' (Roszak, 1969, pp. 128, 141). Roszak stressed the attempt across the counter-culture to arrest processes of alienation (of individual from individual) which threatened to result in the objectification of the individual (ibid., p. 58). Charles Reich insisted that this very attempt resulted from a new consciousness, itself a product of two factors: the promise offered by the American Dream, and the threat offered to it by everything from Vietnam to nuclear war to the degradation of everyday existence (1971, p. 234).

Literature concerning the counter-culture majored on this idea of a new consciousness: thus, Andrew Weil (1975) contrasted 'straight' from 'stoned' thinking, the latter beneficially resulting from psychotropic substances, providing a rational ('straight') argument for the exploits of Timothy Leary, Ken Kesey and others; and the psychiatrist R.D. Laing (1968) challenged the very ground on which 'old' consciousness interpreted behaviour. While this claim for a new consciousness also marked a clear originary point for the New Age mentality (Ferguson (1981) tempers this with reference to such luminaries as Buckminster Fuller), for Reich, it was built on the foundation of personal liberation 'from the automatic acceptance of the imperatives of society and the false consciousness which society imposes' (1971, p. 241) – a liberation in which personal responsibility to effect change was crucial (ibid., p. 248),[3] and which was marked particularly by one's appearance (and thus ultimately degenerated into simply an issue of fashion). The change was towards reconnection, towards undoing the 'disembedding' of the individual from context which, for Giddens (1990, p. 21ff), is symptomatic of modernity.

Thus, to return to the terms used above, we should expect a realist, rather than a modernist, aesthetic to underpin the artistic expression of this culture (although such an assumption, of course, underlies almost all work in popular culture). Nowhere, it seems to me, is this more apparent than in Jimi Hendrix's mauling of the US national anthem at the close of his own set at Woodstock (see Chapter 2). The notes of the tune are attacked, distorted, interrupted with imitations of gunfire and sirens, in an aural equivalent of burning the flag.[4] Individuality, social responsibility, freedom of expression, a separation from the corporate mentality – to what extent can we find these cultural beliefs expressed in the music which was performed at Woodstock?

Heterogeneity

In a telling passage, Reich notes that the music of the Woodstock generation lacked uniformity: 'no single form of music can really claim pre-eminence. It is the richness and variety and continually changing quality of the new music that is its essence' (1971, p. 271). His immediately subsequent insistence that it 'defies analysis and explication . . . because it never stands still to be analyzed' only panders to the refusal to submit experience to rational critique which he has already cited as a hallmark feature. Weil (1975) typifies the difficulty of carrying out such a critique with both personal and cultural integrity. Deena Weinstein argues that it was this heterogeneity which 'demonstrated youth's cohesiveness as a social group defined by age' (1999, p. 107). Indeed, this variety is an immediately perceived feature of both the video and the extant recordings of the Woodstock festival.[5] Thus we find the acoustic (quasi-'folk') singer (Richie Havens, Arlo Guthrie, Joan Baez), retro rock 'n' roll (Sha-Na-Na), progressive blues (The Paul Butterfield Blues Band, Canned Heat, Ten Years After), blue-eyed soul (Joe Cocker, Janis Joplin, Blood, Sweat and Tears), psychedelia (Jimi Hendrix, the Grateful Dead, Jefferson Airplane), 'country' rock (Creedence Clearwater Revival, The Band), soul funk (Sly and the Family Stone), straight-ahead rock (The Who, Mountain) and even the unrestrainedly exotic (Ravi Shankar). Moreover, there is a crazy mixture of performers with actual or potential singles chart viability (Creedence, Cocker, Melanie, The Who, Crosby, Stills and Nash, John Sebastian) and those who wouldn't be seen dead in such charts (even Keef Hartley and Tim Hardin). As I shall suggest below, this stylistic richness is fundamentally contradictory. It is inherently necessary in its valorization of individual taste, without concern for any greater coherent structure of feeling. It also demonstrates aspects of that greater coherence which prevents any simple interpretation of the Woodstock aesthetic as implying a lack of desire, or ability, to discriminate.

By the time Michael Wadleigh's cameras fix on Richie Havens, he had been on stage well in excess of two hours.[6] Although now largely forgotten, in 1968 he was one of few black singers (Otis Redding, Sly Stone and, of course, Jimi Hendrix also come to mind) generally accepted by the counter-culture. His final song, 'Freedom', during the playing of which he simply gets up and walks to the back of the stage as if in disgust, was improvised. Just prior to this exit, he instructs his audience to 'clap your hands' (in time, not in applause) – a traditional gesture of solidarity through communal action. In the context of the festival, however, it seems to have greater significance. First, members of the audience stand, one by one, a shared act felt appropriate at just that moment. Second, many of them would have encountered the advance publicity inviting them to a 'weekend in the country', where the ticket also bought camping space (for which, read 'temporary commune'), an experience which would have been new, and therefore exciting, to many. Third, the reason for Havens' mammoth set was the non-arrival of subsequent performers, itself a result of the organizers' total failure to adequately judge the festival's popularity – roads were jammed for miles around.

This lack of control over arrangements is mirrored by the lack of control shown over admission; somehow, ticket booths were never set up and, once the perimeter fence was stormed, the festival became, to all intents and purposes, free – a powerful subversion of social norms (a basic tenet of which is that all acquisitions are to be paid for). Yet, there were contradictions among the organizers over the degree to which these norms were to be subverted. On the Friday the MC, Chip Monck, announced to the crowd that, just because it is a 'free concert' now, 'doesn't mean anything goes'. This total loss of gate money was of no concern to the festival's driving force: Michael Lang. Barefooted (especially riding his motorcycle), fresh-faced and long-haired, although he was the initiator of the festival and therefore, by definition, one with some appreciable power in the situation, he came across like an archetypal hippy. He argues on film that music's importance lies in the directness with which it communicates with people, and in any case it means much more than just money. Surprisingly, not all his audience agreed. At one point on the film,[7] a long interview with a young male (identified as 'Gerry') and a female, already in a commune, reveals that they feel the attitude of many of the audience to be 'contrived', particularly in relation to the necessity of taking drugs. For them, the music is less important than 'answers' to the ills of industrial society, which the festival is highly unlikely to supply. And, judging from some of the film's eavesdroppings into phone calls 'home', it didn't – some festivalgoers bemoaned the poor facilities, the ubiquitous mud and the failure of supplies. The disagreement with Lang's view moved in the other direction, too. Of the four festival organizers, only Lang and Capitol vice-president, Artie

Kornfeld, appear in the film. John Roberts and Joel Rosenman, who supplied the funding, are nowhere to be seen and, having bought out Lang and Kornfeld within weeks of Woodstock closing, had no further contact for 20 years (see Tiber, 1994).

Performance

I want to bring together observations about the attributes of the Woodstock Nation with some analysis of what actually happened on the stage at Woodstock. If we recall Ginsberg's focus on the creative act's impulse, on the moment itself, we can clearly find this epitomized in Havens' closing song. This focus, I think, is an important clue to the difference between the new consciousness (personal liberation from the imperatives of society) and the old consciousness (marked by alienation and the objectification of the individual) posited by Reich. Whereas the old was concerned for the future, the new was concerned only for the present. This radical departure in terms of temporal sense is crucial to music, an art form utterly dependent on the passage of time. In practical terms, it becomes visible through the notion of free expression. Of the cultural beliefs enumerated above, this is probably the simplest feature to locate in a performance: its most obvious site is in improvisatory passages. Here, so it seems, a player takes flight over some sort of rhythmic/bass support, leaving behind the accepted norms (the melody, probably the phrase structure, certainly the lyrics) of a song, and allowing his or her own expression to arise *ab nihilo* as an exploration of the present moment. The ideology at work specifies that improvisation arises from the emotion of the player, being transferred directly, in unmediated form (well, it has to be translated into sound, but that's so obvious as to be able to be completely ignored), to the emotional receptors of the listener (see Moore, 2001, pp. 83–88). Little could be further from the truth. Improvisation consists of the regurgitation of pre-learnt formulae, recast on the spot to serve the exigencies of the moment, but entirely subject to both the technique of the player and, normally, conforming to the musical substrate provided harmonically and metrically by the bass and drum kit (if nothing else). Even where a player improvises totally unaccompanied, formula and technique remain paramount. And we all experience a very close analogue, of course, when we converse. It is therefore not surprising that, in wishing to preserve the illusion of magic, listeners denied anything so mundane. In the case of Havens' 'Freedom', however, the cause seems less his desire to express himself than his much more prosaic need to continue to play in the absence of subsequent acts. We can see such improvisation operating through a number of very varied examples, in a range of different modes. This very variety implies the lack of coherence mentioned above.

Although Janis Joplin is backed by her Kozmic Blues Band, they make no appearance in the film – the focus is very much on Joplin's highly expressive performance. Her singing of 'Work me Lord' is taken at a very slow speed, giving her plenty of space to indulge her particular vocal approach, which consists of the repetition of very short phrases, with the use of extreme melismas, which are often either wordless or simply repeat just one or two words as if she is struggling with their inadequacy to express her needs fully. When taken with the extremely raucous tone of her voice and the doubt inherent in what lyrics we can make out (is her man remaining with her or not?), her desperate uncertainty is intensified. After all, there is no regular, identifiable melody to be found in her performance here. Indeed, there is very little happening, musically. At some points she is accompanied by protracted organ and horn chords, while throughout there is a steady, unfussy groove in the bass and drum kit. She is therefore able to give free rein to her expression which comes across as straight from the heart, as intensely felt, and as particular to that situation, special to that audience. Only at one moment is this carefully built presentation challenged: towards the end of her quasi-preached improvisation, undertaken with no accompanimental support whatsoever, a single note on the organ momentarily interrupts her singing. She turns her head, with what appears to be a slight smile, but doesn't lose her thread.[8] This continuity could imply two things: either her complete self-involvement in her own expression (although she does seem to acknowledge the bum note), or a greater measure of rehearsal of this improvisatory ending than an audience would otherwise want to believe.

Alvin Lee's improvisatory performance of 'I'm Going Home' represents another approach. Like Joplin, he is in supreme control of the performance which represents his own expression as singer and guitarist rather than that of the band (Ten Years After). It is a fine example of how inherently musical such expression is – although this is a 'song', and although it employs words, those words are no more than a vehicle for Lee's own manner of performance and a contrast to his use of the guitar. They really have no semantic content. In this performance the song runs to almost ten minutes in length and is in four phases. Lee first inserts verses from other 12-bar blues ('Baby Please Don't Go', 'Blue Suede Shoes', 'Whole Lotta Shakin') into his song, without changing key or tempo (the whole performance moves at a terrific speed, ultimately consisting of more than 50 repetitions of the basic 12-bar pattern). There is clear vocal virtuosity at play here, of a different order to Joplin's (the rhythm section maintains a rigid beat throughout – Lee simply alights on particular beats and spaces between, rather than seeming to stretch that space, as Joplin does). This is succeeded by a series of verses over which he improvises, at breakneck speed, but using established improvisatory formulae. Much as he had done in the first phase, he is manipulating already-formed material rather than appearing to create it from nowhere. The third phase is marked by a return to the (minimal) lyrics (which consist of little more than 'I'm Goin' Home To My Baby'), while the final phase combines this with various improvisatory licks, the whole coming to a surprisingly uncoordinated conclusion. This performance contains much evidence of planning.[9] There is the mere fact that it can be broken down into these broad periods. There is the careful way in which the emotional intensity is manipulated: the latter part of the first phase is marked by a decrease of intensity; the latter part of the second is marked similarly, but here the decrease is sustained through much of the third phase; and the final phase therefore begins with a well-prepared explosion of activity. There is the use of established patterns of playing. So, although it is easy to see how an audience can interpret such improvisatory approaches as evidence that performers are expressing themselves by escaping the rigid confines of song, there is plenty of room for doubt as to how free from observation of external structures such expression actually is.

Let's look briefly at the improvisation within three other performances. Joe Cocker's rendition of the Lennon/McCartney 'With A Little Help From My Friends' is regarded as a classic, as an embodiment of the 'sanctified speed' already a staple of bands like Vanilla Fudge, where uptempo mainstream pop songs had their tempi shattered to create immense space for gospel-derived improvisation. What is interesting in Cocker's performance is not only the immense space he traverses within the beat, but his strange stage persona. His movements are awkward in the way his hips control his legs. This stretches to his arms as he returns again and again to miming an intense guitar solo. This difficulty of movement is transferred to his voice as, again raucous in tone, there is pain evident in his singing. The speed of the song allows him almost to flounder within the beat – the help needed from his friends is there for all to hear as, without them, he is temporally nowhere. The help is nonetheless supplied, such that by the climactic second bridge, he no longer needs the lyrics. This performance like that of Joplin, conveys the impression that he is totally immersed but, yet again, the film implies that it is very easily turned off at the end – the passage back to everyday reality is surprisingly short, as Cocker simply leaves the microphone and, although clearly out of breath, within ten seconds is chatting with those towards the back of the stage.

On the other hand, Mike Shrieve's display, although he is equally immersed, seems far less self-seeking. Shrieve, only 16 at the time, was drummer for Carlos Santana's band, and he takes a solo in 'Soul Sacrifice'. He has immense technique, not only displaying virtuosity within the very regular beat (rather as I have described Alvin Lee as doing), but controlling changes of speed – first accelerating, then slowing.[10] The effect of real, physical effort is visible on his face. On Santana's, however, it is metaphorical effort which is visible as he screws his face up on reaching his solo's highest, bent, note. This emotional effort is undertaken empathetically for the audience – they are moving with him, while bassist David Brown looks on in apparent awe. A better visual example of the Romantic myth of the artist as hero would be hard to find.

Jimi Hendrix's improvisations on the final day are of a different order, however. Prior to 'The Star Spangled Banner', he moves into some free invention. This is led partly by the shape of his hand, falling into patterns he has established, but also by a chain of sheer inventiveness based partly on the blues scale, partly on the cycle of fifths harmonic sequence (which clearly appears in two separate locations). Technically, this is outstanding, not least in the immense coordination demonstrated between his hands. Emotionally it is pretty devastating, too,[11] as he leaves bassist Billy Cox musically behind. There is, however, a suspicion of disdain on his face as he plays (he looks unabashedly into the camera, openly aware of the larger audience to whom he is playing) – the audience for his finale was a fraction of that earlier in the weekend.

One thing not to be forgotten is the degree to which the audience outnumbered the performers, and how many of the former were some distance from the stage for large periods of time. There were amateur performers galore at Woodstock, making their own music (perhaps more in the spirit of the counter-culture), using tins and whatever else came to hand. One fine example can be seen at around 1h.30' on the first video (*Woodstock: The Director's Cut*). An elemental chant is accompanied by whatever instruments are to hand – tins, sticks, hand-claps – in a manner reminiscent of the Fugs' revolutionary 'Exorcising the Evil Spirits from the Pentagon October 21, 1967'.[12] Indeed, the individuality prized by these experiments in free expression is supported by the individual nature of the responses of some of the participants. John Street argues that the emphasis on improvisation, and on the exploration of individual subjectivity which this enables, derives from jazz practice. (The other contemporary source of improvisation, that of the experimental art music tradition, while apparent in avant garde rock such as Henry Cow, Kevin Ayres and King Crimson, was not part of the hippy ethos.) There is, however, a vital difference of significance: 'For the white rock artist, "freedom" meant release from parental and school control, and from materialism. For the jazz player, freedom meant freedom from racial oppression and from poverty' (Street, 1986, p. 170). From the evidence above, we can see this as less the racial divide implied by Street and more a purely stylistic one. With the possible exception of Havens' performance, it is personal and spiritual freedom which was being celebrated here, by Santana and Hendrix as much as by Cocker and Lee.

Contradiction

Two extremes of performance were present on the Woodstock stage. On the one hand, there was the intimacy of the solo performer (Joan Baez, John Sebastian), communing, as it were, with each individual separately! Such performers had all graduated from the coffee-bar and folk-club circuit where it was possible, and often necessary, to establish eye contact with individual listeners (and listeners they were, giving far more attention than comes from a dancing audience). On the other hand, there was the level of volume, and hence distancing, associated with electrified bands – whether aimed at listeners (The Who) or dancers (Sly and the Family Stone). In comparison with previous forms of popular music, this music was identified by its propensity for noise. Sound is far harder to shut out, to ignore, than vision, touch or taste and has therefore acted as a site of conflict ever since the public became aware of rock 'n' roll. Although one might assume that this would be a cause of conflict with local residents, interviewees caught on camera complain much more about the inauthenticity of revellers: that the politics had 'nothing to do with Vietnam'; that people were simply 'all on pot'; and that they had 'no conception of money' (and were, therefore, undermining quite fundamental cultural values).

Wadleigh tries to provide a balanced picture. The film opens giving the clear impression of a lack of conflict, at least at the point at which festivalgoers begin to arrive. Locals found the presence, and attitude, of all these 'beautiful people' to be 'overwhelming', despite a great deal of controversy which had already surfaced over whether the festival should be allowed to take place in that neighbourhood at all. Even the local chief of police was happy to be caught on camera claiming to be 'proud of these kids', who he regarded as 'good American citizens', presumably on account of their assertion of their individual rights.

Such identification of beauty is a little difficult to sustain in the face of the mass of detritus left on the camping field, which required an army of those remaining simply to clear up. Indeed, more than one attender inter-viewed talks about the temporary 'city' which has been created – indicating perhaps that such squalor needs to be assumed and accepted. Christopher Small, contextualizing events such as this within both contemporary society and a whole range of other Western musical practices, argues that it is of the nature of music to create, while it is being heard, an 'ideal temporary society or community' (1977, p. 171). Woodstock provides a clear instance of such a community: for three days, a temporary city was in existence, functioning (after a fashion) as a microcosm of a more egalitarian society. Monetary transactions were the exception; support was provided on the basis of need; guarding of individual (alienated) space appears to have been at a minimum; and social mores concerning dress and gesture, inherited from established society, carried no hegemonic force. To quote from Small again: 'something did take place; there *was* a new kind of experience that had nothing to do with the world of the concert hall or . . . dance hall or . . .' and, speaking of the slightly later Isle of Wight Festival in 1970:

> . . . there came into at least partial existence the potential society which lies otherwise beyond our grasp; young people released from the stresses and restrictions of their everyday life were engaging in the celebration of a common myth, a common life-style . . . music became . . . the centre of a communal ritual . . . illusion . . . but real enough at the time. (Ibid.)

This society was clearly totally out of kilter with a corporate mentality in which viability is founded on the bottom line. By failing to ensure that an entrance fee was collected, the organizers failed to ensure that, as an event, Woodstock would repay those who had made a financial investment in it. John Street points out that this was a result of 'administrative mistakes' rather than 'political commitment' (1986, p. 74). Roberts and Rosenmann had made every effort to place the event on a sound financial footing but, from the available evidence, it is certainly possible to argue that this was undermined by Lang – theirs represented only a temporary merger of differing interests.

Yet, there is much more to such an analysis than just this. The 'old consciousness' (to revert to Reich's term), we may assume, includes an interest in maintaining social order. The war in Vietnam can be seen as an outcome of such a position, as a desire to maintain capitalism within Southeast Asia, in order to foster markets. I have already quoted one local resident as claiming that, as far as he was concerned, arguments put forward by the counter-culture against the involvement in Vietnam were simply a front. However, it is difficult not to accept that there was an authentic call against the war, particularly from some of the performances, if not from the anarchist groups who embedded themselves within the festival. (In making this distinction, it is worth recalling Robin Denselow's insistence that 'British pop singers in the sixties . . . were never as politically involved as many of their followers supposed' (1989, p. 97).) Examples include: Country Joe's 'Cheer', whose irony is vitriolic against the patriotism involved in supporting the war; Jefferson Airplane's 'Uncle Sam's Blues', in which Uncle Sam, although 'not a woman', nonetheless can 'take your man'; and also Richie Havens' 'Handsome Johnny', which situates Vietnam in a long line of similarly unnecessary conflicts and which, as a song, gains power through its formal links to the English ballad tradition. There is a clear difference made between the conflict as a political act and the role of those individuals who are involved in it. Prior to Country Joe's performance, one well-dressed attender is interviewed as arguing that the rain is due to the 'Fascist pigs seeding the clouds' (in an outburst which does not seem ironic). However, the use of the army to drop in food and raincoats in the face of the organizational disaster is readily accepted and lauded, while the help brought in by army medical teams is celebrated in terms of 'They're with us, man, they are not against us'.[13] Individual soldiers, even working together, are not the target of the counter-culture's ire here: it is, rather, the politicians directing the war. The acceptance of establishment figures as individuals extends to others: doctors on site were working without pay because 'they dig what we are into'. The care with which this 'conflict' has to be negotiated is made clear by John Sebastian's comment that generations need to understand each other, and are in the process of doing just that.

However, this was a society rife with contradictions that go beyond the easy coexistence of stylistic differences. 'Capitalism isn't that weird,' pronounces the MC, asking people to patronize the owner of the hamburger stand which had burnt down the previous evening, having only just previously announced that 'breakfast in bed' would be provided free to the 400 000 guests.[14] On one part of the site, a group of makeshift canoeists sing, of all things, the 'Eton Boat Song'. A clearer reference to the celebration of class-riven society would be hard to find, and the singing of it in canon, a learned device, merely emphasizes the apparent ignorance in the appropriation. On another part of the site (and presumably at another time, so possibly even involving the same participants), a young yogi instructs a group of initiates in kundalini exercises, pointing (as so much of the counter-culture did) towards the individuality-dissolving practices of Eastern religions (in this context, note the raga-like turns of phrase in Stephen Stills' solo in Crosby, Stills and Nash's 'Suite: Judy Blue Eyes'). Sly Stone encourages participation in his performance by declaring that they didn't need anyone's approval – that 'sing-along' is not unfashionable – this, relating to a practice most closely identified with nostalgic longing.

To have sung along with the aggression of The Who, however, would not have been possible. Unusually among the guitarists featured at Woodstock, Townshend holds his guitar at waist height. This has become the 'normal' position today, allowing the expression of aggression both through the speed of right arm movement and also because the left arm, being fully extended, can shift the guitar some distance away from the body. This position was very rare in the 1960s – most guitarists were still holding their guitars in the more ergonomically sound way, with the body of the guitar in front of the lower part of the chest, almost as an extension of the body. Townshend's aggression, of course, mirrors that of vocalist Roger Daltrey. Whether The Who are included in the 'Beautiful People' of Melanie Safka's show-stopping performance is a moot point.

At two, highly telling, points in Wadleigh's film, the power exhibited in The Who's performance can be seen to relate to a more subtle acceptance of its use. It is here, I think, that identifying Bill Graham's 'hypocrisy' becomes crucial. The first of these is the idealistic delight expressed by Kornfeld and Lang, in conversation, claiming that, even in such a large gathering, police are unnecessary and thus that their society had escaped the control of established forces. The second, and certainly the most depressing moment of the entire film, is a throw-away comment by Arlo Guthrie, coming in to perform, that the festival had succeeding in closing the New York throughway. Here, by force of might, the new society was imposing its will on the old. Nothing new there, then.

Conclusion

Perhaps it is asking too much of such a heterogeneous set of events to display a great deal of coherence – or, at least, to display a coherent philosophy of life, of action, or even of art. But that seems to me to be just the point. In the contradictions which shoot through the performances at Woodstock ('we all had caught the same disease', as Melanie Safka's paean to the festival puts it[15]), both in terms of stylistic parameters and in terms of their expression of social values, these performances do indeed express the social values of the counter-culture, which we may summarize as the longing for free expression and for individuality, and the difficulty of maintaining those within any social structure worthy of the name. These alone, aside from any inherent strength in established modes of acting, suggest why Reich's 'old consciousness', to our continuing detriment, remains our birthright.

Notes

1. Clearly Graham had never paid attention to Grand Funk Railroad, for one.
2. One artistic working-through of this dichotomy is explored in Moore (1995).
3. It is this loss of social conscience which surely marks the degeneration of the hippy ideal into the New Age reality.
4. And yet, Keith Emerson's similar treatment of an excerpt from Sibelius's *Karelia* suite, released in 1968 on the Nice's *Arts Longa, Vita Brevis*, was read as homage. Interpretive context, as here, is all-important.
5. *Woodstock: The Director's Cut*, dir. Michael Wadleigh (Warner, 1994 [1969]), to which I refer continuously. Aside from the many bootleg albums, CDs, and video footage of some individual bands released separately (for example, The Who, Jimi Hendrix), the other key sources are the CDs *Woodstock*, *Woodstock Two* and the 25th Anniversary box set. The most authoritative account of the running order is probably that of Kees de Lange (1999), on whom I rely for this information.

6. For details of the festival organization, as here, I refer largely to Elliott Tiber's firsthand account (1994).
7. At 1 hour 5 mins into tape 1 of *The Director's Cut*.
8. This appears at 1h.19'25" of tape 2 of *The Director's Cut*. The organ note is quite probably an accident – with such little lighting, it is all too easy a matter for a player to clip the keys when walking away from the instrument at the end of a performance.
9. I am not implying that some procedure has been written down, but that previous performing experience, and anticipation of the need to provide a strong close to the set for publicity reasons if no other, have structured this performance prior to its taking place.
10. This may seem a simple comment, but control of such gradual changes of speed is beyond the technique of many otherwise competent drummers, making them the butt of many 'in' jokes.
11. For participants at Woodstock, this performance seems to have appeared rather lacklustre. The running order of the performance is not that displayed on the film – I rely here on Shaar-Murray's account (1989, pp. 194–5), in which the improvisation leads into 'Banner' and then into 'Purple Haze'.
12. A location recording, released in 1968 on *Tenderness Junction*.
13. These occur at the end of Part 1 of Wadleigh's video, and after about 29 mins of Part 2.
14. This announcement appears to have been made on the final, Monday, morning, prior to Jimi Hendrix's appearance.
15. From the Melanie Safka song 'Lay Down' on the album *Candles in the Rain* (Buddah, 1970).

References

Cook, N. (1998), *Analysing Musical Multimedia*, Oxford: Clarendon Press.

de Lange, K. (1999), *The Actual Schedule of Woodstock*, http://home.Columbus.rr.com/woodstock1969/set_lists.html.

Denselow, R. (1989), *When the Music's Over: The Story of Political Pop*, London: Faber.

Ferguson, M. (1981), *The Aquarian Conspiracy: Personal and Social Transformation in the 1980s*, London: Granada.

Giddens, A. (1990), *The Consequences of Modernity*, Stanford, CT: Stanford University Press.

Laing, R.D. (1968), *The Politics of Experience*, New York: Ballantine.

Merriam, A. (1964), *The Anthropology of Music*, Evanston, IL: Northwestern University Press.

Monelle, R. (2000), *The Sense of Music*, Princeton, NJ: Princeton University Press.

Moore, A.F. (1995), 'Serialism and its Contradictions', *International Review of the Aesthetics and Sociology of Music*, **26**(1), pp. 79–95.

Moore, A.F. (2001), *Rock: The Primary Text*, 2nd edn, Aldershot: Ashgate.

Palmer, T. (1976), *All You Need is Love: The Story of Popular Music*, London: Futura.

Reich, C. (1971), *The Greening of America*, Toronto: Bantam.

Roszak, T. (1969), *The Making of a Counter Culture: Reflections on the Technocratic Society and its Youthful Opposition*, London: Faber and Faber.

Shaar-Murray, C. (1989), *Crosstown Traffic: Jimi Hendrix and Post-War Pop*, London: Faber and Faber.

Small, C. (1977), *Music – Society – Education*, London: John Calder.

Street, J. (1986), *Rebel Rock: The Politics of Popular Music*, Oxford: Blackwell.

Tiber, E. (1994), *How Woodstock Happened*, http://www.woodstock69.com/wsrprnt. htm [last accessed 17 January 2002].

Walser, R. (2003), 'Popular Music Analysis: Ten Apothegms and Four Instances', in A.F. Moore (ed.), *Analysing Popular Music*, Cambridge: Cambridge University Press.

Weil, A. (1975), *The Natural Mind*, London: Penguin. First published in 1972.

Weinstein, D. (1999), 'Youth', in B. Horner and T. Swiss (eds), *Key Terms in Popular Music and Culture*, Oxford: Blackwell.

Chapter 7

'Unsafe things like youth and jazz': Beaulieu Jazz Festivals (1956–61), and the origins of pop festival culture in Britain[1]

George McKay

. . . primitive mini-Woodstocks . . . (Mick Farren, counter-cultural organizer
of the 1970 Phun City Festival, on the Beaulieu Jazz Festivals cited in Farren
and Barker, 1972, no pagination.)

We're festival crazy!
In the past five years, we have gone Festival crazy. From Lord Montagu's
late-lamented brainchild, the Beaulieu Jazz Festival, a whole industry has
grown. Bands, which used to look upon the summer as the slack season, now
find themselves on a dozen or more well-paid Festival dates . . . The National
Jazz Festivals at Richmond, Earlswood and Ringwood are now among the
firmly established annual events. ('Guide', 1962.)[2]

This chapter looks at the origins of pop festival culture in Britain, the relatively under-researched phenomenon of the early jazz festivals in the New
Forest during the 1950s. It explores subcultural contestation and negotiation,
with particular attention to the 1960 festival, at which traditional ('trad') jazz
fans and modernists confronted each other during the (mediated) so-called
Battle of Beaulieu. It introduces issues relevant to the later festival movement, and to Woodstock: the significance of the deep green pastoral location,
links (strong or weak) with the burgeoning peace movement of the Campaign
for Nuclear Disarmament, the suggestion from a London beatnik of a free
festival in the forest, the question of atavism and the revival of the past. It
also considers the problematic issue of Americanization in the imitation of
the recently founded Newport Jazz Festival, as well as some of the innova-
tions of Beaulieu.

Beaulieu Jazz Festivals and 1950s Britain

It is no coincidence that some of the first seeds of alternative/youth culture in the context of festival were themselves beginning to germinate, even sprout, during the late 1950s.[3] It is easy to lose sight of that decade, the 1950s, either caricaturing it as one of austerity or conformity, or being blinded by the psychedelia that came after it. Yet it is important to consider the extent to which festival culture as it is understood today (and not exclusively in Britain) originates during that time. Music (trad jazz, later skiffle), youth, radical politics (CND, direct action), and festival/carnival itself (Beaulieu Jazz Festival, the Aldermaston CND marches) – all four familiar features found a crucial early expression and combination in Britain during the 1950s. In 1956 Edward John Barrington Douglas-Scott-Montagu, known as Lord Montagu of Beaulieu, established the annual Beaulieu Jazz Festival in the grounds of his stately home within the ancient royal English landscape of the New Forest, in Hampshire. Over the next five years Beaulieu would become one of Europe's earliest and highest-profile jazz festivals, and certainly the prototype for many of the events and problems associated with pop festivals and youth music gatherings in Britain over the following decades. What follows are glimpses of an alternative originary narrative of British pop, not from The Beatles via Germany and Liverpool, but from deepest green Hampshire, not so much through the blues and rock 'n' roll, but through trad jazz, not so much embodied by Teddy Boys as by the 'rave gear' of tradders. Although they have generally been overlooked, the Beaulieu Festivals fit the carnivalesque template of youth, music, protest or identity developments of the time (in approximate chronological order): the Soho Fair, Teddy Boys, the Aldermaston CND marches, the beginnings of Trinidadian carnival in London, early Mod and Rocker scenes. Iain Chambers describes some of the developing youth cultures of the period as:

> An attempt, if you like, to show that what is recognizable in British life need not be bound to [George Orwell's] 'solid breakfasts and gloomy Sundays, smoky towns and winding roads, green fields and red pillar boxes' . . . [T]hese youth groups adapted their styles from consumer objects, . . . their cultural insubordination was allied to consumerism that touched a very un-British hedonism as it 'squandered' its money on extravagant clothing, pop records, scooters, over-priced frothy coffee, motor bikes, drugs, clubs, and attempts to create a perpetual 'weekend.' (Chambers, 1986, p. 53.)

Beaulieu touched, and was touched by, both of these versions of Britain – the past and the future, rural nostalgia and urban clubbing, sensible breakfasts at party weekends.

The stately home of Beaulieu is better known today for its motor museum than for its early flourish of festival culture. Yet Beaulieu, like Woburn in the 1960s and the better-known Knebworth Festivals of the 1970s (Cobbold, 1986), began a connection of aristocratic privilege and pop music, of private means and mass entertainment, that characterized a certain social stratum of those swinging times.[4] 'A combination of blue blood and the blues' was the 1957 Beaulieu motto, while a slogan over the festival stage read 'Harmless amusement for all classes'. Partly, it was generational (Montagu was around 30 years old at the time of the first Beaulieu Jazz Festival) and partly a social shift. As Christopher Booker recognizes, there was 'intimate cooperation between members of the crumbling old order and of the rising new – each fascinated by the powerful image of the other: the insecure lower or less "established" group longing for the style and stability of culture and breeding, the insecure upper group mesmerised by the life and vitality of the *arriviste*' (Booker, 1969, p. 95). Symptoms of this apparent class blurring ranged from the new satire movement calling its London comedy club *The Establishment* to Lord Snowdon, society photographer and brother-in-law of the Queen, holding swinging celebrity-packed parties at Kensington Palace, from Teddy Boys ironically adorning themselves in upper-class Edwardian-style long jackets in the 1950s to Albert Finney and John Lennon swapping their E-Type Jaguars for Rolls-Royces in the 1960s. According to Neil Nehring:

> In the fifties, the ambiguities and contradictions of claims for the 'affluent' society immediately bred 'a diffuse social unease, [experienced] as an unnaturally accelerated pace of social change', eroding reference points in both class and morality. The anxieties of that decade seized 'on the hedonistic culture of youth', in particular, and its presumed verification of the disappearance of the class structure. (Nehring, 1993, p. 179.)[5]

For Jeremy Sandford, in the first book to chronicle the British pop festival movement, *Tomorrow's People*, the 1958 Beaulieu Jazz Festival was 'the first British festival proper, a two-day event that attracted 4,000 people' (Sandford and Reid, 1974, p. 14). The following year 5–10 000 people attended, and the first vocal complaints about the inconvenience and the type of person the festival was attracting were heard from Beaulieu and other nearby villages. The trad boom, with bandleaders such as Acker Bilk, Kenny Ball and Chris Barber featuring high in the charts in Britain and sometimes in the US, was in full swing in the few years either side of the decade (see Berg and Yeomans, 1962; Matthew, 1962; Wallis, 1987). Trad's subcultural *and* commercial success even rivalled that of rock 'n' roll for a while, the hit records beginning with Monty Sunshine playing 'Petite fleur' with Chris Barber's Band in 1959. This had been preceded by the skiffle craze, Lonnie Donegan having a hit with 'Rock Island Line' in 1956, and Chas McDevitt playing his hit 'Freight Train' on *The Ed Sullivan Show* on

American television in June 1957 (McDevitt, 1997, p. 102). The Beaulieu Jazz Festivals contributed to, as well as benefited from, this new music craze. Not too much imagination was required to jump on the, well, bandwagon: the BBC broadcast a series featuring live bands called *Trad Fad*, while the final boom year of 1962 saw books such as Brian Matthew's *Trad Mad* and Richard Lester's film *It's Trad, Dad!* By this time, British jazz was torn not only between revivalists and traditionalist purists, but between both these and the relatively new modernists, so much so that trouble among fans at the 1959 Beaulieu Jazz Festival merely presaged the 1960 festival's Saturday night riot between fans of tradder Acker Bilk and modernist Johnny Dankworth.

For Mick Farren, self-styled (British) White Panther, alternative press journalist, leader of the free festival band the Deviants, and organizer of the 1970 Phun City Festival, 'the scarcely plausible figure of Acker Bilk' during the trad craze could be ignored because:

> Although trad was nowhere as solid as Elvis or Jerry Lee or Little Richard, it did at least bop along in a jolly manner, you could get drunk on cider, and nobody got uptight, although the older patrons did refer to the teenage invaders as 'ravers'. This was all this group was looking for. It was a collective title, it defined them and they could at last rejoice in a separate identity. (Farren and Barker, 1972, no pagination.)

The Beaulieu subculture was indeed eccentric: a group of 15 teenage boys from Worthing, Sussex, called themselves the Barbarians. For the weekend they wore caveman gear – fur loincloths, presumably cut from old fur coats – and carried wooden clubs. The back of one girl's long white shirt was painted with 'IDIOTS OF THE WORLD UNITE!' and many other fans wore clothes sporting slogans. A Movietone newsreel of one festival shows how, as the newsreader says, 'fans forget the conventional life . . . [and] act like crazy!' (*Movietone*, 1961). On the other hand, Kenneth Allsop of the *Daily Mail* (1 August 1960) saw in the term 'raver' 'an ugly new word for an ugly new menace'.

Sandford recaps the story of festival culture to date in the mid-1970s, and traces pop music and identity through the festival:

> What sort of people go to pop festivals? To start with the audience were fairly elitist; trad jazz enthusiasts and, later, trad and modern jazz enthusiasts . . . It is no longer like that now. 'Hippy' ideas, ideals, customs and costumes have spread into large areas of the culture of the young, and the influence of the 'alternative society' can very clearly be seen at festivals; the influence of the underground, flower-power scene, heads, freaks, bohemians, drop-outs, ravers, or whatever title you or fashion prefer to call them by, stretches fairly far; furthest in its music, stimulants and clothing, but far also in other ways. (Sandford and Reid, 1974, p. 10.)

From the beginning of the 1960s, Harold Pendleton's work in particular shows this trajectory of jazz as precursor of festival culture, with his Richmond Jazz Festivals organized under the aegis of the National Jazz Federation (NJF). Not unlike Michael Eavis in subsequent decades with his Glastonbury Festival (see McKay, 2000a, ch. 5; Elstob and Howes, 1987), Pendleton was skilled in identifying changing tastes in popular music and in booking newer bands. As he observed on the 1965 Richmond Festival, 'Over the past year or so the hit parade has been getting crowded with groups whose roots are in jazz' (quoted in Sandford and Reid, 1974, p. 20). He learned this through his involvement with both the Marquee Club in Soho, London, and some of the later Beaulieu Jazz Festivals. The Richmond Festivals are interesting as they encapsulate the musical and social transformation of the time; in the space of a few years in the early 1960s, musical tastes shifted from retro trad jazz and blues of Acker Bilk, Ken Colyer, Alex Welsh, towards the new popular music – and audience – of the blues-oriented bands such as The Rolling Stones, The Yardbirds and Manfred Mann. The 1965 NJF festival was the moment when this change in youth consciousness, music, instrumentation and style became most clear, as the festival publicity articulated: 'Something unheard of is happening at Richmond . . . for the first time . . . the pure jazz-men are outnumbered by beat and rhythm-and-blues groups who are no stranger to the hit parade . . . [The festival is] something of a teenagers' Ascot, the only social occasion on a national scale when they can "try out" new clothes' (quoted in Sandford and Reid, 1974, p. 20). The shift from jazz to rock music is identified as a wider manifestation by Dennis Dworkin:

> Rock music in the sixties and seventies came to express the experience of a generation as powerfully as any form of artistic experience in the twentieth century; during the same period, jazz was more acclaimed in art circles than in the urban neighbourhoods in which it originated. (Dworkin, 1997, p. 120.)

The guitarist with The Who, Pete Townshend, perhaps combining nostalgia with retrospective self-criticism, saw weaknesses in this move:

> Something happened between the trad age and rock. In the trad age there were great people doing great things, founding CND or Amnesty, and trying to mobilize young people. But then the whole subject of politics and the power of the individual to affect change was buried under this tidal wave of rock. (Quoted in Denselow, 1989, p. 93.)

The events at Richmond featured most of the familiar elements of festival culture, for both its proponents and opponents, as outlined by Michael Clarke in *The Politics of Pop Festivals*:

The invasion of large numbers of young people into the pleasanter parts of the countryside for a weekend or a week in the summer, to camp in the open, listen to music, usually loud, sometimes to consume drugs, and in the context of the espousal of overtly bohemian values, involving attitudes to property and sexuality, for example, that are at gross variance with those of the local population, is inevitably a strong base for opposition. (Clarke, 1982, p. 11.)

It should be emphasized, though, that the majority of these common features were inherited from Beaulieu; they were expected by audiences as a result of their experiences at, or their mediated images of, Beaulieu. Christopher Booker's claim in 1961 that: 'The prospect for the promoters of jazz festivals during the sober sixties seems happily "cool"' was only partly correct: jazz festivals did indeed wane, but the decade was hardly to be characterized (or mythicized) by sobriety, and festivals were to become a central form of social expression and gathering (*Sunday Telegraph*, 23 July 1961).

The past and the pastoral, from Beaulieu to Aldermaston

I have written elsewhere of the revivalist aspects of pop festival culture in Britain, of the ways in which many new festivals and carnivals sought to authenticate and *atavise* their existence by echoing or re-presenting previous now-lost traditional events or rituals or, indeed, myths (McKay, 1996, ch. 1). This is evident in some of the most significant urban and rural festival events in Britain today (see McKay, 2000a). For example, in London from 1959 onwards, the Notting Hill Carnival has twin early strands of Trinidadian carnival organized by West Indian immigrants and the revived (with a twist) Victorian-style fair at Notting Hill, in part organized by the alternative community in the mid-1960s. Glastonbury Festival, first held in minor form in 1970, but really an event of the 1980s and 1990s, was invariably timed for the weekend nearest to the summer solstice (21 June), and (subtly) marketed with a heady mixture of medievalism, from Arthurian legend and Avalon to ley lines and, in the 1990s, even a newly constructed Neolithic-style stone circle. Such gestures of reference or invention are not only variously ahistorical or nostalgic or utopian – or even just cod-folkloric – they can also be signs of competing versions of Englishness, reclamations of alternative traditions or visions of the past/present (I know that sounds a bit hippy-dippy) and statements of the significance of place (which helps explain the importance of the Stonehenge Free Festival each summer solstice for a decade up to 1985, and indeed the fact that Stonehenge became an ideological battlefield between travellers and festivalgoers on the one hand and the rightwing authorities on the other during the Thatcher years).

The first Beaulieu Jazz Festival was something of an echo, a conscious revival of the local Beaulieu Fairs of the nineteenth century which had, perhaps ominously, been finally ended due to 'loosely organised rowdyism' of fairgoers (Montagu, 1973, p. 72). *Melody Maker*, keen to promote the jazz festival because of its own organizational links with it, identified some of its retro appeal in 1958 in its description of festival as '[t]he blending of the music of today with memories of centuries gone by' (9 August, 1958). But Montagu, taking control of the estate at the age of 25 after it had been held in trust for two decades following his father's death, was keen to revive other old and now-defunct local customs as well: in 1959 an audit dinner was held again for tenant farmers on the estate, and plans for the revival of the Beaulieu Easter Fair were announced in November 1960. For Montagu, reaching into the past was a way of bridging the interregnum – the lengthy wait until he inherited direct control and responsibility had effectively magnified the past's significance. His motivation for such gestures was strongly to revive manorial authority and his position at the centre of that: after all, in the interwar period other stately homes had been hit by financial crisis, or had architecturally crumbled, or, worse, had been handed over to the state in lieu of taxes. The young Montagu – newly married, lately released from prison for homosexuality following a *cause célèbre* trial,[6] peer of the realm and with a short career in public relations behind him (see Montagu, 2001) – would have to be flexible if he was to survive and prosper through the partial 'collapse' of the upper class and the 'relative decline of the significance of landed wealth, and the increasing diversity of wealth' (McKibbin, 1998, p. 42). He saw those twin icons of transatlantic modernity, cars and jazz, as the means of diversification to protect his 8000-acre privileged patch of historic England. Old English and New World cultures would be brought together at the festival – not quite the dairy imperative and pastoral promise of Max Yasgur's farm at Bethel, or even Michael Eavis's farm at Glastonbury come to that. But for a time it worked, to the extent that jazz critic Benny Green could observe in 1962 that: 'It seems likely that the festival has now superseded the concert as the highest degree of respectability in the jazz world. To the evolutionary progress from brothel to ginmill to dancehall to podium must now be added the greensward' (*Observer*, 19 August, 1962).[7]

Of course, the past was everywhere at Beaulieu, in the New Forest – a landscape and community that was an atavistic social and cultural space all of its own. Beaulieu was an extraordinary, and extraordinarily rural, site for the continued negotiation with modernity that was taking place in Britain (possibly more especially England) during the period: a slow embracing of speed cultures. A key visual and functional icon of modernity (the motor car) was championed, but for its vintage, its heritage; a key sonic signifier of modernity (jazz music) was championed, but with a major glance to its past forms, specifically traditional and revivalist jazz, which Kevin Morgan describes neatly as 'the newest and the oldest sound in British jazz' (Morgan, 1998, p. 123).[8] This incongruity, achronology, remains part of Beaulieu's charm today, for motor car enthusiasts at least: visitors to the motor museum gaze at a record-breaking speed machine inside; outside, framed in the picture glazing, a New Forest pony walks through a wooded glade. For other visitors, the extraordinarily romantic landscape of wild ponies, open heathland and willow, oak and birch forests and glades is a powerful touristic experience of a *special, boundaried* and *historic* rurality.

At this time, too, other, more socially democratic and politically engaged countermodernisms were being expressed and explored in the increasingly shifting society of Britain. Meredith Veldman argues that:

> Whether it was E.P. Thompson's alternative version of history with its stress on the antiauthoritarian tradition of the freeborn Englishman or the more familiar orthodoxy of the Whig interpretation of the steady unfolding of democratic rights within a stable democratic system, the British, or at least *the English past could be and was used to criticize and challenge the nuclear present.* (Veldman, 1994, p. 203; emphasis added.)

The Campaign for Nuclear Disarmament was founded in 1958 and, as Ian Campbell has written, 'The jazz revival and the rise of CND were more than coincidental; they were almost two sides of the same coin' (1983, p. 115; see also McKay, 2003). Sandford notes that the third annual Beaulieu Jazz Festival in the summer of 1958 was 'the first British festival proper' – the first to be held over an entire weekend, with extensive professional amplification for the many bands, and crash tents and other formal camping facilities. The concurrence of the first Aldermaston CND march of 1958 with the first 'proper' festival at Beaulieu *is* as important and connected as Campbell suggests: trad bands playing for the camping marchers, packed with youth, through green and leafy Berkshire at Easter 1958; trad bands playing for new audiences, packed with youth, in the ancient New Forest of rural Hampshire a few months later in the summer of the same year. David Widgery has described the first Aldermaston march as 'a student movement before its time, mobile sit-in or marching pop festival; in its midst could be found the first embers of the hashish underground and premature members of the Love Generation' (Widgery, 1976, p. 104). He describes the traddy soundtrack to the 'decent British sort of protest', 'an awkward mix of gaiety and grimness', that the Aldermaston march presented:

Alongside it, pick-up trad bands blasted out variations of 'The Saints' and 'Oh, Didn't He Ramble', usually with so little unanimity about time signature as to make the business of being in tune quite superfluous. Although somewhere in the centre a determined figure, often on cornet, could be found remorselessly blazing away at his own authorised version of the tune. (Ibid., pp. 103–104.)

The second national CND march took place during Easter 1959, this time from Aldermaston to London rather than the other way round. The 3000 marchers covered 50-odd miles over several days, and were joined for the last part in London, from the Albert Hall to Trafalgar Square, by 12 000 others in a national demonstration on Easter Monday. CND historians John Minnion and Philip Bolsover describe how the protest had all the paraphernalia of a moving festival, including 'jazz bands and guitars, songs and slogans, banners, placards and pamphlets . . . luggage vans, banner wagons, litter collectors and Elsan toilet teams; stewards, dispatch riders, first aid teams' (Minnion and Bolsover, 1983, p. 18). Jazz historian Val Wilmer told me that she experienced the jazzy festival-style events of Aldermaston *and* Beaulieu in 1960 and 1961: for her, they were part of the same social and musical scene. This conjunction was more widely acknowledged as well: the *Glasgow Herald* wrote of 'all the usual Aldermaston-cum-Jazz-Festival uniforms – tight jeans, baggy sweaters painted with the CND symbol, bowler hats, long hair for all sexes' (31 July, 1961). On the march, remembers Wilmer,

> . . . there were always bands playing. They made the event more appealing. I did go for CND, but the bands were an exciting extra. We'd always try to be behind a band on the march, we'd position ourselves with an ear on the music . . . I went to Beaulieu with [Johnny Dankworth's] band, on their bus with a friend. I saw Tubby Hayes there, too . . . The following year I went again, stayed overnight. (Wilmer, personal interview, 24 January, 2002.)

According to George Melly, who sang at the festival regularly with the Mick Mulligan Band, sometimes worked there as a compere and was also an intelligent commentator on pop music and the changing world of Britain, the eccentric 'rave gear' fashion worn by subcultural members:

> . . . came into its own at the festivals or at the gargantuan all-night raves which were held under the echoing dome of the Albert Hall or among the icy wastes of the Alexandra Palace. Another marker of the raver was the CND symbol. Among the musicians there were some, myself among them, who were actively committed to the cause of nuclear disarmament, but I rather felt that for most of them the symbol was anti-authoritarian rather than anti-nuclear, not that I found this in any way unsympathetic. (Melly, 1965, pp. 221–22.)

There were, then, significant connections between the developing scene around Beaulieu (as its audience began to take over) and the Aldermaston marches, in terms of youth, music, subcultural identity, and to an extent a political articulation (see McKay, 2000b). This last would soon be shaped and more forcefully articulated within the New Left as well as in the counter-culture more generally. In *Bomb Culture*, Jeff Nuttall traces some of the motivations and context for the embracing of trad jazz, which he views as part of a post-war 'cult of the primitive'. For Nuttall, British musicians and activists choosing the 'small-band collective improvization of twenties New Orleans jazz . . . was a natural reaction after the harsh metal of war. It was a hungering for the green and intuitive life, almost for the pastoral' (Nuttall, 1968, pp. 41–42). The eccentric tribal gathering in the deep green ancient New Forest that began to characterize the Beaulieu Jazz Festivals, the collective excursion through the English Home Counties countryside that was the Aldermaston march – both satisfied the 'hungering . . . for the pastoral' identified by Nuttall. He elaborated to me on '*primitivism* as a mode of the times':

> For trad, for CND-ers, it signified in the nomadic gesture of Aldermaston, in the barefoot dancing to acoustic music . . . A great cult of dirt – black jeans, duffle coats or donkey jackets, straggly hair, unkempt . . . And this is the case even though trad's authenticity was totally spurious! You can tap in here to the *comic* ruralism of Acker Bilk, and more interestingly to the anti-commercialism of some of the culture (not least [the purist New Orleans music of Ken] Colyer). (Nuttall, personal interview, 13 December 2001.)

Go wild in the country! Subcultural contestation, carnivalesque transgression

> The near riot at the Beaulieu Jazz Festival on Saturday . . . was a disgraceful affair. There are those who criticise Africans and who say that such people will never be fit to govern themselves. But a tribal dance to the sound of a tom-tom has a more civilised air than this modern wreck and roll to the beat of the jazz drum. (*Bradford Telegraph and Argus*, 1 August 1960.)

However, the new romantic lifestyles, rural excursions and incursions, musics and fashions, temporary communities of festivals and marches, competing versions of Englishness and the past that I am writing of, and have linked as Beaulieu and Aldermaston, do not always behave. For peace is not always easy during carnival.

At the 1960 Beaulieu Jazz Festival, the trad clarinetist and somehow pop star Acker Bilk entered on a Model T Ford, courtesy of the Motor Museum. By the end of Saturday night, vehicles had been targeted by festivalgoers for destruction (I am resisting calling this an early anti-car protest – that is too utopian an argument, even for me!). While Acker played, jazzed-up youths removed wooden horses from the roundabout stage and climbed a scaffolding lighting rig, mounting horses on the rigging as they climbed. A storage shed was set ablaze, and a 1921 14-seater charabanc had its hood burned. During the Saturday-night riot 39 people were injured, none seriously, although two people were subsequently imprisoned for assaulting police officers. For George Melly, though, '[i]t wasn't a vicious riot. It was stupid. The traddies in rave gear booing the [modern jazz] Dankworth Band. A young man climbing up the outside of the palace in the floodlights waving a bowler hat from the battlements. Cheers and scuffles' (Melly, 1965, p. 239). Others viewed the exuberant youths quite differently. Kenneth Allsop in the *Daily Mail* asked his readers:

> Why do the Ravers rave? At which point do enthusiasm and high jinks twist into the urge to hate and destroy? . . .
> Whacky dress and wild fun do not necessarily spell delinquency. Yet for a certain product of our Affluent Society this seems to have become a rebel's uniform of viciousness – and the degree is fine between beating-up a jazz festival and beating-up Negroes in Notting Hill and Jews in Germany. (*Daily Mail*, 1 August 1960.)

For some of those activists and idealistic jazz fans who had been on the Aldermaston march a few months earlier it must have come as a surprise to be compared now to racists and fascists. But Allsop's point is perhaps more a symptom of a common English unease with American popular culture (it was Teddy Boys, inflamed by the new sounds of rock 'n' roll, that beat up London's black youth), or with unfamiliar mass events such as these new youth festivals. Lord Montagu himself was to say that: 'You'd need a policeman in every garden' in Beaulieu village if the festival was held again (*Movietone*, 1961) – hardly the image of pastoral promise he would have wanted to transmit.

In 1960 Beaulieu was also important as an example of the mediation of subcultural panic. Jazz from the festival was filmed and broadcast live both on BBC television and the BBC Light Programme radio network. During the Saturday-night riot the live broadcast was cut by six minutes, an interruption prefaced by an anxious BBC commentator saying: 'Things are getting quite out of hand. [pause] It is obvious things cannot continue like this.' A commandeered BBC microphone was used to broadcast a shout from one fan for 'More beer for the workers!'. An apologetic BBC spokesperson was quoted in the next morning's press: 'We have had a lot of telephone calls from viewers who thought the scenes were disgraceful' (quoted in *Sunday Express*, 31 July 1960). On the other hand, the *News of the World* (31 July 1960) was happy to report to its readers that its switchboard had been jammed with calls from television viewers wanting to know what was happening. The 'BEATNIK BEAT-UP', as it was headlined in one newspaper, was reported in the Commonwealth and world press – in South Africa, the US, Argentina, Gibraltar, Australia, Kenya, Canada, Italy, Germany and France. The combination of aristocracy and jazz madness was an outstanding popular story of English eccentricity run, quite literally, riot.

We would do well here to remember that, as E. Taylor Atkins observes wryly, '[o]ur comfortable characterization of jazz as a "universal language" fails to do justice to the conflicts the music ignited around the world' (Atkins, 2001, p. 121). The Battle of Beaulieu was partly a symptom of jazz purists' investment in their particular artform: subcultural tensions between traditional jazz fans and modernists were evident – by this stage, 'Go home dirty bopper' was a favoured insult used by tradders (see Turner 1984, p. 132 for the origin; see also Gendron, 1995). This may also explain the irreparable damage inflicted on Acker Bilk's banjoist's instrument – the banjo was truly despised by modernists. The riot was also a demonstration of the cumulative sense of empowerment developed by the collective identities of groups attending the event each year – the carnival beginning to blur the distinction between participant and observer as well as to challenge and invert the social hierarchy. Here the minor manifestations of transgression at the 1959 and 1961 festivals should be acknowledged, too. Also important, though, was the presence of the media – the camera as inflammatory device – and its privileged space at the 1960 event – the camera as intrusion, as noted by Jeremy Sandford:

> Montagu had been criticised for giving too much space to T.V. cameras, and of thinking too much of the T.V. technicians and too little of his audiences . . . The BBC had also been accused of a prissy and somewhat condescending attitude 'to unsafe things like Youth and Jazz. (Sandford and Reid, 1974, p. 14.)

For Mick Farren too, the Beaulieu Festivals were 'primitive mini-Woodstocks that reached media attention when *the audience took offence at being filmed as though they were sociological exhibits* and turned over BBC TV cameras' (Farren and Barker, 1972, no pagination; emphasis added).

There is a (retrospectively) intriguing coda to the Beaulieu Jazz Festivals. In 1962, a *Daily Mail* article describes the extraordinary early invention of a proto-free festival, of the kind organized extensively in Britain in the 1970s and early 1980s. The article points to the growing distance between festival organizers and festivalgoers, as well as the increasing autonomy of carnival:

> Like Frankenstein, Lord Montagu of Beaulieu has created a monster from which, it seems, there is no escape.
> After the beatnik riots last year Lord Montagu vowed: 'There will never again be a jazz festival at Beaulieu'.

But last night he told me that he has had to appeal to the police for protection from the jazz beatniks, who threaten to descend on the picturesque, Hampshire village again. Thousands of leaflets have been distributed in Chelsea exhorting the 'trads' and 'moderns' to turn up in force on August 4 'for a free rave to the bitter end'.

The leaflets, signed 'Pete the Brolly', read: 'If you can play any musical instrument please bring it with you and help make a successful weekend for every one. Spread the news and rave on'. (*Daily Mail*, 16 May 1962.)

The uncertainty of this putative Beaulieu free festival's counter-cultural or subcultural construction – it veers in its embryonic way between an alternative gathering or 'free rave' and a Mods versus Rockers-style showdown between competing jazz fans 'to the bitter end' – should not detract from its importance as an early manifestation of a more radical DIY youth culture. It also provides evidence of the emotional and social investment on the part of the audiences at Beaulieu in making the festival their own over the years it ran, even to the extent of claiming it as their own autonomous event. The newspaper returned to the story a month later, when the identity of white beatnik Pete the Brolly (complete with goatee beard and a small signifier of English eccentricity, a monocle, though no umbrella, I think) became clear at a court appearance following, of course, a drug bust. Outside a London court, following a £10 fine for possession of cannabis found during a raid on the candlelit Chelsea jazz club, *Café des Artistes*, Pete the Brolly owned up: 'I am the cat who has been distributing thousands of leaflets in Chelsea and throughout the country exhorting anyone who can play a musical instrument to come to an unofficial Beaulieu jazz festival on August 4' (*Daily Mail*, 9 June 1962). Pete the Brolly, aka 30-year old Peter Dawson, said from his Holborn office, having just been visited by two police officers:

This is really awful man, but awful . . . [The police] told me if I persisted with the plan I would be the first to be carried off. When I wrote to Lord Montagu I pointed out that to combat any trouble I would organise a beatnik police force. There would be little risk of damage. This rave would have lasted a while. We planned to live in the forest while it was on. (Quoted in the *Scottish Daily Mail*, 16 June 1962.)

Wild pastoral living, self-policing, DIY music-making and a non-commercial economy – many of the ingredients of the free festival movement are glimpsed here up to a decade before its popularization in Britain, and long before the inspiration of Woodstock. The poor or political in the free community of Desolation/Devastation Hill outside the fences of the 1970 Isle of Wight Festival, the 1970 *IT* financial 'fuck up' (*IT*'s own description quoted in Nelson, 1989, p. 98)[9] that became the free festival of Phun City, the 1971 free festival of Glastonbury Fayre organized and financed by upper-class drop-outs such as Andrew Kerr and Arabella Churchill – these were the early manifestations. But, as a British ideological social movement of sorts, free festivals came into their own with Windsor People's Free in 1972 and then the best-known, Stonehenge Free, from 1974 onwards. In a way, with Pete the Brolly, Beaulieu was present at the lost beginning of the movement and also at its notorious end, the 'Battle of the Beanfield' near Stonehenge, where the large convoy of New Travellers on its way to the stones for the 1985 festival was violently ambushed and broken up by police (see McKay, 1996, chs 1–2). As head of English Heritage at that time, Montagu was responsible for the preservation of national monuments such as Stonehenge, although he was not absolutely opposed to some sort of gathering:

> My desire was to turn the festival into some sort of controlled event, which meant it could still have happened. I would have loved to have made a sensible event – in fact, one year we offered 400 tickets to the alternative community to attend the stones during the solstice, but they said no, we'd rather stay outside. I did then think they were anarchists, you see: they'd rather riot really. Were there anarchists at Beaulieu, too, among the trad jazzers, beatniks, and CND-ers? Oh yes, quite possibly. (Montagu, personal interview, 1999.)

At Beaulieu in 1960 and (in leaflet form at least) 1962, as well as at Stonehenge after 1985, the aristocratic imperative to grant and control freedom of festival was challenged and rejected. As is its wont, carnival would not be so easily limited;' it *required* the fulfilment of its potential for social inversion. And so it was fulfilled. The *Daily Mail* delineated the carnivalesque trajectory of the Beaulieu Jazz Festivals for its readers:

> At first audiences were sprinkled with famous faces. Gerald Lascelles, cousin of the Queen, was one who made the trip to Beaulieu.
> Then the rowdies moved in and last August [*sic*: July] there were riots, nude bathing parties, fights with broken bottles, beatings-up of innocent bystanders and drunken orgies. Fifteen ambulances were called.
> 'I was disgusted and flabbergasted by the drunken youths and girls lying on the ground,' said Lord Montagu. (*Daily Mail*, 16 May 1962.)

Just as in the Victorian Beaulieu Fairs banned by his grandfather, the transgressive purpose of carnival, in the highly encoded and hierarchical social setting of an English stately home, burst out with energy, without apology, once more. That the febrile Americanisms of jazz should now be carnival's accompaniment, compounded the 'disgust', and/or the pleasure for, as Baz Kershaw reminds us:

> . . . carnival inverts the everyday, workaday world of rules, regulations and laws, challenging the hierarchies of normality in a counterhegemonic, satirical

and sartorial parody of power. And, like the counter-culture, carnival *appears to be* totally anti-structural, opposed to all order, anarchic and liberating in its wilful refusal of systematic governance. (Kershaw, 1992, pp. 72–73, emphasis added.)

Conclusion: Americanization and Englishness in early festival culture

What [Britain] did develop, however, probably in close association with American New Deal radicalism, was a powerful bonding of jazz, blues, folk and the extreme left, mainly communist but also, marginally, anarchist. For such people jazz and blues were essentially 'people's music' in three senses: a music of folk roots and capable of appealing to the masses, a do-it-yourself music which could be practised by ordinary people, as distinct from those with technical training, and lastly a music for protest, demonstration and collective celebration. (Hobsbawm, 1998, p. 272.)

For Andrew Blake, 'the notion of a popular festival [can be] a way of proposing, trying to create, a truly vital cultural politics, one which has involved thousands of people and their pleasures, generating a far greater level of enthusiasm than other political events' (1997, p. 191). The Beaulieu Jazz Festivals of 1956–61 did no such thing, of course – arguably, it was not only the aristocratic mien of Montagu, peer of the realm, and the topos of Palace House that maintained privilege and Little Englanderism,[10] but also the annual presence of other signifiers of traditional Englishness: for example, the 1959 commission of 'Festival Suite' written by Kenny Graham, one part of which depicted the hunting of a fox (the fox's part was played by the tenor saxophone), or the 1960 Sunday afternoon cricket match of Lord Montagu's XI versus Jazz/Showbiz personalities XI. Nonetheless, a 'people's music [of] . . . protest, demonstration and collective celebration' *could* be heard, even here.

Montagu explained to me that he was aiming for 'a British version of the American Newport Jazz Festival, if you like, but I think I saw the festival ideally as the Glyndebourne of Jazz, or hoped it might become that' (personal interview, 1999).[11] So, although musically looking across the Atlantic, Montagu's ambitions were modelled much nearer home. Despite the American origin of virtually all of the music played at the festivals, as well as the partial US template of the Newport Jazz Festival, signifiers of Englishness at Beaulieu would differentiate its identity. In these ways, Beaulieu became more than 'a watery imitation of their American counterparts' (*Observer*, 19 August 1962), in Benny Green's harsh but not unfair judgement of other British attempts at festivals of the time. And yet, in what became the final festival, during 1961, Anita O'Day appeared on Saturday evening and Sunday afternoon. For fans such as Val Wilmer there was a direct echo here of the 1958 Newport Jazz Festival, as seen in O'Day's memorable performance in the film *Jazz on a Summer's Day*. Wilmer elaborates on the imitative aspect of the UK jazz scene:

> It wasn't just Beaulieu that was imitative, UK jazz as a whole was. In fact, all people on the jazz scene *were* essentially imitators at that time. But that can also be seen positively – jazz is (partly) about the development of an individual style, so there became the possibility of developing through the stage of imitation towards something more individual, more original. But lots of copying too. British musicians played under a cloud, and were trying to shift it, but I'd say it wasn't until the early 1960s that they began to move away from the strictly American model really. (Wilmer, personal interview, 24 January 2002.)

Even the Battle of Beaulieu in 1960 was understood in this imitative framework by many. A few weeks before the troubled British festival, there had been violence at the Newport Jazz Festival in the US. Over 1–2 July, martial law was declared following 150 injuries and one fatality, as a result of large numbers of fans being unable to gain admittance. A British correspondent for the *Washington Post* wrote of Beaulieu that '[t]he riot was a fair copy of America's recent Newport, R.I, bangup. And the doings at Newport probably contributed to the British brawl. *Almost everything in popular music in the United States is repeated here*' (1 August 1960, emphasis added).

In the jazz setting of the earliest festivals at Beaulieu and the NJF events at Richmond the energy was sparked by transatlantic cultural exchange that combined with an eccentric indigenous take on tradition and an atavistically located desire for, and pastoral articulation of, the new. The ideals of what would soon become counter-culture, interwoven with its petty capitalism and its avowed political internationalism, circulated comfortably and rapidly via mass media and popular music: Arthur Marwick even suggests that: '[i]n some ways the hippies were the most international of all the phenomena associated with the sixties' (1998, pp. 480–81). Harry Shapiro maps things as he saw them then:

> The Beatles also helped to put London on the psychedelic map and there were many attempts to re-create Haight Ashbury in W10 and NW6. For the *Berkeley Barb* and the *Oracle* read *International Times* and *Oz*; the Round-house, UFO and Middle Earth for the Fillmore and the Avalon Ballroom; Ally Pally for the Be-In; Pink Floyd, Soft Machine and Cream for the Dead, Airplane and Quicksilver. Cream and Hendrix straddled both continents. (Shapiro, 1988, p. 146.)

Shapiro, too, implies that the British counter-culture is the imitative one – the secondary 're-creation' – which is also how George Melly saw it during the Summer of Love: 'San Francisco became the capital of British pop, and

British pop became in consequence provincial' (1970, p. 107). It has been argued, too, that:

> . . . festivals reflected a new kind of consumerism . . . [M]any of those 'in' the counter-culture were there chiefly as consumers, spectators more than participants, perhaps ultimately spectators more than anything. And ironically for the British counter-culture, which was trying to reject what it saw as straight society's acceptance of the 'American way of life' – including American 'consumerism' – it became imbued itself to a large extent with what might be termed the 'American view of the alternative future'. (Nelson, 1989, p. 99.)

On the other hand, at least one American perspective reverses the transatlantic pop cultural influence. *Rolling Stone* writer Jerry Hopkins describes the burgeoning scene in Haight Ashbury in 1965 as follows: 'San Francisco became known as "America's Liverpool"' (quoted in Marshall, et al., 1970, p. 22). Nevertheless, it remains true also that nobody ever said Woodstock was America's Beaulieu . . .

Finally, what is important in the context of this book is the *absence* of Woodstock as a template or inspiration in much of what I have discussed. Chronologically, this is an obvious omission, since the Beaulieu Jazz Festivals began in the decade before Woodstock took place. Yet there remains a frequent urge to reference the high-visibility event of Woodstock, and the still higher-visibility text of the subsequent film(s), in narratives of pop festival culture, even on the European side of the Atlantic. This is understandable, justifiable even, but it should not entirely obstruct the role played by earlier festival moments, with different (American) soundtracks, on different landscapes.

Notes

1. This research was made possible in part by an Arts and Humanities Research Board small research grant in the creative and performing arts, awarded in 2001. I am very grateful for the board's support. I would also like to thank Professor Andrew Blake, Robert Greenwood, David Nathan of the National Jazz Foundation Archive at Loughton, Essex, Dr Graham Taylor, Professor Helen Taylor, Susan Tomkins and other staff of the Beaulieu Motor Museum archives, the editors of *Just Jazz* magazine. Also sincere thanks are due to those involved from the scene who kindly agreed to be interviewed, and whose thoughts are quoted above: George Melly, Jeff Nuttall and Val Wilmer. Edited transcriptions of all the interviews, interspersed with images, on issues within the traditional jazz scene of the 1950s in Britain, can be found at: www.uclan.ac.uk/facs/class/cultstud/staff/mckaytext.doc.

I also thank Lord Montagu of Beaulieu for a telephone interview in 1999.

2. All newspaper and magazine quotations in this chapter are taken from the Beaulieu Jazz Festival press cuttings files of the Beaulieu Motor Museum Archive, Hampshire.

3. Books devoted exclusively to British pop festival culture are: Sandford and Reid (1974); Clarke (1982); Hinton (1995); McKay (2000a).

4. There developed a sense of competition (often uncritically written up in some of the British press) between Montagu and some of the other young aristocratic stately home owners – especially in terms of the various attractions that each devised to maintain the stately pile: Montagu had the motor museum and the jazz festival, the Duke of Bedford had a safari park and played in a skiffle band at Woburn, for instance.

5. Yes, *presumed* disappearance of the class structure. In fact at the time of writing (2002) – that is, half a century on from the social upheavals of the 1950s – Montagu maintains what one employee described to me as a 'manorial' hold on the Beaulieu estate and its allotted territory in the ancient New Forest, while one of the 'street fighting men' of the burgeoning blues scene of the time, Mick Jagger, is awarded a knighthood by the Queen. During the Queen's Golden Jubilee celebrations. Montagu also sits – unelected by the populace – in the House of Lords, while in the 1980s he was the Thatcher government's first head of the new organization to present and preserve certain forms of national culture, English Heritage. With profound irony, bearing in mind his formative role in festival culture in Britain, as we will see that part of his brief at English Heritage involved the control of the Stonehenge Free Festival, which was violently suppressed in 1985 (see McKay, 1996, 2000a.)

6. A police drive against homosexual acts in 1953–54 led to a number of trials and convictions (see The Knitting Circle website). Writing in *The Independent* on 25 October 1999, Philip Hoare called the Montagu case 'the highest profile gay trial since Oscar Wilde's'.

7. Montagu lent his name and the reputation of Beaulieu Jazz Festivals to the Manchester International Jazz Festival of June 1963, which featured the most impressive transatlantic bill of headliners to date for a UK jazz festival (much more ambitious than Beaulieu ever was), including Dizzy Gillespie, Buck Clayton and Bud Freeman. It was a financial flop, for reasons including the fact that the jazz boom was at an end and the headliners may have been too modern for some tastes. In addition, it may have been an indication of the importance of the *genius loci* of Beaulieu and the New Forest: when offered the industrial urban north of Manchester instead, audiences, ironically prompted by Montagu's presence in the publicity material, connecting this festival with the earlier Beaulieu ones, refused.

8. Montagu's enthusiasm for linking music and motor cars reached new heights (or depths) a few weeks before the 1958 festival. With an eye on publicity for his ambitiously expanding motor museum, on 17 July 1958, Montagu performed at what was billed as a 'Midsummer Madness' event, a pre-Prom romp at the Royal Albert Hall in London. Antony Hopkins' 'Concerto for Motor Car and Orchestra' includes two movements called 'Ritual Tyre Dance' and 'Carburettor Waltz'. For the first, Montagu danced round a car; for the second,

he played the car, which was specially fitted with six tuned horns. Surprisingly critical, the *Daily Express* (28 June 1958) called the performance 'a new low in musical buffoonery'.

9. *IT* stands for *International Times*, a leading underground publication at that time.
10. It is important not to overstate the purity of the English aristocracy, particularly in the context of the reception of US cultural exports such as jazz music. As long ago as 1933, a certain Lady Londonderry was complaining that 'Society' was becoming 'Americanised' (McKibbin, 1998, p. 24), while Ross McKibbin writes that, throughout the twentieth century, society hostesses increasingly 'saw their role as the integration of Anglo-American elites. "Society", as it was understood at the time, was in any case a significantly Anglo-American affair' (1998, p. 27).
11. Glyndebourne Festival Theatre was opened in 1934 in a private estate in Sussex. Its critically acclaimed opera festivals started again after the Second World War, in 1950.

References

Atkins, E.T. (2001), *Blue Nippon: Authenticating Jazz in Japan*, Durham, NC: Duke University Press.

Berg, I. and Yeomans, I. (1962), *Trad: An A to Z Who's Who of the Traditional British Jazz Scene*, London: Foulsham.

Blake, A. (1997), *The Land Without Music: Music, Culture and Society in Twentieth Century Britain*, Manchester: Manchester University Press.

Booker, C. (1969), *The Neophiliacs: A Study of the Revolution in English Life in the Fifties and Sixties*, London: Fontana.

Campbell, I. (1983), 'Music against the Bomb', in J. Minnion and P. Bolsover (eds), *The CND Story: The First 25 Years of CND in the Words of the People Involved*, London: Allison and Busby.

Chambers, I. (1986), *Popular Culture: The Metropolitan Experience*, London: Routledge.

Clarke, M. (1982), *The Politics of Pop Festivals*, London: Junction Books.

Cobbold, C.L. (1986), *Knebworth Rock Festivals*, London: Omnibus.

Denselow, R. (1989), *When the Music's Over: The Story of Political Pop*, London: Faber.

Dworkin, D. (1997), *Cultural Marxism in Postwar Britain: History, the New Left, and the Origins of Cultural Studies*, Durham, NC: Duke University Press.

Elstob, L. and Howes, A. (1987), *The Glastonbury Festivals*, Glastonbury: Gothic Image Publications.

Farren, M. and Barker, E. (1972), *Watch Out Kids*, London: Open Gate Books.

Gendron, B. (1995), '"Moldy Figs" and Modernists: Jazz at War (1942–1946)', in K. Gabbard (ed.), *Jazz Among the Discourses*, Durham, NC: Duke University Press.

'Guide to a Swinging Summer' (1962), *Melody Maker*, 2 June.

Hinton, B. (1995), *Message to Love: The Isle of Wight Festivals 1968–70*, Chessington: Castle Communications.

Hobsbawm, E. (1998), *Uncommon People: Resistance, Rebellion and Jazz*, London: Weidenfeld and Nicolson.

Kershaw, B. (1992), *The Politics of Performance: Radical Theatre as Cultural Intervention*, London: Routledge.

The Knitting Circle, www.southbank-university.ac.uk/stafflag/purge1950s.html [accessed 25 June 2002].

McDevitt, C. (1997), *Skiffle: The Definitive Inside Story*, London: Robson.

McKay, G. (1996), *Senseless Acts of Beauty: Cultures of Resistance Since the Sixties*, London: Verso.

McKay, G. (2000a), *Glastonbury: A Very English Fair*, London: Gollancz.

McKay, G. (2000b), 'Anti-Americanism, Youth and Popular Music, and the Campaign for Nuclear Disarmament in Britain', in S. Mathé (ed.), *Anti-Americanism at Home and Abroad*, Aix-Marseille: Publications de l'Université de Provence.

McKay, G. (2003), 'Just a Closer Walk With Thee: New Orleans-Style Jazz and the Campaign for Nuclear Disarmament in 1950s Britain', *Popular Music*, **22**(3), pp. 261–81.

McKibbin, R. (1998), *Classes and Cultures: England 1918–1951*, Oxford: Oxford University Press.

Marshall, J., Wolman, B. and Hopkins, J. (1970), *Festival! The Book of American Music Celebrations*, New York: Macmillan.

Marwick, A. (1998), *The Sixties: Cultural Revolution in Britain, France, Italy, and the United States, c. 1958–1974*, Oxford: Oxford University Press.

Matthew, B. (1962), *Trad Mad*, London: Consul.

Melly, G. (1965), *Owning-Up*, Harmondsworth: Penguin.

Melly, G. (1970), *Revolt Into Style: The Pop Arts in Britain*, Harmondsworth: Penguin.

Minnion, J. and Bolsover, P. (1983), 'Introduction', in J. Minnion and P. Bolsover (eds), *The CND Story: The First 25 Years of CND in the Words of the People Involved*, London: Allison and Busby.

Montagu, E. (1973), *The Gilt and the Gingerbread*, London: Michael Joseph.

Montagu, E. (2001), *Wheels Within Wheels: An Unconventional Life*, London: Weidenfeld and Nicolson.

Morgan, K. (1998), 'King Street Blues: Jazz and the Left in the 1930s–1940s', in A. Croft (ed.), *A Weapon in the Struggle: The Cultural History of the Communist Party in Britain*, London: Pluto.

Nehring, N. (1993), *Flowers in the Dustbin: Culture, Anarchy, and Postwar England*, Ann Arbor: University of Michigan Press.

Nelson, E. (1989), *The British Counter-Culture, 1966–73: A Study of the Underground Press*, London: Macmillan.

Nuttall, J. (1968), *Bomb Culture*, London: MacGibbon and Kee.

Sandford, J. and Reid, R. (1974), *Tomorrow's People*, London: Jerome Publishing.

Shapiro, H. (1988), *Waiting for the Man: The Story of Drugs and Popular Music*, London: Quartet.

Turner, B. (1984), *Hot Air, Cool Music*, London: Quartet.

Veldman, M. (1994), *Fantasy, the Bomb, and the Greening of Britain: Romantic Protest, 1945–1980*, Cambridge: Cambridge University Press.

Wallis, B. (1987), 'Revivalism to Commercialism: A Study of Influences on the Developing Styles of Ken Colyer and Acker Bilk', unpublished undergraduate dissertation, held at the National Jazz Foundation Archive, Loughton, Essex.

Widgery, D. (ed.) (1976), *The Left in Britain 1956–68*, Harmondsworth: Penguin.

Movietone (1961), newsreel compilation tape no. 7, Beaulieu Film Archive.

Other sources of material

Beaulieu Film Archive, Beaulieu Motor Museum, Hampshire.
Beaulieu Jazz Festival cuttings files, Beaulieu Motor Museum Archive, Hampshire.

Chapter 8

A public transition: Acoustic and electric performances at the Woodstock festival

Dave Allen

Introduction

In this chapter I wish to argue that, during the 1960s, the broad field of popular music was enriched by a variety of different styles and approaches by different performers. To a large extent I want to focus on the differences between acoustic and electric music, partly in terms of rapid technological developments (instruments, amplifiers and recording equipment), but also essentially in terms of musical genres and lyrical contents. The consideration of acoustic music will relate it partially to the waning influence of the rural in popular music in the twentieth century. I will suggest that the Woodstock festival was almost the last very public celebration of the rural within popular music and that it was also the last occasion on which acoustic performers shared a major public stage with electric acts on equal terms.

In that context I will focus on the two performances by Country Joe McDonald at Woodstock and examine his subsequent career and the effect that his appearance at the festival – and more significantly in the film – has had on that career. I will suggest that Country Joe's two appearances at Woodstock represent the two sides in this transitional moment in popular music. I will further suggest that his subsequent career has been limited because his main representation in the film has caused him to be identified principally with an acoustic and political 'old guard' rather than the electric revolution which made myths and heroes of so many of his contemporaries.

The antecedents of Woodstock and other major festivals of the late 1960s lay in the jazz, blues and folk festivals held at Newport and Ann Arbor (US), Beaulieu and Richmond (UK) and elsewhere (McKay, 2000; see also Chapter 7). Most of the performers at these earlier festivals came from outside mainstream pop music, representing older traditions of blues, jazz, country and folk music. As a consequence, apart from some of the more 'modern' blues performers like Muddy Waters or Howlin' Wolf, most of the performers played acoustic instruments – an apparent sign of 'authenticity' in contrast to the perceived artificiality of modern pop music.

When Bob Dylan appeared at the Newport folk festival of 1965 wearing leathers, playing an electric guitar and backed by members of The Paul Butterfield Blues Band, some folk fans saw it as a betrayal of their ideals and booed the performance (Hajdu, 2001, p. 263). It is reported that folklorist Alan Lomax, outraged by the sound, fought backstage with Dylan's manager. Similarly, when Dylan plugged in at Manchester's Free Trade Hall in 1966 the famous cry of 'Judas!' echoed across the hall and – on record – down the years.

This was not the first occasion on which Dylan had upset the audience at the Newport Festival. Hadju reports that in the previous year he had disappointed 'the political old guard of the folk world' by moving away from apparently political songs to more introspective work which the editor of *Sing Out!* described in a note to Dylan in the following terms:

> Your new songs seem to be inner-directed now, innerprobing, self-conscious – maybe even a little maudlin or a little cruel on occasions . . . You're a different Bob Dylan from the one we knew. The old one never wasted our precious time. (Hajdu, 2001, p. 211.)

Bob Dylan did not appear at the Woodstock festival, but exactly two weeks later he was the main attraction at the second Isle of Wight festival in Britain. There he appeared with The Band in an electric performance which he nonetheless fronted playing acoustic guitars. When Dylan played there, his latest release was the album *Nashville Skyline*, described by Gray as 'his first sustained leap into country music' (2000, p. 6) and the point at which 'he began to deconstruct himself' (ibid., p. xvii). At the festival he played some of his songs from earlier albums but none of the early 'political' titles and not in the contemporary electric style of *Highway 61 Revisited* or *Blonde on Blonde*. The more general transition from acoustic to electric music was central to Dylan's work throughout the 1960s but, at what I wish to suggest is one of its pivotal moments, he took a typically oblique turn and literally left the stage to others.

In that context, Country Joe McDonald was perhaps the most interesting performer at Woodstock – not least because he was the only performer to appear twice, once acoustically and once with his electric rock band, The Fish. Unlike Dylan at the same moment, McDonald still performed political songs and one of them 'I-Feel-Like-I'm-Fixin'-to-Die-Rag' was featured in the film in such a way that it, more than any other of his songs, has determined his subsequent reputation. Like Dylan, McDonald's music had developed through the folk revival of the late 1950s and early 1960s. The two men shared a passion for the music of Woody Guthrie and after early careers as solo acoustic performers, both began playing with electric bands in the mid-1960s.

Acoustic Woodstock

Although he was then playing with an electric band, Country Joe McDonald's first appearance at the festival was as a solo, acoustic act. One of the striking things about Michael Wadleigh's film, *Woodstock*, is how many of the performers play acoustic guitars, which connect them with the older musical traditions of the USA. Before Elvis, the acoustic guitar was played mainly by folk, country or blues musicians, not least the itinerant, mainly rural performers who enjoyed its portability such as Robert Johnson, Jimmie Rodgers, Blind Lemon Jefferson or Hank Williams. In contrast to the popular crooners of the 1940s such as Sinatra or Crosby, early performance photographs of Elvis Presley show him with a jumbo acoustic guitar, which does little to inhibit the visual impact of his performance, as he uses it to enhance the provocative sexuality of his impact. Behind him the embryonic classic band was forming: guitar, (string) bass and drums,[1] and in many respects the 'authenticity' of the acoustic guitar adds to the impact of this young performer, not yet tainted by any projection of showbiz artifice.

In little more than a decade, the fully electric version of this line-up had been exploited and developed by bands such as The Beatles, The Rolling Stones, Cream (with Eric Clapton) and Jimi Hendrix in his famous appearance at the 1967 Monterey festival (which might be seen as the Woodstock prototype). On stage there, he presented an unambiguously sexual relationship with his Fender Stratocaster before burning it, smashing it and throwing it to the crowd. Despite the sensuous shape of acoustic jumbo guitars such a performance was only possible with a solid-bodied, bright electric guitar; it wouldn't have worked with an acoustic.

But the solid-bodied electric guitar was not always so provocative. In pop's 'second' phase, around 1960, many prominent electric guitarists (for example, Duane Eddy, Hank Marvin or Bob Bogle) seemed more polite, more 'showbiz' than many of their acoustic contemporaries – a good example is shown in the performances of the Shadows in the film, *The Young Ones*. At the turn of the 1960s, the acoustic guitar and its link to blues, folk and country traditions attracted an alternative audience who were seeking an apparent authenticity denied them by the carefully controlled images and choreographed performances of mainstream 'pop' acts (including post-army Elvis). Within a few years, however, a new electric energy in the performances of guitarists like Hendrix, Pete Townshend,

Carlos Santana and others seemed to have rendered the acoustic models obsolete. Yet, at Woodstock, the acoustic guitar flourished alongside those electric performers as an equal partner for the last time in the history of popular music.

Appropriately, the reasons were in part ecological. The unexpected size of the audience at the Woodstock festival clogged the roads and delayed the arrival of many of the main electric bands and their equipment. As a consequence, the festival opened with a number of performers playing acoustic sets, including Richie Havens, John Sebastian and Country Joe McDonald. The film is misleading as a strict *documentary* account of what occurred, since it places Country Joe's solo performance in the middle. In fact he was there to appear with his rock band Country Joe and The Fish but his manager suggested that he might help out by playing an acoustic set on that first afternoon. He was thus the only performer to appear twice at the festival.

We might see the presence of so many acoustic guitars as one element of the Woodstock generation's brief desire to get back to the garden.[2] Woodstock (like Glastonbury) was staged in a farmer's field. The film opens with the festival recollections of a local tavern owner before offering a montage of the agricultural environment and the construction of the wooden stage. The first act we hear from the stage is Canned Heat performing an amplified, but rural, blues (after Henry Thomas) entitled 'Goin' Up The Country'. This theme is sustained with images – people swimming in the river, making love in the fields, walking in the woods, smoking 'weed' (the most *natural* drug?) and eating brown rice. The names of some of the organizations supporting the event, such as the Hog Farm or the Ohio Mountain Family, enhanced the rural feel although it would be an exaggeration to suggest that Woodstock was simply or deliberately a back-to-the-roots movement. The festival needed modern amplification, and most of the performers had to be flown in by helicopter from their comfortable New England hotels. We know as much as we do about Woodstock because of the film and other mass-media representations. Although some members of the Woodstock audience returned to the commune-style life depicted in *Easy Rider*, most went back to modern American living. The same audience who sang along with Country Joe and cheered the acoustic performers also enjoyed the electric sounds of The Who, Jimi Hendrix and Santana, as well as the highly polished performances of Sly and the Family Stone and Sha Na Na.

In this way, Woodstock represents the final moments in that transitional musical period before the dominance of electric rock music in the early 1970s. In the 1960s there was a more discernible shifting between the vernacular traditions of mainly acoustic music which had been indispensable to the development of popular music, and the excitement and (literal) *power* of electric instruments and huge PA systems. Led Zeppelin was the last major act to draw extensively upon the vernacular traditions which had been central to the development of the music of figures like Elvis Presley, Bob Dylan and The Rolling Stones. The group continued to rework the vernacular acoustic music of Britain and America in the 1970s but, even with them, their electric power, their stage performances and their behavioural excesses cut the ties to those older styles.

Of course, acoustic music has survived – partly through the contrivance of MTV's *Unplugged* series – but it has never since been an *equal* partner in the production of popular music. Since 1970 all major styles including pop, progressive rock, reggae, punk, new wave, new romantic, rap, grunge, techno and Brit-pop have been *mainly* electric, if not technological. The acoustic pre-1950 vernacular musical styles such as blues or country music have not maintained the impact they exercised on the popular music of the 1950s and 1960s, even though more of this music is now available through reissue programmes than was ever available before. Rather, the exotic 'other' music which has been popularized in more recent years has often been contemporary 'world' music rather than historical styles – and this 'world' music is often amplified electric music.

In the original film of Woodstock there are almost as many acoustic performers as electric ones. The electric acts are The Who, Jimi Hendrix, Sha Na Na, Joe Cocker, Country Joe and The Fish, Ten Years After, Santana, and Sly and the Family Stone. The following artists performed (amplified) acoustic sets: Richie Havens, Joan Baez, Arlo Guthrie, Crosby, Stills and Nash, John Sebastian and Country Joe McDonald. The decision about which acts were included in the film of Woodstock was not simply a matter for the film-makers. We have reports of financial and artistic decisions preventing the inclusion of other acts. There were a significant number of electric acts who were not shown (including the Grateful Dead, Jefferson Airplane and Creedence Clearwater Revival) but there were also other acoustic performers including Melanie, the Incredible String Band, Tim Hardin and Ben Sommer. Apart from differing in terms of performance from electric bands, many of the acoustic songs in the film are also more explicitly political. As a consequence, the film offers a representation of a point in popular music when the acoustic guitar, and the resonances surrounding it, still had a certain status with a particular audience – the Woodstock 'generation'.

The electric–acoustic transition

Popular music tolerated a shifting relationship between acoustic and electrical sounds in the 1950s and early 1960s (with orchestras and big bands as other elements) but became increasingly electric and amplified from the mid-1950s. By the late 1960s electric rock music seized the dominant position which it has never relinquished. Initially, amplification was often simply added to acoustic instruments but, technologically, the key developments were the solid electric guitars made by firms like Fender and Burns and the more powerful amplifiers of Fender, Vox and later Marshall, in particular. These instruments enabled guitarists to produce sounds which had previously been impossible and which, in the film, are most apparent in performances such as Jimi Hendrix's 'The Star Spangled Banner', Santana's 'Soul Sacrifice' or The Who's 'Summertime Blues'. In terms of rock music in the cinema perhaps the first example of such a sound is Jeff Beck's feedback and guitar-smashing sequence in the Yardbirds' performance in Antonioni's film of 'swinging London', *Blow Up* (1966).

Before this, much of the early music of major artists such as Elvis Presley, Bob Dylan or The Beatles was written or performed using acoustic instruments. As late as the summer of 1965, Paul McCartney was performing 'Yesterday' as an acoustic solo number in live Beatles shows. By the time The Who or Jimi Hendrix appeared at the Woodstock festival we were regularly listening to music which could only be made electrically. This was as public a demonstration of the new dominance of live electric rock music as we might find anywhere in the history of popular music, since the live audience of half a million was swelled hugely by those who saw the film.

This very public demonstration occurred at the end of a period when the music of young white performers had shifted almost completely from acoustic, vernacular styles to electric rock music. In Britain this had centred on the transition from skiffle – derived from pre-war American jug, blues and string bands – to the British 'pop-rock' of performers such as Marty Wilde or Cliff Richard and the Shadows. In the US, pop-rock performers like Bobby Vee, Fabian or the Ventures had been somewhat ousted by the folk revival of the early 1960s. By the middle of that decade, however, many of those young folk musicians were plugging in and creating a new form of rock music. Many black musicians such as Muddy Waters and Chuck Berry had been playing amplified music for some years, but Muddy Waters had a particularly interesting experience when he first toured England. In 1958 he performed a number of concerts with the Chris Barber Band playing a Fender Telecaster electric guitar and some British blues fans were disconcerted by the volume of his 'rock' style. When he returned just a few years later, Muddy planned to play acoustically but discovered that his new audience, weaned on bands like The Rolling Stones, now wanted his electric style (see Brunning, 1986).

In addition to the electrification of Bob Dylan we know that bands like the Lovin' Spoonful, the Byrds, Jefferson Airplane, the Grateful Dead and Country Joe and the Fish began as acoustic folk/blues/jug bands. Despite their roots in American vernacular music, in many cases they attributed their encouragement to play electrically to the impact of British bands such as The Beatles and The Animals. Nonetheless Shaar-Murray reports Robert Wyatt's view that 'they remained very loud folk bands' (1989, p. 196). Furthermore, this was not a one-way shift. The Rolling Stones began life in the early 1960s as the loudest British rhythm and blues band but when Mick Jagger and Keith Richard began songwriting, songs such as 'Tell Me', 'Play With Fire', 'Ruby Tuesday', 'As Tears Go By' and 'Lady Jane' had a gentle acoustic feel. Even in 1968, 'Sympathy for the Devil' is shown starting life as a slow, acoustic song in Godard's film, *One Plus One*.

While some festivals created a significant space for live acoustic performers, many of the major recordings of the period were increasingly electric – not merely in the use of instruments and amplifiers but in their dependence on the techniques of multitracking and studio effects. For example, mid-1960s albums such as *Revolver, Sergeant Pepper's Lonely Hearts Club Band* and *Pet Sounds* are often considered among the 'greatest' of the pop albums (see, for example, Larkin, 1999), and they comprise material which had been worked out and manipulated in the studio rather than 'on the road' at live gigs. The same is true of albums like *Troutmask Replica* by Captain Beefheart and his Magic Band, *Astral Weeks* by Van Morrison, or the inclusion of Nico on the first Velvet Underground album. In each case, the continuing status of such albums in the critical canon signals that studio construction and technical manipulation became a respected process in the creation of serious popular music during the 1960s.

Albums such as these have to be understood as the product of increasingly powerful instruments and amplification, and improved studio facilities (especially multitracking), as much as the new relationship between songwriting and performance. Some of the albums contain songs that were never performed live and others combine songs from live sets with studio productions. Record production was increasingly sophisticated and the long player (LP) made it possible for acts to record longer songs – sometimes with a thematic approach to the whole album. These were, then, carefully constructed and essentially electric artefacts. They featured songs but, crucially, they also featured sounds.

In some respects, objects that remain, like records and films, have a status beyond their contemporary significance. Albums and the filmed *record* of events like Woodstock or Monterey have become increasingly powerful simply because we have them and can refer to them again and again – they contribute significantly to our understanding of the 1960s. For example, in *Woodstock*, John Sebastian gives an archetypal tie-dyed, stoned-hippie performance. He then commented, 25 years later:

I've always kicked myself in retrospect. It's disappointing that ... future generations have that as my most highly visible performance! Especially when I had put in so many years of good, long, sober shows. I mean, the Lovin' Spoonful kicked most of the West Coast bands asses *bad* when we went out and played live, and nobody knows that! (Sebastian, 1994, p. 83.)

In this respect, many of the contemporary live performances of acoustic music in the 1960s – particularly in the coffee bars and folk clubs – are now little more than a distant memory and are probably underrated in terms of their contemporary impact by comparison with studio albums and surviving films.

Country Joe McDonald

In pre-Woodstock America, a major source of the earlier music of the 1920s and 1930s were the songs assembled by Harry Smith on his *Anthology of American Folk Music*. Smith created his anthology from 78s, which he collected wherever he went. In 1952 Folkways issued his collection of LPs which introduced many young Americans to the acoustic performances of black and white performers of the 1920s and 1930s. Through these LPs, many young musicians heard Doc Boggs, Uncle Dave Macon, the Carter Family, Sleepy John Estes, the Alabama Sacred Harp Singers and many others for the first time. One of those young singers, Dave Van Ronk, recalled: 'We all knew every word of every song on it, including the ones we hated' (Marcus, 1997a, p. 5).

Country Joe McDonald came to front a psychedelic rock band from a background of performing in an acoustic band rooted in these sounds of the 'old weird America' (Marcus, 1997b). At school he had studied music and performed in the school's orchestra and jazz band. He joined the navy at 17 where he played guitar and learned to love, in particular, the songs of Woody Guthrie. He soon left the navy and moved to Berkeley, across the bay from San Francisco where he has lived ever since. Country Joe and the Fish are associated with the San Francisco scene but they were in fact the main band from Berkeley. The University at Berkeley was a major reason for the spirit of political activism in the area and, with his background, Joe McDonald was a natural contributor to such a move.

Joe's father, Worden McDonald, was the son of a 'hardheaded Scotch Presbyterian preacher-farmer' (McDonald, 1987, p. 26). In the 1930s Worden 'hoboed' the trains through the Dust Bowl regions looking for work. In the 1940s he married Florence Plotnick and they began to raise a family. In 1946 they moved to Los Angeles where he worked for a telephone company and also became a council delegate to his union. In January 1954 he was summoned to appear before the Californian Un-American Committee, and the *Los Angeles Examiner* reported that he refused to reply to questions about communism. He became one of three employees 'who together had more than sixty years of experience' to be fired and blacklisted (McDonald, 1987, p. 122). At the age of 48 he found a new occupation as a mobile egg salesman and then became a gardener. Joe was in his teens when this happened and, if you meet him today, he still expresses anger and resentment over this experience.

By 1965 Joe had his first acoustic version of Country Joe and the Fish including washboard and harmonica and wrote 'I-Feel-Like-I'm-Fixin'-to-Die-Rag' reputedly for the Berkeley Vietnam protest in the autumn of 1965. That event is immortalized in Tom Wolfe's chapter on 'The Frozen Jug Band', in his account of Ken Kesey's Merry Pranksters, *The Electric Kool-Aid Acid Test*. Wolfe reports that, while the protesters took cover from a police tear-gas assault, the band were too stoned to move and the combination of drugs and tear-gas literally 'petrified them'! The band continued to play at major public events, not just Woodstock but also the Monterey festival and San Francisco's Human Be-In (both 1967). They recorded their first four-track EP in December 1965 and, in the following year, began playing electrically.

Psychedelic roots

From their beginnings, Country Joe and the Fish drew upon a variety of styles. The first EP, recorded in 1965, opens with the ragtime polemic of 'Fixin'-to-Die', its title borrowed from Mississippi bluesman Bukka White. 'Superbird' is the pseudonym for Lyndon B. Johnson, the American president who was escalating the war in Vietnam, and this first recorded version is crude, young, white jug-band music with a noisy backbeat tambourine and undisciplined harmonica. By contrast, '(Thing Called) Love' from the following year is 1960s funk – West Coast white James Brown. Then 'Bass Strings' and 'Section 43' presage the increasingly intricate, contemplative and more electrically psychedelic music which grew from these 12-bar 4/4 roots. In this sense I am using the term psychedelic not merely as a loose aesthetic category but to describe music which was both produced and consumed around the use of cannabis and LSD at a particular period in history. Bromell, for example, records that:

> Rock 'n' Roll brought psychedelics into popular culture even for the millions of Americans who never knew what marijuana smelled like. For better and for worse, the fusion of rock and psychedelics helped change fashion, art, politics, and social attitudes about everything from sex to schooling. (Bromell, 2000, p. 61.)

More specifically, Country Joe and the Fish consumed psychedelic drugs during the period when they were making their music, and many of their fans did so too. The conditions of that production and consumption were highly specific and, if there was the broader impact that Bromell describes, it cannot have been qualitatively the same as making and hearing this music under the influence of those particular drugs at that particular moment in history.

While I am content to use the broad term 'psychedelic', it is useful to acknowledge that the range of music often described as psychedelic subsumes a range of different sounds and influences. For example, the music of Country Joe and the Fish, like that of the Grateful Dead, is psychedelic music *rooted* in the acoustic traditions of folk and blues music. The songs of Country Joe and the Fish are more explicitly political than those of the Grateful Dead partly because of the influence that Woody Guthrie has exerted on McDonald's career but Guthrie, in turn, was not simply a political singer. There are many recordings of Guthrie with folk-blues performers like Sonny Terry and Brownie McGhee, Leadbelly and Cisco Houston, and these influences and connections are also apparent in McDonald's music.

The psychedelia of Country Joe and the Fish is, in this sense, interestingly different from the more 'pop' psychedelia of songs like 'Incense and Peppermints' (Strawberry Alarm Clock) or 'Arnold Layne' (Pink Floyd). It is also different in kind from the blues/soul influenced recordings of the Jimi Hendrix Experience and Cream, and from the psychedelic rock of Steppenwolf or Moby Grape. Moby Grape are considered to be part of the San Francisco scene which itself contained a number of different approaches to psychedelia. The Charlatans who are generally credited with being the first of the San Francisco psychedelic bands (see, for example, Hoskyns, 1997 or Selvin, 1995) recorded versions of a number of traditional American folk and blues songs. They featured electric guitar and drums but the rhythm section was not heavily bass-dependent and the drums are lightly percussive – typical of the electrification of folk groups in the mid-1960s. They did not develop the more powerful electric sound of, for example, San Francisco's Quicksilver Messenger Service, as is evident by comparing the two bands' versions of Buffy Sainte Marie's 'Codine'.[3]

As a part of the rush to sign up the West Coast bands, Country Joe and the Fish joined Vanguard Records. This was not quite the same as the Grateful Dead on Warner Brothers, or Jefferson Airplane on RCA because those were major multimedia companies locked into the conventions of mainstream American politics and commerce. Vanguard was a smaller label which had been releasing specialist classical, blues, folk and jazz recordings, many of which were explicitly political. Country Joe and the Fish followed folk and blues acts such as Odetta, Richard and Mimi Farina, Joan Baez, the Weavers, the Kingston Trio, Big Mama Thornton and Mississippi John

Hurt to Vanguard and were allocated Sam Charters as a producer. He had written about and produced many blues artists (see, for example, Charters, 1961) and continued in this vein so that, in another respect, the electric Country Joe and the Fish recordings never lost that connection with older forms and styles.

The first Haight Ashbury 'pop' success was Jefferson Airplane who later reinvented themselves as avant-garde experimenters (*After Bathing at Baxters*) and 'revolutionaries' (*Volunteers*) before settling for the rock mainstream with Jefferson Starship. They made good pop singles, but the band's political impulse can be discerned by reading Grace Slick's banal socialite autobiography (Slick, 1998). From the early 1970s, Jefferson Starship included only Grace Slick and Paul Kantner. Bass player Jack Casady, as well as recording with Jimi Hendrix, continued to work with guitarist Jorma Kaukonen in the folk blues band Hot Tuna – not psyche-delic, but a back-to-the-roots band. Casady and Kaukonen also work occasionally with Country Joe McDonald and, in 2002, Kaukonen released a very well-received acoustic album of blues, folk and roots songs, *Blue Country Heart*.

My point here, by way of comparison, is that the music of Country Joe and the Fish is particularly interesting for simultaneously and explicitly revisiting the roots of American popular music while exploring the new possibilities inherent in the developing technology, the political climate and the effects of 'new' drugs. Their songwriting combined sincerity and satire, the political and the personal. This multilayered approach gives their music a sophistication achieved by few other contemporary acts, but the band changed personnel rapidly and had split by the autumn of 1970 without achieving the success of some of their contemporaries. There have been many discussions about the concept of authenticity in relation to the popular music of the past 50 years and I don't think it will help consider-ation of the music of Country Joe and the Fish to revisit those debates. Nonetheless I find it useful to approach their work, and Country Joe McDonald's subsequent work, through the idea of integrity. I use it in its sense of meaning unity or wholeness – a judgement which is modernist in that its wholeness is defined predominantly in its own terms.

This is not a simple aesthetic judgement. I do not dissent from the common view that Country Joe McDonald's greatest achievements were in the first two Vanguard albums and were partly the result of ensemble playing – not least the musical relationship between McDonald and guitarist Barry Melton. Nonetheless his later work also has an integrity, a wholeness, because he is clear about his role as a modern day 'troubadour' (*Evening Standard*, 2001), and his purpose in singing about war, army veterans, nursing[4] and other political, social and personal issues. In addition, my experience of making music with him is that he approaches ensemble playing with a natural openness and receptiveness which I take to be characteristic of the psychedelic attitude. I have no space to develop this idea here, but I would be interested to pursue the question of integrity in terms of the production and reception of psychedelic (and other) music at another time.

Politics

I have pointed out that by no means all psychedelic music was political, but the filmed performances in *Woodstock* offer interesting examples of different approaches to political music at that time. I have already suggested that, as well as differences in style and volume between the electric and acoustic performers at Woodstock, many of the acoustic performers in the film sing explicitly political songs. This, of course, was at a time when many of the Woodstock generation in the US were taking a political stand against America's war in Vietnam but it is interesting that the increasingly dominant electric music was also less political.

Of the acoustic performers on the Woodstock stage, Joan Baez brought a greeting from her husband David, imprisoned for refusing the draft before singing the old union song 'Joe Hill', Richie Havens performed the anti-war song 'Handsome Johnny' and Country Joe's assault on Vietnam was a ragtime sing-along with a bitter, angry twist. Elsewhere John Sebastian's 'Younger Generation', Crosby, Stills and Nash's 'Wooden Ships' and Richie Havens' improvised 'Freedom'[5] speak more directly to the audience about their own social agendas. Woody Guthrie's son, Arlo, implies an historical political presence even though he presents himself as the archetypal stoned hippie ('I was rapping to the fuzz – can you dig it?').

We know now that the conditions for such political music changed dramatically and rapidly after Woodstock, and the circumstances for the production of political–psychedelic music were already on the wane by August 1969. Within a year or two the Grateful Dead (*Workingman's Dead* and *American Beauty*) and Country Joe McDonald (*Thinking of Woody Guthrie*) had followed the lead of The Band and the Byrds (*Sweetheart of the Rodeo*) and moved away from inventive psychedelia in favour of a return to the old America. In addition, while Woodstock itself may be construed as a social/'political' moment, with the significant exception of Hendrix's savage electric version of 'The Star Spangled Banner' (see also Chapter 3), the political performances in the film soon appeared somewhat old-fashioned and even irrelevant to a new generation of rock fans. In England, the acoustic folk revival of the early 1960s was supplanted by electric folk-rock acts like Fairport Convention, Pentangle, Steeleye Span, the Albion Country Band or the Strawbs. After 30 years, most of the old folk clubs have disappeared or struggle to survive. The more popular folk festivals remain, but most feature electric folk, blues and world performers alongside traditional acoustic English folk musicians.

Country Joe McDonald has performed with other musicians since the final demise of the Fish but, for the most part, he has been a solo act for 30 years. In that period major singer-songwriters like Joni Mitchell, Paul Simon or Van Morrison have not generally pursued a political agenda, but have rather taken Dylan's more 'self-conscious' lead. Meanwhile, McDonald has been content to sing his various songs and make his various points while younger and more public 'political' acts such as the Clash, Public Enemy, the Specials or the Manic Street Preachers have played amplified group music in modern styles and genres.[6]

Conclusion: touring with Country Joe

In 1999 I obtained Country Joe's business address from his website and sent him a couple of albums by my band, Reet Petite and Gone, which for a decade played amplified acoustic versions of old blues, country and jug-band music. My band might be seen as the modern inheritors of the essentially English tradition of skiffle (McDevitt, 1997) which developed within the 1950s jazz revival, and into the folk boom of the early 1960s. The latter was a direct parallel to the American developments, informed by visits from American musicians as notable as the youthful Bob Dylan and Paul Simon. With the albums, I attached a message about always enjoying his music and sending mine by way of thanks.

Many months later he responded, telling me he had enjoyed the music very much. I told a local promoter friend the story, he developed a plan to bring Joe to England to tour with us and – to my astonishment – the tour took place with eight gigs in the summer of 2001. Joe always performed a solo set but we played with him on stage for a substantial part of the evening.

I think there might be an interesting story to be told about that tour, but this is not the place. In the context of this chapter and book, two things interested me in particular. First, Joe was usually marketed by the individual promoters as the Woodstock legend and was more relaxed about that 30 years later than he had been at times during the interim period.[7] Second, Joe played a wide variety of songs on the tour but was entirely content to rework his 'classic' psychedelic songs with an English skiffle band which, in instrumentation and sound, was closer to the original Fish than the Vanguard album versions.[8]

The tour was very happy and a great success in terms of the hopes and expectations of its participants. The gigs took place mainly in clubs or arts centres, and we visited Manchester, Leeds, Norwich, Sheffield and London, as well as the Trowbridge Festival and a Sunday afternoon free concert on Southsea seafront. At the first, it rained and the second was one of the hottest days of the year so we had a flavour of the full range of Woodstock experiences! The audiences were fairly full throughout, generally attentive, very receptive and delighted to participate in the 'Fuck Cheer'. The *Evening Standard*, reviewing the Borderline gig, described how the 'memories flooded back' as the 'well-worn' musical mix 'won everyone over'. And yet there was very little broader interest from the media – not even from specialist nostalgia publications like *Mojo* which rejected more than one offer of an article or report.

I can only speculate as to why that might be. In this chapter I have suggested that it might be Joe's persistence in performing acoustically, retaining a political agenda and touring in 2001 with an amplified acoustic band consisting of mandolin, dobro, guitar, harmonica and washboard. Perhaps Woodstock persists mainly as a film and album while only its major performers (perhaps only Carlos Santana and what remains of The Who) can still command large regular audiences.

I have to say that Joe was largely unconcerned about the absence of coverage and since Reet Petite and Gone had otherwise ceased to exist by then, it did not matter to us either. The broader problem lies in the construction and representation of a tale of the late 1960s. It is a tale which has created cult heroes out of artists such as Arthur Lee, Nick Drake, Jimi Hendrix, Janis Joplin and Syd Barrett, of whom only Hendrix produced a *substantial* body of great work. The others all had their moments, but so did Country Joe McDonald and there is a worrying equation between mythical status and the social casualty – a role which McDonald refuses to play. In career terms, the cynical view might be that his mistake was to go on living, recording and playing the acoustic guitar with integrity, rather than vanishing into a netherworld of death, drugs, insanity or prison, which might have assured him of cult status. One of his great achievements is to continue as a working musician in the tradition of the vernacular musicians. Major black performers like James Brown and BB King have always done this despite their substantial success. Bob Dylan, The Rolling Stones and Van Morrison, whose musical roots are also in pre-rock styles, are similar, but the regular *live* performers are relatively few.

The 1960s were a time of great invention against a backdrop of rapidly changing technologies, new social alignments and drug-related experiments with consciousness. Many of the musicians and audiences at the heart of those experiments were also absorbed by earlier musical forms – especially early blues and country music which occupied a position at the interface between popular recordings and older vernacular traditions. To some extent 'world music' now fulfils a similar role, although it is less historical and less of a musical antecedent of current popular music. Otherwise, in recent pop's archaeological efforts there is a certain solipsism in the reworking of earlier pop by bands as various as Oasis, the Strokes, the Coral or Beachwood Sparks.

I have no idea whether the music of Country Joe and the Fish will ever exercise a significant influence on new bands although, stylistically, I think it would be improbable. However, in this chapter, I have suggested that they produced fascinating work at a key transitional moment in the history of popular music. Taken as a whole, their approach offers a fascinating model for the creation of popular music that incorporates the strengths of acoustic *and* electric music; it draws upon vernacular, classical and rock traditions and, lyrically, combines satire, romance, politics and straight-up fun. The integrating style is psychedelic, and the band combined all these elements in innovative approaches to new technologies and ensemble playing. Country Joe McDonald is no longer located at the heart of the popular audience. Nonetheless, he and his band offer a treasure trove of largely unexplored and underdeveloped musical possibilities, and their recordings, as well as Country Joe's two performances at Woodstock, remind us of a significant moment of achievement and transition in popular music. More broadly, I wonder whether acoustic music is now simply a backwater of popular music or whether it might still have a significant role in the music of the future.

Notes

1. In this respect, I am identifying a key moment in the development of modern popular music as the formation of blues and country bands with amplified guitars, string bass and drums in the period around 1940. My examples would include the Chicago blues bands recording notably on the Bluebird label and Western Swing acts. Within 20 years the string bass had been almost wholly replaced by the electric bass guitar.
2. From Joni Mitchell's song of the festival, 'Woodstock' in which she urges her generation that we must get 'back to the garden' with all its ecological resonances and implications of simplicity and innocence (Eden).
3. I have excluded Janis Joplin from this brief summary because I do not see her as a psychedelic performer in the terms I have described. This is not a judgement about the quality of her work.
4. He has a massive interest in Florence Nightingale, war nursing, and nursing in general. He has established a website dedicated to the work of Florence Nightingale and also works extensively for military veterans.
5. Included in *Woodstock: The Director's Cut*.
6. I am aware that black urban acts in the US, Jamaica and Britain have also produced many political songs during the past 30 years. I believe this is a different tale and one that I am not especially well-equipped to tell.

7. For example, on the *Oprah Winfrey Show* in 1989 he commented that his solo appearance at Woodstock had ruined his career.
8. Except that at the Borderline we performed three songs with the guitarist and bass guitarist of the Bevis Frond who played faithfully in the style of Melton and Barthol.

References

Bromell, N. (2000), *Tomorrow Never Knows*, Chicago: University of Chicago Press.

Brunning, B. (1986), *Blues in Britain: 1950s to the Present*, London: Blandford Press.

Charters, S. (1961), *The Country Blues*, London: Michael Joseph.

Gray, M. (2000), *Song and Dance Man III: The Art of Bob Dylan*, London: Continuum.

Hajdu, D. (2001), *Positively 4th Street*, London: Bloomsbury.

Hoskyns, B. (1997), *Beneath the Diamond Sky: Haight Ashbury 1965–1970*, London: Bloomsbury.

Larkin, C. (1999), *All-Time Top 1000 Albums*, London: Virgin.

McDevitt, C. (1997), *Skiffle: The Definitive Inside Story*, London: Robson Books.

McDonald, W. (1987), *An Old Guy Who Feels Good*, 6th edn, Berkeley: Ol' McDonald Press.

McKay, G. (2000), *Glastonbury: A Very English Fair*, London: Victor Gollancz.

Marcus, G. (1997a), 'The Old, Weird America', booklet accompanying the *Anthology of American Folk Music*, New York: Smithsonian Folkways Recordings.

Marcus, G. (1997b), *Invisible Republic: Bob Dylan's Basement Tapes*, London: Picador.

Sebastian, J. (1994), ' "A Spectacular Accident" (Woodstock)', *Mojo* (8), July.

Selvin, J. (1995), *Summer of Love*, New York: Plume/Penguin.

Shaar-Murray, C. (1989), *Crosstown Traffic: Jimi Hendrix and Post-War Pop*, London: Faber and Faber.

Slick, G. with Cagan, A. (1998), *Somebody to Love? A Rock-and-Roll Memoir*, New York: Warner Books.

Wolfe, T. (1968), *The Electric Kool-Aid Acid Test*, London: Black Swan Books.

Chapter 9

Still picking children from the trees? Reimagining Woodstock in twenty-first-century Australia

Gerry Bloustien

This is your Woodstock and it's long overdue (Joan Baez, Live Aid Concert, cited in Garofalo, 1992, p. 15).

Spike: Oh, *please*! If every vampire who said he was at the crucifixion was actually there, it would have been like Woodstock ... I was actually at Woodstock. That was a weird gig. I fed off a flower-person, and I spent the next six hours watching my hand move.[1]

I more or less wandered around the arena spellbound for three nights and two full days. This was what I had been missing in my life since I attended the great rock festivals of the 60s and 70s, the same good times feeling of peace and harmony was alive and well in this crowd, absolutely uplifting to find it again after so long an absence.[2]

From Woodstock to WOMAD: the wilting of flower power?

The legacy of the original Woodstock, the US's quintessential music festival clearly still reverberates in time and space, far from its original source. In the quotations above, Joan Baez invokes its political power at a charity rock concert, 15 years after the original event while a fictional (vampire) character at the end of the twentieth century humorously recounts his own experience at the 'weird gig'. Two different generations and venues, and yet members of both audiences would understand the allusion and make the connection (and, in the case of *Buffy*, share the joke).[3] The last example, given above, is from Womadelaide, a music event held every two years, in the lush and broad-sweeping Botanic Parklands of Adelaide, South Australia.[4] In this chapter, I argue that this remarkable Australian event can be read as a deliberate and self-conscious re-enactment of the spirit of a reimagined utopia. In fact, I would argue that the main appeal of Womadelaide, particularly in the twenty-first century, is its nostalgic yearning for an imagined experiential community – a return to the Woodstock dream, if not the reality. Yet, clearly, such a statement needs a fuller explanation, for even a cursory glance renders the two events very far apart in intention and ideology.

In the original 1969 Woodstock, rock music rode on the back of the politics and not vice versa. The event was envisioned as participatory, non-commercial and counter-cultural, with music being the cultural prism for already existing social movements. Abbie Hoffman, notorious political activist of that period, saw it as epitomizing a part of an ongoing social revolution which was 'not something fixed in ideology, nor is it something fashioned to a particular decade. It is a perpetual process embedded in the human spirit.'[5] Yet, of course, there were issues specific to the period: at that time, 'the civil rights and anti-war movements engaged millions of people in the politics of direct action primarily on the strength of the issues themselves' (Garofalo, 1992, p. 16). In turn, the politics influenced the style and form of the music itself. Today's world is very different. With the decline in trust and belief in the political power of social movements,[6] popular music has come to the fore. It fills the gap, often serving as the main vehicle to organize large masses of people and raising social awareness. Furthermore, the original simplicity has gone: like so many other contemporary cultural events, WOMAD festivals, including the ones held in Adelaide, rely increasingly on the use of the latest technologies for their wide impact. They are 'mega-events' (Garofalo, 1992) coalescing a variety of cultural products to form something that can be produced, marketed and consumed in a number of ways simultaneously. Of course, mega-events can have their own political impact and power through a wide range of interrelated activities, including the harnessing of the media itself.[7]

Womadelaide as a mega-event: sharing the vision?

WOMAD is the acronym for World of Music, Arts and Dance. The original British 1982 event founded by Peter Gabriel and a small group of fellow musicians attracted 15 000 people. The original aim was to celebrate and showcase the many different forms of music, arts and dance from countries and cultures all over the world, raising awareness of the global value of self-expression and community festivity through music and dance. Since the first WOMAD festival, more than 90 similar events have been presented in 21 countries and islands around the globe. From the initial 'offspring' events in Denmark and Canada in the late 1980s, WOMAD's reputation grew rapidly. Now WOMAD events are staged worldwide in locations including

Figure 9.1 Crowds at Womadelaide (Photo: Gerry Bloustien)

Australia, South Africa, North America, Canada, Japan, Singapore, Spain and a number of other European countries every year. The festivals usually take place over a whole weekend, encouraging family groups through special participatory events for children (see also Chapter 1). At most events there are at least three stages of simultaneous performances and often several other workshops and sessions run by the visiting artists themselves. This easy mixing between performers and audience is perceived to be one of the keys to the events' success. As singer Peter Gabriel, who originally conceived the WOMAD concept, puts it: 'There are two boxes, Them and US. Womad puts everybody into the box marked US'.[8]

My particular fascination and personal experience of WOMAD began in 1993. It was the first outdoor music festival that I had experienced since my teens. Along with the crowd, I delighted in what appeared to be the sudden transformation of the usually peaceful open parkland with its shady fig trees, into a swirling, crowded mass of people, stages and exotic music. And everything was strangely and delightfully unfamiliar – the sounds, faces, smells and dress rendered the place I had lived in for 20 years a totally different somewhere else. As in later Womadelaide events, I was to observe what appeared to be a communal step back in time, as thousands of participants of all ages flocked to the outside arena. It was, it seemed, a

Figure 9.2   Man dancing at
Womadelaide
(Photo: Gerry Bloustien)

biennial reawakening of the neo tribes, in their deep-seated desire for
'*communitas*' (Turner, 1982) or mimetic play (Schechner, 1993), for, indeed,
there was no self-mocking critique here as the participants over the weekend
came adorned in resurrected neo-hippie gear complete with flowing kaftans,
brown roman sandals and flowers in their hair. And as the music played
long into the night, men and women of all ages created symbolic 'free
spaces' (Bey, 1991), some lying stretched out on the grass while others
danced ritualistically, moving in self-contained, self-absorbed concentration
to the music. Above the heads of the adults, small children climbed the trees
and swayed contentedly to the music until, at the end of the night, they
were plucked again from the branches by their parents like strange, ripe
fruit.

   While the original concept of WOMAD was perceived as a vehicle to
broaden the international market for many different types of music and
artist from around the globe, Peter Gabriel equally saw the festival as
having an explicitly political purpose. He argued that it would enable 'many
different audiences to gain an insight into cultures other than their own
through the enjoyment of music. Music is a universal language; it draws
people together and proves, as well as anything, the stupidity of racism.'
Apart from Gabriel's vision, WOMAD's official website also offers the
event's 'mission statement' asserting that it 'aim(s) to excite, to inform, and
to create awareness of the worth and potential of a multicultural society'.[9]

In addition to the festival itself, in 1983, the WOMAD Foundation was established to produce a variety of educational projects in the UK and around the globe. Its stated purpose was to offer cultural exchange, educational experiences and active participation: a clear attempt to realize a democratic 'global village'.[10]

So mega-events are more than just large 'money spinners'. Reebee Garofalo, drawing on producer Tom Hollingsworth's categorizations, cites fund-raising, consciousness-raising, artist activism and agitation as four ways in which the political impact of mega-events can be evaluated (1992, p. 26).[11] All these categories seem to underpin some of the attraction of WOMAD. For example, the WOMAD Foundation, noted above, has explicitly highlighted fund-raising for political purposes as one of its core activities through the use of well-known musicians and music practitioners as a fund-raising resource. Specifically, at Womadelaide 2003, several organizations, such as Urban Ecology Australia used WOMAD as the platform both for launching their own fund-raising event (*PEACEBEATS* – a fundraising event for peace!)[12] and for their own publicity at a stall at WOMAD itself. By their very nature, the WOMAD festivals everywhere attempt to raise social consciousness, particularly through exposing participants to the cornucopia of diverse global musics, dances and performances. Inevitably, an essential part of those performances means that the political concerns, issues and yearnings behind the lyrics and the melodies are explicitly highlighted; it is commonplace for artists to explain the background context to, and political inspiration for, their compositions through their performances and more intimate workshops. At some WOMAD festivals, however, a deliberate link has been made to topical political themes. In 1995, for example, the Womadelaide committee chose to firmly link the music festival event with the International Year for Tolerance. Paul Keating, the Australian prime minister at that time, made the following public statement heading his comments with the title 'The global music event of the International Year for Tolerance':

> The International Year for Tolerance provides an opportunity to discuss what makes Australia a tolerant nation, and to listen to and learn from each other's experiences. Tolerance also is a particularly appropriate theme for the first year of the International Decade for the World's Indigenous People – furthering our achievements of reconciliation between Aboriginal and Torres Strait Islanders and other Australians. By supporting the objectives of the International Year for Tolerance, my Government is demonstrating its commitment to justice, inclusion, acknowledging rights and responsibilities, and respect for difference and diversity. The objectives of the WOMADELAIDE Festival, gathering such richly talented artists, musicians and performers from all over the world, will further the aims of the International Year for Tolerance.[13]

The corporate nature of any music mega-event, such as Womad(elaide), tends to lead to criticism that the commercial involvement takes away 'the selflessness of its motivation' (Marsh, 1985, p. 1, cited in Garofalo, 1992, p. 31). Yet the sheer scale of the phenomenon of the festivals provides the perfect platform for political consciousness-raising about specific and more generalist progressive issues, too. Sandra Vershoor, the current marketing manager for Womadelaide described the aim of the committee as reinforcing a clear vision of social justice. Even the process of the steering committee's decision-making is deliberately designed to be non-hierarchical, inclusive and casual: 'we have no rule-book, no mission statement to work from. Decisions are made collectively' (Vershoor, private conversation, April 2003). Yet beneath that deceptively informal approach is a clear focus upon the main outcomes, underpinned by a commitment to green politics and interracial harmony. In practice, this means that the committee only sanctions the use of biodegradable disposable cups and plates on site; no fast foods, such as those made by transnational corporations and laden with fat or high sugar content, are permitted. Instead of McDonalds or similar fast-food outlets, a range of stalls are selected to sell locally-produced, good-quality food, the majority based on Asian or African cuisine. Similarly, the craft, book and music stalls sell many goods from Third World countries. Of course, however well-meaning, the inevitable paradoxical result is a recurring aura of neocolonialism combined with an almost Disneyesque gathering of generic 'otherness' and 'exoticism' – a step into 'hyper-reality' or mimetic excess (see Soja, 1996; Baudrillard, 1983; Taussig, 1993) for all the stalls are brought together under one arena. Most of the stalls showcase art and cuisine which have originated in the Third World and are brought together under the one umbrella-term 'global'. Umberto Eco could have been describing aspects of the Womadelaide village in his account of Orange County's famous theme parks:

> . . . an ideology realized in the form of a myth, presented as at once absolutely realistic and absolutely fantastic . . . a disguised supermarket, where you buy obsessively, believing that you are still playing . . . Disneyland makes it clear that within its magic enclosure it is fantasy that is being absolutely reproduced . . . But once the 'total fake' is admitted, in order to be enjoyed, it must seem totally real . . . here we not only enjoy a perfect imitation, we also enjoy the conviction that imitation has reached its apex and afterwards reality will always be inferior to it. (Eco, 1986, pp. 43–46.)

Or, put more simply in Soja's words, 'reality is no longer what it used to be' (1996, p. 240). This leads us to ponder why such places and events are so important; why it is so essential for participants to share in the 'sympathetic magic' (Taussig, 1993, p. 16), the (re)creation of the idealized spirit of Woodstock even while accepting that so much of the dream is a 'total fake'.

To do this, I need now to turn to the ways in which both WOMAD and Woodstock fulfil comparative functions as (contemporary) rituals – that is, as celebration of the 'shared mythology and values of a certain group within our deeply fragmented society' (Small, 1987, p. 6).

Like Christopher Small, I take ritual to mean:

> . . . an act which dramatizes and reenacts the shared mythology of a culture or social group, the mythology which unifies and, for its members, justifies that culture or group. (Ibid., p. 7.)

Small, here, is specifically demonstrating the ways in which ritual is embedded in a symphony concert performance, but his observations and analysis are just as valid when applied to the original event of Woodstock and to the more contemporary world music festivals of Womad(elaide). To understand music festivals as rituals or unifying, 'shared mythologies' and therefore the links between them, we need to analyse them as events taking place in a particular society, at a particular historical juncture, in a particular place and involving a particular group of people. None of these elements is arbitrary, of course, even though both of the examples drawn on here have a deliberate appearance of spontaneity and creativity built into their processes and performances. Rather, we can see them as epitomizing aspects of ritual, and hence the seriousness of play, in everyday life.

The role of play in myth, drama and contemporary ritual

Play in this concept, as I have argued elsewhere (for example, Bloustien, 2003) is not trivial but needs to be understood as a lifelong, deadly serious process and, for the players, something potentially threatening and dangerous. It seems extreme to be describing participation in a music festival as menacing or frightening but, as Schechner has noted:

> . . . the perils of playing are often masked or disguised by saying play is 'fun', 'voluntary', a 'leisure activity' or 'ephemeral' – when in fact the fun of playing, when there is fun, is in playing with fire, going over one's head, inverting accepted procedures and hierarchies. (Schechner, 1993, pp. 26–27.)

Part of the difficulty of coming to terms with this meaning of 'play' is that, particularly in Western popular discourse, play becomes synonymous with childish behaviour – trivial actions that we (should) outgrow as we reach maturity and adulthood. It is usually associated with unreality, make-believe and childishness. We tend to talk about 'just playing', keen to relegate this activity to daydreaming, playing with ideas and words. Yet, playing, and the multiple realities it exposes, is a fundamental human activity that crosses all cultures. It is a process of representation and identification through which all people make sense of their worlds and deal with uncertainty.[14] For this reason, we can see that art and ritual, and particularly the performative nature of both, underpin the process of what I refer to as 'serious play'. Richard Schechner reminds us of the link between theatre, drama and ritual for he argues that the relation between them is:

> ... dialectical and braided; there is plenty of entertainment and social critique in many rituals ... conversely theatre in its very processes of training, preparation, display and reception is ritualized. (Schechner, 1993, p. 58.)

Within this conception we can see that carnivals, street demonstrations and (music) festivals are a form of a theatre or drama in everyday life. They are often a conscious step 'into the subjunctive' as it were, into a 'what if?' utopian vision, an expression of seemingly spontaneous '*communitas*' (Turner, 1982), often all the more poignant through the awareness that the utopian realization can only be fleeting and ephemeral. 'Playing' from this perspective is not conceived as separate from everyday life nor as an interruption but is 'the underlying, always-there continuum of experience' (Schechner, 1993, p. 42; see also Handelman, 1990). In events such as street protests (such as the 1989 Tiananmen Square movement in Beijing or Western anti-war protests in 2003), carnivals (such as Mardi Gras) or music festivals (such as Woodstock and WOMAD) we can see the theatrical acting out of political desire. Although often trivialized in everyday life, when our 'playing' becomes part of our more formal public institutions, we recognize it as ritual (Schechner, 1993). Certainly, the media and the military take playing seriously when they report the staging of simulations and war games.[15] In late modernity, with the huge shift in ideas, widespread belief in certainties, law and justice, science, religion, concepts of wholeness and 'Truth' have increasingly wavered and fractured. At the same time, we are increasingly forced to acknowledge that our understandings of the self and reality are splintered into incoherence and anxiety. Our reliance on play to deal with these complexities and paradoxes has become even clearer and more urgent or, in Jerry Rubin's words, 'The power to define is the power to control ... We create reality wherever we go by living our fantasies' (1970, pp. 142–43).

But playing can never occur in a vacuum because imagination and dreams of utopia have to have a specific (material) site in order to be expressed, shared and realized.[16] This recognition leads us back to the concept of 'spaces to play' – arenas that enable and legitimate that political impact through the expression of individual and shared cultural identity. In turn, such symbolic space is increasingly seen as being under threat, and hence events such as Womad(elaide) represent the perceived, even desperate, need to create and maintain them, 'to squeeze as much pleasure as possible from a brief time and a well-defined space' (Schechner, 1993, p. 86).

Space to play

The use of public space, as potentially 'free enclaves' (Bey, 1991, pp. 97–99) and as continually contested 'spaces for (serious) play' (Handelman, 1990; Schechner, 1993; Bourdieu, 1999; Bloustien, 2003) is not peculiar to music events but offers insights into the ways in which all experiential groupings develop and survive. This is particularly true for the most marginalized or disenfranchized in our societies:

> Certain spaces, and in particular the most closed and most select, require not only economic and cultural capital; but also social capital as well. (Bourdieu, 1999, p. 129.)

Here we gain insights into how globalized culture becomes 'glocal' (Robertson, 1995), how cultural products can be reworked and reinscribed with local meanings in a local setting (Bennett, 2000) and, indeed, how imperative this appropriation often seems to be to the participants. As I have argued elsewhere (Bloustien, 2003), any place where one can share in a cultural activity, particularly with large numbers of like-minded others, is particularly exciting, for social space is never neutral. It is always experienced as a space of power relations (Duncan, 1996, p. 4), implicitly classed, aged and gendered. It is frequently contradictory and often exclusive (Shields, 1991; Massey, 1994; Harvey, 1996), particularly for those regarded as being on the margins of social respectability. All space, then, is an arena of potential struggle for symbolic power (Bourdieu, 1991).[17]

But, as indicated above, there has to be a geographical (or in more recent times, a 'virtual') place,[18] for such political expression to be realized – that is, a locale where the realm of the private imagination and vision can infiltrate and appropriate the public domain. Any sense of open and safe 'space to play', does not just happen. For space to be appropriated, even temporarily, three related elements have to successfully intertwine – time, place and subjectivity. In other words, the timing and duration of the event and the physical structure and ambiance of the locale have to enable a sense of free (political) expression. Finally, the participants themselves have to feel *able* to participate. In the case of Womadelaide, there has been a deliberate attempt to create and maintain this winning combination over the past decade of its existence, despite, and sometimes because of, the contradictory demands arising from its being a mega-event. It takes a great deal of careful orchestration to produce such a metaphorical oasis, bringing these three elements of place, time and subjectivity together, particularly in the contemporary climate of cultural and social division.[19] The steering committee for Womadelaide, as an eclectic group composed of high-profile arts, public relations and marketing administrators, has always understood this problem. They are aware that they have to work together, explicitly and implicitly, to create an inclusive performance space for both performers and audience which has become increasingly more challenging every year. As such, the committee acknowledges the need to deploy deliberate strategies within the detailed event – strategies that have to cover every detail in order to create a particular sense of warmth and openness with a core aim of addressing issues of social justice. This is not only quite remarkable for such a high-profile mega-event which clearly must be economically viable to maintain its current level of government and corporate sponsorship, but also inevitably incurs some complex and contradictory consequences. I will now examine the implication of each of the three categories of time, place and subjectivity in relation to Womadelaide as a contemporary ritual. Following this, I will focus on the event as a locus of mimesis and performance, an expression of a nostalgic search for the imagined experiential community of Woodstock.

The creation of performative 'private space'

The 'where' of staging such events is central to their success and the facilitating of their role as contemporary rituals. Music events usually take place in buildings specifically so designed or in spaces appropriated and transformed for that purpose. The aim, as with most art exhibitions and performances, is to create a space that is special, separated from the everyday outside world. To reinforce this sense of separation, however, there are always further distinctions of place within the arena of performance. For example, within these designated buildings there are other carefully separated areas that define what is openly accessible and what is only available for the select few with authority and privilege, including the performers themselves. A concert or play often uses a stage and proscenium arch to distinguish between audience and performers, and the place of the actual performance is usually distinguished from an anteroom for socializing, eating and preparation. Such delineation of areas is still to be found within the WOMAD setting, even though it is outdoors, as we shall see.

The original designated locale for Womadelaide was to be Belair National Park, South Australia's oldest national park situated approximately 15 kilometres outside of the central business district (CBD). It has an extremely well-developed range of services and infrastructure for visitors including a golf course, tennis courts, ovals (large grassed public arenas) and picnic areas. Although apparently eminently suitable in many ways, it was ultimately rejected by the committee as a location for the music festival because of a regular fire ban during the summer months. This ban would mean that no food could be cooked in the area on barbeques or gas burners, which would clearly prove an insurmountable problem for any caterers. The choice of the Botanic Park as an alternative site was in fact quite radical. It had never been used for communal events such as Womadelaide; most community-based festivals, such as the regular sporting events or the yearly celebrations of Greek or Italian culture within the city had been held in one of the four main open parklands which surround the CBD. These locales are mainly characterized by wide, though relatively bare, grassed areas, interspersed with children's playground equipment, barbeques and picnic areas, dedicated sporting ovals or tennis courts.

The Botanic Park was different. Like Belair National Park, it was seen mainly as an 'unspoiled area' thereby retaining an aura of authenticity as 'rural' or 'natural' as opposed to a developed or commercialized urban site. Unlike the Belair National Park, however, it was located in fact in the heart of the CBD and therefore was not affected by the annual fire bans. It boasted huge shady fig trees and was easily accessible by public transport as well as by private cars. It was large enough to provide a sense of openness and freedom and yet simultaneously could provide easy access for participants and equipment for the organizers, caterers and musicians. An additional advantage was that it was framed on all sides by roads, including smaller access paths, and could be confined and made secure, by fencing, thus permitting access to event officials or those who have paid to enter.

As can also be seen from the map in Figure 9.3, the area of Botanic parkland is sandwiched between the more cultivated Botanic Gardens and the majestic North Terrace. Both of these areas carry permanent reminders of the city's colonial past; the Gardens with their formal and ornate flower gardens and domed glass Victorian conservatories and North Terrace, Adelaide's main boulevard which is lined with buildings, monuments and marble statues. The Botanic Park takes on qualities from both of its geographical neighbours. It is a less formal, inclusive and sedate area – no formal gates or financial barriers usually prevent access. The large Morton Bay fig trees provide shade for any visitor and, on many a weekend, one can see groups of picnickers enjoying the peace of the surroundings. Children have no sense of restriction. Unlike the Botanic Gardens and other more formal parks, these trees can be enjoyed at any time as access from the main road is always available.

Of course, as indicated above, access to sites of any ritual, even in late modernity, is an important aspect of distinguishing who has authority and who has not. During Womadelaide and now other types of festivals held in

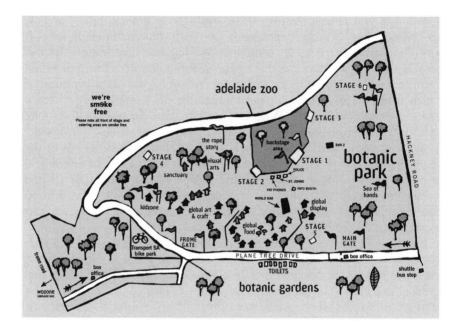

Figure 9.3   Map of Womadelaide

the parklands, access is a privilege not an automatic right, limited to those who are performers or who can afford to pay for entrance. Barriers are erected and gates are monitored by stern security guards. In the case of Womadelaide the cost can be prohibitive for some people. While there are concession and cheaper night and daily rates of entrance, the price of a weekend pass per adult is over Au$200. Not much comparatively, perhaps, for such a wide variety of entertainment, but quite a sum for some families who could usually enjoy the parklands for free. While concession and complementary tickets are provided by the management to specific groups identified as disadvantaged through particular funding by the state government, many people clearly do not see themselves as able to enjoy the festival as firsthand participants.[20]

The importance of time

The second category I want to consider is the question of *when* and *for how long* an event such as Womadelaide takes place, which affects the viability of the festival. Clearly, as indicated above, perceptions of time are never separated from the places where events occur and how the individual feels about that place. In other words, these perceptions are deeply embedded in their immediate ideological and cultural context (Gell, 1992; Hastrup, 1995) with the result that in their everyday lives 'people respond rather than just react. Their motivations are inextricably linked with their self-understanding' (Quinn, 1992 cited in Hastrup, 1995, p. 97). I will return to this notion more specifically below, when I discuss the concept of Womadelaide as a place of mimesis and performance.

Womadelaide began in 1992, originally as part of the biennial Festival of Arts. The original steering committee believed that the same population group who celebrated and welcomed the adventurous and often obscure events of the arts festival would also enjoy an event that focused on world music. On the one hand, the organizers felt that the fact that most of the musicians and performers were not so well known outside their own countries could increase the attraction of the event. On the other hand, to ensure the ongoing success of the festival, after this inaugural 1992 event, there would have to be a particularly big 'star' attraction for the following year.[21] The promoters therefore showcased Peter Gabriel for the 1993 festival hoping that his appearance alone would draw in fans from all over the country. This proved to be the case; that year, the 15 000-strong crowd each night secured the future of WOMAD in Adelaide. Other high-profile, already established artists were also billed to appear that season, including Mahlathini and the Mahotella Queens, Not Drowning Waving, Geoffrey Oreyema, Tiddas and Yothu Yindi, who shared the stages with the less well-known performers.

In keeping with other WOMAD festivals across the world, the committee decided that the festival should take place over a weekend during one of the hotter months of the year. Early February coincides with the school holidays for most of Australia and so the aim, even at that time, was to attract both adults and younger children from Adelaide and interstate. The hope was that audiences would already be in 'holiday mode', primed up for excitement. At this time, children aged 15 and under were admitted free with accompanying adults – part of the aim undoubtedly being to develop an ongoing audience in the future, as well as create an open and inclusive space. The overall effect of the strategy was to create a symbolic 'time out' for the audience, a period when they could slow down their everyday, frenetic lives and relax in the music and the ambiance of the festival.

Subjectivity

The third element that I argue has to be in place for an effective 'space to play' to occur, is that of subjectivity. The participants have to feel that they are *able* to participate freely, to experiment and to take risks. Part of this sense of freedom so far as Womadelaide is concerned stems from the fact that the majority of the audience sees itself as sharing a liberal progressive viewpoint. As noted above, initially at least, the festival was deliberately targeted from the audience usually attracted to the Festival of Arts – a group of people who were seen, and more importantly *perceived themselves*, to be educated and progressive, open to and comfortable with experimental art forms and left-wing political causes, yet not (too) iconoclastic. The audience for most of the major Adelaide Festival of Arts events is characterized not only by its relative affluence (ticket prices, as indicated above, being far from cheap), but also by its willingness to support the younger, more spontaneous sister event, the Adelaide Fringe which originally evolved in the early 1970s as a reaction against the establishment and the more mainstream Adelaide Festival. Nowadays, the two events coexist side-by-side but do seem to target slightly different audiences, even though, in practice, their respective audiences will dabble in both festivals. The Fringe events are often rougher, cheaper and tend to feature more underground and experimental works and, as such, they tend to attract a broader cross-section of participants, particularly in terms of age and socio-economic class. Womadelaide seems to have nervously flirted with both groups of attendees over the ten years of its existence but overall, like Woodstock, it is very much a middle-class affair, the majority of its clientele now being middle-aged.

So what does this mean? It means that this is an audience that *consciously* engages in and re-enacts non-conformist behaviour. It has been socialized into restraint and bodily control. Its acting out of any public behaviours which are regarded as less controlled or less respectable, such as wild dancing in public, has to be 'allowed' and encouraged. The works of Rob Shields and David Chaney are useful here in understanding the transformation that can occur in a site of activity which is perceived as a liminal zone – that is, where the areas for leisure activities become a site of the carnivalesque where the setting or infrastructure not only supports but encourages 'the carnivalization of social relations' (Shields, 1990, p. 40; also Chaney, 1993, p. 150). During Womadelaide, the Botanic Park too can be seen as an 'interstitial space to license the relaxation of conventional norms' (Chaney, 1993, p. 150), but this does not mean that what occurs at Womadelaide is spontaneous free activity. Instead, what occurs, I would argue, is, first the reframing of the physical space into 'a site for playful actions' and, second, the transforming of 'cultural space of relations so that actions and interactions are to be understood as playful' (ibid., p. 151). I suggest that what Chaney describes as the idealizing of 'a vanished community, a social history reconstructed as entertainment' (ibid., p. 173) is being acted out in this space. In this framework, play or mimesis is a segue into a state of practical nostalgia.

Still picking children from the trees?

In this final section I want to return to the concept of nostalgia, the desire and, more importantly, the yearning for a vanished, idealized past. So far, I have argued that Womadelaide, a contemporary music festival, should be understood as a modern ritual that dramatizes the desire for the spirit of Woodstock, a desire for 'a utopian community (or idealised system of social arrangements)' (Chaney, 1993, p. 175). It is important to recognize that the way in which nostalgia is envisioned from this perspective differs in two important respects from the way in which it is often considered as 'a sentimental dramatisation of the past' (ibid., p. 137). First, nostalgia as I am using the term here is far from being a passive activity but is, rather, embodied and efficacious. The second difference is that it is not postulated as a 'physical space outside of the conventionally known world in which a completely new form of social organisation can be inscribed' (ibid., p. 175; see also Kumar, 1991; Levitas, 1990). Rather in this conception, nostalgia requires a reappropriation and redefining of the space itself through the contemporary dramatization of myth.

I began this account of Womadelaide by describing the peaceful setting, the kaftans, the sandals and the sense of harmony. For most people, walking around Womadelaide seems to evoke a sense of 'time out'. People coming to Womadelaide from similar festivals interstate and overseas comment on the serene, friendly atmosphere:

> You don't see anyone drunk or aggressive here. It seems safe for small children even though there are so many people around. (Miriam, visitor to Womadelaide 2003.)

> [It's] [k]ind of like an all-too-short-example of how the world should be – and it's the music and the heart of the masses who attend that makes it so. (Michael Hunter, senior writer, *Greenman review*.)

Perhaps here we reach the point – that is, in Womadelaide, as in Woodstock, we have a representation of the world 'as it should be'. Never mind that, for some people, illicit drugs might be required to reach that state (marijuana is certainly commonly smoked at most music festivals, including WOMAD); never mind that one has to 'dress up' to feel the part. Never mind, too, that the participants know that it is just a short interval of time within their far more mundane existence. What is achieved in this short space of time is a respite, a sense of connectedness and belonging, a sense of being at one with the world. Music is, of course, perceived as a central vehicle in this process:

> It can determine or change one's mood, it can take you places nothing else can, and it can link individuals and whole cultures . . . When an event like

WOMADelaide takes place, these observations become all the more apparent, especially the characteristic of various cultures enjoying, and often finding commonality with, each other. It doesn't have to try to be a successful example of 'one planet' multiculturalism, it just naturally happens that way. (Michael Hunter, senior writer, *Greenman review*.)

Ann Game (2001, p. 230) distinguishes between a sense of nostalgia and a particular form of what she describes as 'at-home belonging'. Referring to a concept of 'sacred time' she argues that 'nostalgia is a desire for re-presentation of a "real" past as it was, . . . a return to an original point of departure or home, whereas belonging is a living in our primitive world, the timelessness or eternal return of mythic being'. Is this what the participants of Womadelaide, myself included, are (re)experiencing – a (re)creating of an idealized past that in fact we never had? To me, Game's concept of belonging which attempts to account for 'the time of lived experience through reworked phenomenology' (May and Thrift, 2001, p. 45) seems to be synonymous with 'practical nostalgia' (Battaglia, 1993) or 'mimetic excess' (Taussig, 1993). All three concepts attempt to describe and account for an embodied, deliberate and theatrical and, most importantly, *shared* step into 'otherness', an often unconscious 'strategy' which all people use in order to have a better, safer grasp on the present (see Bourdieu, 1993, for his explanation of this distinctive use of strategy). Womadelaide enables the players – musicians and audience alike – to experience the myth of '*communitas*', to embody a freedom and a shared political imagination. Even more importantly, perhaps, it allows the participants to remember and revisit their own physicality, to set aside the learned inhibitions of polite (adult) behaviours and recall the adolescent body, through a total engagement with the music. This is achieved not simply through dance, although that is clearly one of its most common manifestations, but through sitting or lying amongst others on the grass, moving or swaying to the rhythms, tapping out the beats with hundreds of like-minded others, sharing the moments. In the processes of musical production and consumption, the body is deployed through specific practices as a cultural resource. At such moments, too, the body becomes not simply a way of experiencing but also a way of knowing 'a site of somatic knowledge' (Willis, 1990, p. 11). This knowledge, this desire, for the shared political imagination is the legacy of Woodstock, still alive and exhilarating in 2003. We know it is ephemeral, we know it is imaginary and, of course, we know, like all 'serious play', it is hard work to maintain – but it is still wonderful to share the moment and to pass it on to our sleepy children, also reluctant to be plucked from the trees, just yet.

Notes

1. *Buffy the Vampire Slayer*, Season 2; 'School Hard', Warner Brothers.
2. http://tinpan.fortunecity.com/ebony/546/womad-1993.html.
3. In fact, it may be not a joke to describe Woodstock as a 'weird gig'. Abbie Hoffman, a counter-cultural icon of the 1960s coined the term the 'Woodstock Nation' and used it as the title of his 1969 book, which was described as a guide to surviving the counter-culture. The book and the term underscored not just the idealized utopian dream but also the unpleasant underbelly – a point to which I will return later in this chapter. For a brief biography of Abbie Hoffman and the political force behind the Woodstock festival and gener-ation, see also http://www.teaching.com/webstock/center/text/webstock19.htm [accessed 5 May 2003].
4. Since 2003 the fesitval has become an annual event.
5. This famous quotation from Abbie Hoffman is cited everywhere in essays, and books but usually with different dates and never page numbers. I read it again on one of the most comprehensive Hoffman websites, http://theaction.com/ Abbie/ [accessed 11 March 2003]. Amazon.com indicates that it can also be found in *Steal this Book* (1971), but I could not find the page number.
6. At first sight, recent peace rallies around the globe in response to the Western coalition's invasion of Iraq seem to have been an exception to this. This phenomenon is discussed in more detail below.
7. It is important to remember, of course, that the original Woodstock was not a 'spontaneous happening' but required a great deal of organization and, more importantly, large amounts of financial backing as it showcased some of the greatest celebrity rock musicians of the period (see Young and Lang, 1979).
8. Patrick McDonald http://tinpan.fortunecity.com/ebony/546/womad93-gabriel. html [accessed 1 May 2003].
9. Information and direct quotes are from WOMAD's official website, http:// www.womad.org [accessed 7 May 2003].
10. The publicity flyer exhorts visitors to WOMAD to experience 'Global eating. Global shopping. Global learning'.
11. Garofalo is drawing on Tom Hollingsworth's original discussion and categor-ization. Hollingsworth, the producer of Nelson Mandela's Seventieth Birthday Tribute, was a panelist on the politics of mega-events, New Music seminar, New York, 17 July 1989.
12. See http://www.urbanecology.org.au/whatsnew/archive/.
13. http://www.va.com.au/womadelaide/intro.html [accessed 12 April 2003].
14. To gain a deeper understanding of this conception of play and its relationship to ritual and myth in both contemporary Western and non-Western contexts, see Schechner (1993) and Taussig (1993).
15. At time of writing, the city of Adelaide has just staged a simulated terrorist attack, acting out possible scenarios through the medical personnel and facili-ties of one of the major hospitals, together with the police and the military. This has been publicized and discussed through the media as an attempt

(through extremely serious stylized play) to learn more about, and attempt to deal strategically with, the uncertainties of modern warfare.

16. In material I include the increasing use of virtual spaces to share views and ideas, for behind every website are real geographic sites where the communicating individuals live and deal with their everyday realities (see Smith and Kollock, 1999).

17. For the relationship of space and serious play see Bloustien (2003).

18. See, for instance, Gurak (1997), Wellman and Gulia (1999) and Mele (1999) for examples of using the Internet as the site of a community action and as a 'tool for political action' (Mele, 1999, p. 290).

19. At the time of writing, the Western Alliance-led war on Iraq and concerns about potential terrorism have led to the Australian government running an advertising campaign urging its citizens to be 'alert but not alarmed' against foreigners, outsiders and invaders.

20. This is in contrast to the Fringe Festival or particular free events staged in other arenas. However, some Womadelaide artists do offer free concerts on a large grassed area over looking Adelaide, at the top of Montefiore Hill.

21. This belief had more to do with interstate rivalry and the (mis)perception that Adelaide itself, as a city, was far more conservative than its sister East Coast metropoli of Melbourne and Sydney. These other cities are far larger and more cosmopolitan.

References

Battaglia, D. (1995), 'On Practical Nostalgia: Self-Protecting among Urban Trobrianders', in D. Battaglia (ed.), *Rhetorics of Self Making*, Berkeley: University of California Press.

Baudrillard, J. (1983), 'The Precession of Simulacra', *Simulations*, New York: Semiotext(e).

Bennett, A. (2000), *Popular Music and Youth Culture: Music Identity and Place*, Basingstoke: Macmillan.

Bey, H. (1991), *T.A.Z.: The Temporary Autonomous Zone, Ontological Anarchy, Poetic Terrorism*, Brooklyn: Autonomedia.

Bloustien, G. (2003), *Girl-Making: A Cross Cultural Ethnography on the Processes of Growing Up Female*, New York: Berghahn.

Bourdieu, P. (1991), *Language and Symbolic Power*, Cambridge: Polity Press.

Bourdieu, P. (1999), 'Site Effects' in P. Bourdieu et al., *The Weight of the World: Social Suffering in Contemporary Society*, Cambridge: Cambridge University Press.

Chaney, D. (1993), *Fictions of Collective Life: Public Drama in Late Modern Culture*, London: Routledge.

Duncan, N. (ed.) (1996), *Bodyspace*, London: Routledge.

Eco, U. (1986), *Travels in Hyperreality*, San Diego: Harcourt.

Game, A. (2001), 'Belonging: Experience in Sacred Time and Space', in J. May and N. Thrift (eds), *Timespace: Geographies of Temporality*, London: Routledge.

Garofalo, R. (ed.) (1992), *Rockin' the Boat: Mass Music and Mass Movements*, Boston, MA: South End Press.

Gell, A. (1992), *The Anthropology of Time: Cultural Constructions of Temporal Maps and Images*, Oxford/Providence, RI: Berg.

Gurak, Lawa J. (1997), *Persuasion and Privacy in Cyberspace: The Online Protests over Lotus Marketplace and the Clipper Chip*, Newhaven, CT: Yale University Press.

Handelman, D. (1990), *Models and Mirrors: Towards an Anthropology of Public Events*, Cambridge: Cambridge University Press.

Harvey, D. (1996), *Justice, Nature and the Geography of Difference*, Blackwell: Oxford.

Hastrup, K. (1995), *A Passage to Anthropology: Between Experience and Theory*, London: Routledge.

Hoffman, A. (1969), *Woodstock Nation*, New York: Vintage Books.

Hoffman, A. (1971), *Steal This Book*, New York: Pirate Editions, Inc.

Hunter, M., *Greenman Review*, http://www.greenmanreview.com/womad.html [accessed 12 May 2003].

Kumar, K. (1991), *Utopianism*, Milton Keynes: Open University Press.

Levitas, R. (1990), *The Concept of Utopia*, London: Prentice-Hall.

Massey, D. (1994), *Space, Place and Gender*, Cambridge: Polity Press.

May, J. and Thrift, N. (eds) (2001), *Timespace: Geographies of Temporality*, London: Routledge.

Mele, Christopher (1999), ' "Cyberspace and Disadvantaged Communities": The Internet as a Tool for Collective Action', in Marc A. Smith and Peter Kollock (eds), *Communities in Cyberspace*, London: Routledge.

Quinn, N. (1992), 'The Motivational Force of Self-Understanding', in R. D'Andrade, and C. Strauss (eds), *Human Motives and Cultural Models*, Cambridge: Cambridge University Press.

Robertson, R. (1995), 'Glocalisation: Time-Space and Homogenity-Heterogenity', in M. Featherstone, S. Lash and R. Robertson (eds), *Global Modernities*, London: Sage.

Rubin, J. (1970), *Do It!*, New York: Simon and Schuster.

Schechner, R. (1993), *The Future of Ritual*, London: Routledge.

Shields, R. (1990), 'The "System of Pleasure": Liminality and the Carnivalesque at Brighton', *Theory, Culture and Society*, 7(1), pp. 39–72.

Shields, R. (1991), *Places on the Margin: Alternative Geographies of Modernity*, London: Routledge.

Small, C. (1987), 'Performance as Ritual: Sketch for an Enquiry into the True Nature of a Symphony Concert', in A.L. White (ed.), *Lost in Music: Culture Style and the Musical Event*, London: Routledge and Kegan Paul.

Smith, M.A. and Kollock, P. (eds) (1999), *Communities in Cyberspace*, London: Routledge.

Soja, E.W. (1996), *Thirdspace: Journeys to Los Angeles and Other Real-and-Imagined Places*, Oxford: Blackwell.

Taussig, M. (1993), *Mimesis and Alterity*, London: Routledge.

Turner, V. (1982), *From Ritual to Theatre: The Human Seriousness of Play*, New York: Performing Arts Journal Publications.

Wellman, Barry and Guria, Milena (1999), 'Virtual Communities as Communities: Net Surfers Don't Ride Alone', in Marc A. Smith and Peter Kollock (eds), *Communities in Cyberspace*, London: Routledge.

Willis, P. (1990), *Common Culture: Symbolic Work at Play in the Everyday Culture of the Young*, Milton Keynes: Open University Press.

Young J. and Lang, M. (1979), *Woodstock Festival Remembered*, New York: Ballantine Books.

Afterword

Country Joe McDonald remembering Woodstock[1]

Country Joe McDonald with Dave Allen

It was as Country Joe McDonald that I earned world fame during the Vietnam era for writing and singing a song whose chorus goes:

> And it's 1, 2, 3 what are we fighting for?
> Don't ask me I don't give a damn, next stop is Viet Nam –
> And its 5, 6, 7 open up the pearly gates.
> There ain't no time to wonder why – Whoopee! we're all gonna die.

This was the same song that I sang on the stage at Woodstock in 1969, in front of 400 000 people, on the *Woodstock* film and for audiences all over the world ever since. I am an honourably discharged Vietnam veteran having served three years in the regular navy. I also grew up in Southern California with American Communist Party members as parents. I had an early realization that not all Americans agree on things. Having had both these experiences in my background left me feeling victimized. I had no love for the leaders of the American military or the American Left – I was neither enamoured of, or mystified by, either. Consequently, a life mission emerged from these experiences that I was never to abandon:

> Dedication to the cause of justice.
> A dream of peace.
> To try and help those who cannot defend themselves.

I was born on 1 January 1942 in Washington DC. My grandparents fled the oppression of czarist Russia in the early years of the century, and my parents were both committed politically to socialist ideals. I was named after Joe Stalin. My father, Worden, grew up in Oklahoma during the economic depression. He was a very interesting, adventurous man who eventually wrote his life story, *An Old Guy Who Feels Good*.

From an early age I played music. I played the harmonica and, at school, the trombone. I would practise every day, which gave me a good musical grounding. I played trombone in the school band and traditional jazz after school. I also played in a classic dance band on weekends for fun and in the school marching band at the football games. I loved the new sounds of 'cool' jazz coming out of LA including Howard Rumsey and the Lighthouse Allstars from Hermosa Beach and Buddy Collette, J.J. Johnson and Kai Winding on trombone. Through my parents, I also heard the music of the ordinary working folks of America, and that influence has stayed with me – I especially remember Woody Guthrie and Pete Seeger.

I was very fortunate to spend my teenage years in Los Angeles County in the little town of El Monte. There was an incredible mix of music to listen to at that time on both the radio and TV, and even in live acts. I joined the Columbia Record Club and I distinctly remember buying LPs by Blind Lemon Jefferson and the Dave Brubeck Quartet.

On the radio I listened to rhythm and blues and traditional Dixieland jazz. On the TV I watched country and western music and Los Angeles gospel music on Sundays. Johnny Otis, the classic rhythm and blues bandleader, had a TV show, and I had the pleasure of seeing his live show at the American Legion Hall in my home town where I also saw Fats Domino live.

I saw a rhythm and blues show in Los Angeles at a big theatre with many classic 1950s acts including the great R & B sax player Big Jay McNeeeley and his band. I loved the Leslie sound of their organist Bo Rambo. On another occasion, I saw the Maddox Brothers and Rose, Joe Maphis, The Collins Kids and Lefty Frizzel on the Town Hall Party country and western TV show. There were two rock 'n' roll TV shows on the weekends, one white and one black, and I used to watch both. I heard, but did not like so much, the new white rock 'n' roll and rockabilly. Mostly, I loved the R & B sounds of Don and Dewey, Little Willie John, La Verne Baker and all the Doo-Wop groups.

In high school I began to play the guitar and had a couple of bands that did a few folk clubs and coffee house gigs with but in 1959, when I was 17, I joined the navy because it seemed like a good idea at the time. I was posted to Japan and took my guitar with me, playing mostly versions of rock 'n' roll tunes, or folk music, which was becoming more popular at that time. Often, a group of us would play together, just for pleasure.

When my time was up I left the navy and returned to the US where I began travelling around, playing at folk clubs and coffee bars. I went back to college, but that was not a happy experience, so I took a few other jobs. In 1964 I got married and moved to San Francisco and then to Berkeley where I played in a band called the Berkeley String Quartet. We played acoustic guitars, mandolin, banjos, washtub bass, washboard and our music had a certain old-timey feel. Then Nina Serrano asked me to write a song for an anti-Vietnam War play. I wrote 'Who Am I?' and then immediately began working on a tune influenced by my old Dixieland college tunes. The melody and lyrics came to me very quickly and it became 'I-Feel-Like-I'm-

Fixin'-to-Die-Rag'. In that same year I recorded some songs with Blair Hardman. A little later, I met a young guitar player Barry Melton and we began playing together in a band called the Instant Action Jug Band, which eventually became Country Joe and the Fish. At this point we were still playing mainly acoustic music, and our first real gig was at the Berkeley Folk Festival of 1965. Then we were invited to entertain the crowd at a Vietnam rally in Berkeley. Someone started throwing tear gas, and Tom Wolfe wrote that famous piece about the band being literally petrified by the effects of the gas and whatever else we had been taking!

Country Joe and the Fish were really born when we went electric. Until the mid-1960s many American musicians played acoustic folk music – the Byrds, Jerry Garcia, Barry Melton and me. But then Dylan went electric and we all went electric. The whole electric sound was becoming really popular and to play at bigger venues we had to be amplified, but the truth was we weren't always sure what we were doing with that equipment. David Cohen started out as a guitar player but he got an electric organ, which sounded very strange but was part of the famous Fish sound. It had switches on it, which were supposed to make it sound like other instruments but it never did. It just sounded like Country Joe and the Fish.

We became part of the Haight Ashbury scene and lived there for a while, although we were always a Berkeley band and Berkeley was that bit more political than San Francisco. Country Joe and the Fish made two locally produced EPs and I did another solo one. After this, Country Joe and the Fish made five studio albums together (see discography). Most of the other San Francisco bands like the Charlatans, Grateful Dead, Jefferson Airplane, Big Brother and the Holding Company or Quicksilver (Messenger Service) recorded songs by other artists as well as their own stuff, but we wrote everything ourselves right from the start. This was important but it was tough. When you signed a record deal they expected so many albums and our five albums were released over just three years (April 1967–May 1970). When you are playing, travelling, rehearsing, recording and doing inter-views and promotional things it can be difficult to find time to write. When we started recording we had a stock of songs. 'Fixin'-To-Die', 'Superbird', 'Love', 'Bass Strings' and 'Section 43' which we had done on the EPs but which we could re-record on the first two albums. I also had 'Who Am I', a song originally written for a radical theatre group in Berkeley, who were staging an anti-Vietnam War play called *Change Over*.

We signed a record deal with Vanguard Records of New York who were known for recording classical, jazz, folk and blues rather than more popular acts. Vanguard asked Sam Charters to produce our albums, he had been working mainly with blues singers and this was his first psychedelic album. They didn't want 'I-Feel-Like-I'm-Fixin'-to-Die-Rag' on the first album because they thought it might be too controversial.

We were definitely playing psychedelic music. Some of our songs were based around old blues or country things, sometimes we would try more complex arrangements and sometimes we wrote in time signatures other than the usual 4/4 time. Janis Joplin asked me to write a song for her, which I did in waltz time. We recorded it on the second album ('Janis'). Whatever we did, the sound was definitely psychedelic.

This was partly, as I have said, because we were learning to use electric equipment and the sound of Barry's guitar and David's organ was quite distinctive. It was also because we took lots of psychedelic drugs – marijuana, LSD, peyote and so on. That was happening all over Haight Ashbury at that time, we were a part of it and we used to have a lot of fun with it. We even recorded some little tunes about that – especially on the second album.

The Summer of Love, in 1967, really began in January with the Human Be-In, also known as the Gathering of the Tribes in San Francisco's Golden Gate Park. I went there on my own and sat in on a song with the acoustic trio, The New Age. As well as musicians like ourselves and the Dead, there were the poets Lawrence Ferlinghetti, Allen Ginsberg and Gary Snyder and Owsley, the LSD man. Around 15 000 people attended.

Later that year we played at the Monterey Festival and then appeared in D.A. Pennebaker's film of the event. By this time there was a real sense of community in San Francisco, not just among the musicians, but with everybody who was really involved in that whole 'hippy' thing. The bands were fairly suspicious of people who seemed to represent the old values and, although most of the San Francisco acts appeared at Monterey, we were wary of the Los Angeles business promoters. We played on Saturday afternoon alongside Steve Miller, Quicksilver Messenger Service, Paul Butterfield, Canned Heat and Janis Joplin. I was enjoying some of Owsley's new concoction, STP, and we played 'Section 43', 'Fixin'-to-Die' and 'Please Don't Drop That H-Bomb on Me'. After the set we went over to the auxiliary stage and played there. There had been jazz and folk festivals in America for some years but this was the first big rock festival and it set a pattern for later ones, including Woodstock. After the Monterey Festival the San Francisco music scene was featured on the front cover of *Time Magazine* and things were never quite the same again.

By the summer of 1967 our first album, *Electric Music for the Mind and Body* had been released and Vanguard were promoting 'Not So Sweet Martha Lorraine', a single taken from the album. It was getting airplay and, with the reviews from Monterey, the band was attracting interest outside the Bay Area although, in truth, we never enjoyed touring. We had a very successful launch party for the album at Bill Graham's Fillmore West Auditorium and we continued to play there regularly and at the Fillmore East in New York. The other major San Francisco venue was the Avalon Ballroom.

Country Joe and the Fish were responsible for the great smoking banana skins hoax. Chicken, our drummer, had the idea; he told us that he'd read about how smoking the scrapings from the inside of banana skins would get you stoned. We tried it one day when we had already taken some acid and we kept going across the street to buy more bananas. We forgot we were tripping, and when we told the storekeepers the word spread. It never really worked.

Chicken was a great one for ideas. We had been doing the F-I-S-H Cheer for some time live on stage and getting the audience to join in and then playing the 'I-Feel-Like-I'm-Fixin'-to-Die-Rag'. It didn't make much sense, but that's the way it went. We got hired to play the Shaefer beer festival and *The Ed Sullivan Show* in New York and got paid in advance, which was always great. We played the beer festival in New York in front of about 40 000 people in Central Park and, in the dressing room before the gig, Chicken said 'Why don't we change it to the F-U-C-K cheer?' I said, 'Whoa, that's a good one', so we did it for the first time that night. There was a near riot, which is always a good sign at a rock festival!

Afterwards we were sitting in the dressing room congratulating ourselves on our new idea and a guy from the beer company stuck his head around the door and said, 'You'll never play the Shaefer Beer Festival again in your lives.' Then a guy from *The Ed Sullivan Show* stuck his head round the door and said, 'You can keep the money but you'll never play *The Ed Sullivan Show*.'

But we continued to do the F-U-C-K cheer. We went up to Worcester, Massachusetts and played in front of a couple of rather jumpy cops because Jim Morrison and Janis Joplin had been misbehaving on stage recently. We did the F-U-C-K cheer but nothing much happened until we arrived in Boston for the next gig where we were met by around 100 uniformed cops with guns, clubs, helmets, shields and maces, and I was summoned to meet the local police captain.

The Boston police captain told us that the Worcester police had called up about the show. I thought this was great until he said, 'You don't understand, pal. Don't say it here.'

'What's that?'

'You know what I mean.'

'I don't know what you mean.'

'Yes you do know what I mean.'

So the sergeant called me into the corner urging me to be a little cooperative. I said, 'that's no problem.'

'Well don't say it here,' he said.

'What do you mean?' I said.

'You know what I mean,' he said.

There was a law in Boston that cops could not say 'fuck' on duty, so the captain threatened dire consequences if we said it. I went back to the dressing room where we had one of those terrible things called a band meeting. As a generation of young Americans we were experimenting with something called participatory democracy.

On-stage the 100 cops were facing us, the captain was pacing up and down and there were 25 guys with trench coats, crew cuts and sunglasses behind the stage who were definitely not our roadies. So we did the L-O-V-E cheer, which thoroughly confused the audience, but we got away okay.

When that tour finished, the band split up again because we never much liked touring and I started doing solo gigs, including one in Worcester. When I arrived there, I was issued with a summons for leading the audience in a lewd, lascivious and wanton cheer. The police called a couple of witnesses who testified that they had not been offended, so the judge put me on the stand and told me that he could not understand the connection between this cheer and the Vietnam War. I told him that on learning you were being sent to Vietnam you would certainly say, 'Oh fuck.' So he fined me $50 and I appealed, and eventually the whole thing cost me $2500 but I got this story out of it anyway.

In 1968 we released our third album, *Together*, which included 'Rock & Soul Music' which was eventually the band's featured song on the *Woodstock* film. That was our third album and the final one with the original band. In the spring of 1969 Country Joe and the Fish toured England. Barry and David were still with us but Bruce and Chicken had left. We had recorded *Here We Are Again* and featured songs from that album on the live show, as well as older stuff.

I knew very little about Woodstock until three weeks before the event when we were added to the show. We were added so late that our name was not on the publicity and I had no idea about the size of the event until I arrived. I got there before the band because I wanted to see some other performers and I hitched a ride with one of the festival workers. Backstage I realized just how many people were there.

Bill Belmont had a backstage conversation with John Morris, one of the organizers. Richie Havens had played first because none of the bands had not got their gear yet, and John asked Bill if I could play a solo set. I didn't even have a guitar but someone found one without a strap. I tied it on with string and went up and played a few songs. Nobody was too excited so I did the F-U-C-K cheer and 'Fixin'-to-Die' and the crowd loved it. When it was included in the film with the lyrics subtitled and the little bouncing ball I had an international reputation for a gig that was never planned! Country Joe and the Fish were paid $2500 for the gig, but I was never paid for the solo set. I was the only performer to play twice at the festival – once with Country Joe and the Fish and once by myself.

A few months after Woodstock, Country Joe and the Fish appeared on

The David Frost Show. We played 'Fixin' to Die' to a prime-time national audience, and Frost received so many angry letters about the band that he sent them to me. One of the letters suggested that the 'unbathed folk group who sung about Vietnam should be shipped to any country of their choice'. That was fairly typical.

In 1970 at around the time that the *Woodstock* film came out, we released the final Country Joe and the Fish album, *CJ Fish*, produced by Tom Wilson. Only Barry and I were left from the original band and I had already released my first solo album, *Thinking of Woody Guthrie*. In the 30-odd years since then I have played all over the world and recorded many more albums – sometimes as a solo artist, sometimes with other musicians. Occasionally I play with former members of the band but Country Joe and the Fish, as a band, was together during the second half of the 1960s. When that momentous decade ended, the band ceased to exist.

In recent years I have realized that my generation has not been allowed to grow up together and I felt bad that some of my peers have never had the experience of going to rock dances and love-ins in the 1960s. Since I was a US navy veteran, a hippie and a known anti-war protester – who never lacked respect for the GIs – I had an entrée into both worlds. I began to see that the biggest difference was between the individuals who did nothing during the war and those who did something. Those motivated to serve joined the military or the anti-war movement. Others joined the Red Cross or some other public service. Those motivated to make a moral stand sometimes left the country at great sacrifice and under government intimidation, some became conscientious objectors or did hard jail time for refusing the draft. Others just dropped out and became hippies to be disowned by their parents.

The vast majority of the 50 million people making up the Vietnam generation did nothing but wait the war out. Ten million people – 9 million men and 1 million women – served in the Vietnam-era military, and several million were in the peace movement or the counter-culture, as it is sometimes called. Many of those who did nothing were able to move up the social economic ladder into positions of power and leadership, leaving those who experienced the trauma of the era on the outside looking in.

At times I have resisted my connection to the Vietnam War. It has been consistently bad for business and I have been warned and cautioned by many of my peers for constantly bringing up the issues of the Vietnam War in my songs and in my chats to my audiences. Over the years I have accepted this as my fate. Ever since I sang 'I-Feel-Like-I'm-Fixin'-to-Die-Rag' at Woodstock I cannot escape a connection with the Vietnam War. Whether or not I chose to make Vietnam a focus of my life, it seems to have chosen me. My efforts to help veterans and the country heal from the war have been both reviled and honoured, just like the war itself. There were times when I thought I would lose my mind. The worst of times came for me during the wars in El Salvador and Nicaragua. Extremists on the nation's political left and right wings squandered huge resources while Vietnam vets suffered in VA hospitals, on the streets, or in their homes with families sharing their burdens with little outside help or support.

To America's credit we seem, at the turn of the century, to finally be healing and accepting that the Vietnam War, as McNamara now suggests, was a horrible mistake. It was certainly not the fault of those who fought the war or those who resisted it.[2]

In 1989 I appeared on the *Oprah Winfrey Show* as part of the 'celebration' of the 20th anniversary of the Woodstock festival. On air I said:

> My appearance at Woodstock essentially ruined my career and I have never recovered but it was motivated by the same reasons that I enlisted in the navy at 17 years old, which were patriotism and altruism . . . I don't think it is that important and I'm amazed it's getting as much attention as it is.

Since then I have come to realize that Woodstock is what it is, and I am at peace with it now. At that time, I wanted it to be something other than it was. We all have our own personal history and I am pretty much at peace with mine now. Woodstock was great fun! I loved it!

Notes

1. This chapter was written by Country Joe McDonald with Dave Allen. It is the product of conversations, email correspondence and known history of Country Joe. The latter includes items from his website (www.countryjoe.com) notably a biography by a former navy buddy, Ron Cabral.
2. Taken from Joe's website and written before 11 September 2001 and its outcomes. Since it refers specifically to Vietnam we agreed to leave this statement as it was.

Country Joe and the Fish LP discography

Vanguard VSD 79244, *Electric Music for the Mind and Body*, April 1967.
Vanguard VSD 79266, *I Feel Like I'm Fixin' to Die*, November 1967.
Vanguard VSD 79277, *Together*, August 1968.
Vanguard VSD 79299, *Here We Are Again*, July 1969.
Vanguard VSD 6545, *Greatest Hits*, December 1969.
Vanguard VSD 6555, *C.J. Fish*, May 1970.
Vanguard SD 27/26, *Life and Times of Country Joe and the Fish*, November 1971.
Vanguard VCD 111/12, *Collected Country Joe and the Fish*, 1988.
Vanguard VCD 139/40–2, *Live! Fillmore West 1966*, May 1996.

Index